BURGUNDY
AND
BEAUJOLAIS
ON A BUDGET

ROSTERS LTD.

To Jill

About the Author

Patrick Delaforce was educated at Winchester, served as a troop Commander from Normandy to the Baltic in the 1939/1945 War. Became a Port Wine Shipper in Portugal, and also worked in New York and the City of London.

He recently returned to Brighton after seven years as a vineyard owner in France and is now fully occupied as an author. Among his recent writing are books on historical research, French regional wines and Lady Frances 'Fanny' Nelson.

Also available in this series:

Champagne On A Budget
Gascony And Armagnac On A Budget
French Riviera On A Budget
Travel Money
Talking Turkey
Viva Espana

BURGUNDY
AND
BEAUJOLAIS
ON A BUDGET

PATRICK DELAFORCE

ROSTERS LTD.

Published by ROSTERS LTD.
60 Welbeck Street,
London W1M 7HB.

ISBN 0 948032 82 0
First Edition 1989
Copyright © Patrick Delaforce 1989
All rights reserved.
Previously published as Burgundy on a budget.

Designed and published by ROSTERS
Maps by Marlborough Design.
Typeset by Lovell Baines Print Ltd, Newbury, Berkshire.
Printed and bound in Great Britain by Cox & Wyman Ltd, Reading, Berkshire.

Acknowledgements
I would like to thank Carolyn Eardley for her helpful advice during the preparation and editing of this book. This new edition has been expanded and updated to include prices for the Spring 1989 season. P.D.

Every care has been taken to ensure that all the information in this book is accurate. The author and publisher cannot accept any responsibility for any errors that appear or their consequences.

CONTENTS

CHAPTER ONE:
DISCOVERING THE REGION

The beauties of Burgundy are many and varied. Small medieval towns, often with ramparts intact, perch jauntily on little hilltops, curiously undisturbed by wars of long ago. Peaceful, well-scrubbed, white Charollais cows munch contentedly in the lush green valley pastures. The countryside is watered by wide, dignified rivers and a network of canals which crisscross the four départements of the region. There are over a thousand Romanesque churches to be found in Burgundy, tucked away in modest little villages, and over fifty châteaux and castles to be visited. Nowhere in France is there a richer, more complete mélange of beautiful sights, scenery and good living than in beautiful Burgundy.

The great architectural sights of Burgundy must rank with the finest in the world: proud Vézelay, where the huge church boasts relics of Mary Magdalene, and where Richard the Lion Heart planned his crusade against the Saracen; classic Cluny, the abbey of the Benedictines, where poor Abelard once studied; the amazingly beautiful Hospice de Beaune, with its famous polychrome roof tiles; the great ducal palace in Dijon; the medieval city of Auxerre; and lonely, dignified Pontigny, the twelfth-century abbey church which gave refuge to three English primates.

The rolling green vineyards of Chablis and Auxois are the first to be seen on the drive south from Paris. Then the Côtes-de-Nuits, the Hautes-Côtes de Beaune and the Mâconnais, and further west the vineyards of Pouilly. The region has been famous throughout the ages for its good food — *'la bonne table'*. There is game from Châtillon and Puisaye. Try Morvan smoked pork and bacon, fine beef from the Charollais,

Nivernais and Auxois, and poultry from Bresse. There are many local cheeses, including Epoisses, Gevrey, Soumaintrain and the Mâcon Chevrotons. Lake and river fish of all varieties abound — along with snails for those who like them! There are fine fruits, particularly blackcurrants from Beaune, and most people have heard of Dijon mustard.

Over the centuries, Burgundian fortunes have waxed and waned. The considerable empire of the great dukes of Burgundy which included all of the Low Countries and all northern France, was diminished in the fifteenth century. The Burgundy we know today comprises, very neatly, four départements. Yonne (postal code 89) is the northern, Nièvre (58) is the western, Côte d'Or (21) is the eastern, and Saône-et-Loire (71) is the southern département. All have roughly the same land area of 7,000 to 8,750 square kilometres, but the populations vary from 300,000 in the Nièvre to 580,000 in the Saône-et-Loire. The capital of Burgundy is Dijon, and the other main towns are Chalon-sur-Saône, Auxerre, Nevers, Beaune, Mâcon, Sens and Autun.

Budget brief

About a thousand years ago my family were petty feudal princes in Gascony. Until recently my wife and I owned an old stone Quercy-style farmhouse, complete with vineyard and fruit trees, on the borders of Gascony. For twenty years we have journeyed with the utmost pleasure on many of the minor roads of France, and more recently of Burgundy in particular. My object in this book is to document accurately, and as interestingly as possible, all that first-time visitors need to know, particularly if they are of slender means, in order to visit and enjoy Burgundy and Beaujolais.

First, the budget. For a couple travelling by car, it would be sensible to allow approximately 400 francs per day, which might be broken down as follows:

		Francs
1.	Double bedroom in modest hotel	100
2.	Continental breakfast for two	35
3.	Picnic lunch of bread, butter, paté, cheese, fruit and bottle of local wine from the supermarket	60

7

4.	Petrol	25
5.	Château entry charge	30
6.	*Prix fixe* dinner	100
7.	One bottle or *pichet* of local wine at hotel price	25
8.	Coffee, apéritifs or soft drinks	25
	Total	400

It is a matter of luck and taste whether this budget is exceeded or not. In a modest Citroen, my wife and I, on a recent visit averaged rather less than 350 francs per day.

The main part of this book covers, one by one, the four Burgundian départements. Apart from a short summary of the main attractions of each département and some suggested regional tours, I have covered four topics: towns and villages, along with local 'curiosities' such as grottoes, dolmens, battlefields and archaeological sites; buildings of historical or other interest, including castles, châteaux, major ecclesiastical buildings and museums; wine co-operatives, with a description of the local wines; and accommodation and food, which lists modest hotels, camp sites, and restaurants which offer good meals at reasonable prices. There is also a two-week 'grand tour' designed for those with a limited amount of time. The book includes a short piece on the delightful Morvan National Park in the centre of Burgundy (the ideal spot for an open-air holiday); a description of the wines of Beaujolais; and suggestions for alternative ways to enjoy Burgundy, such as boating holidays and coach tours, with useful addresses for those planning their visit.

Helpful hints

In case the reader of this book has not visited France before, the following few basic suggestions may be of use:—

• A green card for car insurance is essential, even for those coming from EEC countries, as the statutory coverage available is, frankly, minimal.

• Most of the many modest hotels mentioned in this book are located on busy roads, and, though the traffic usually diminishes by about 7.00 p.m., try to select an inside, quieter room. The very sensitive might even take ear plugs in case of emergency! Make sure the room is fairly close to the bathroom and w.c. on the landing, but preferably not next door, since walls can be wafer-thin. French hotels in this category do not usually provide soap, so bring some with you.

• As the night in provincial towns is unlikely to be very exciting, and the television downstairs may not be to your taste, you may have to create your own amusement — and what better than to plan the travel details for the morrow? With this in mind, note that the electric light in the bedroom is often insufficient for reading, so a small, portable, folding lamp with a two-pin plug is recommended.

• Hotel bedroom prices are fixed individually each year with the local authorities. They are net prices for the rooms, which may hold one, two, or more people, and are not negotiable. A schedule of individual room prices should be clearly displayed at the reception desk. Preferably, then, do not ask simply whether there is a room available for the night, for hotel owners naturally endeavour to fill their most expensive rooms. Ask, for example, to see 'the double room no. 15 priced at 85 francs'. The price will also be displayed in the bedroom, probably on the back of the door, so that you will know precisely what the charge is. Always — and this is the custom — ask to see the room offered before you decide whether or not to accept it. If you are travelling in high season, it is advisable to telephone in advance to make a room reservation, and be as specific as possible about your requirements. Most small family-owned hotels close for two weeks either in the autumn or after Christmas. Remember that substantial old town houses and mansions in the cities and larger towns are also called 'Hôtel'.

• Breakfast is always extra, and is usually served in the bar, not in the restaurant, from about 7.00 or 7.30 a.m. English breakfast is rarely available in modest hotels. A choice of coffee, tea or chocolate, with plenty of delicious bread (occasionally croissants), butter and jam is the standard breakfast throughout France. The two main meals of the day conform to a *prix fixe* (fixed price) set menu of three or four courses, which usually includes tax and service, but excludes wine. Most hotel restaurants listed in this book have inclusive menus in the range of 40 to 55 francs and local wine at reasonable prices.

● If you are staying in the same hotel for three days or longer ask for the *pension* or *demi-pension* rates. This is a discounted price which includes the room, breakfast, and one or both *prix fixe* meals, and is usually very good value. *Pension* means taking the two main meals, and *demi-pension* only one — but you should specify to the proprietor whether this is to be lunch or dinner. The restaurant times are likely to be 12.00 noon to 1.30 p.m. for lunch, and 7.30 to 8.45 p.m. for dinner. If you are given a handsome menu which by some 'oversight' omits a reasonable *prix fixe* meal, ask for the appropriate *carte* politely and firmly.

● Car parking can often be a problem, since few hotels have their own parking area. In Dijon and Auxerre, the recommended hotels either have a car park or are near a small, secluded square suitable for parking. Of course, lock your car on every occasion, and leave no valuables visible inside it — although standards of honesty, thank goodness, are still remarkably high in France, particularly in the country areas.

● The region's roads are well surfaced and well signposted. If you see a sign saying 'Toutes directions', do not despair; follow it, and soon the direction you want will be indicated. You will need to know, however, not only the minor town you are heading for, but also the major town some distance ahead on the same road, since often only the latter will be signposted to start with. The Burgundy region is approximately 180 kilometres square. Daily road journeys are probably unlikely to exceed 80 kilometres, since there is a cluster of local sights around the key towns.

● The best times of year to visit the region are from very early spring to early summer, and during the autumn months of September, October and November.

CHAPTER TWO:
PLANNING YOUR HOLIDAY

Since most visitors to Burgundy arrive from the north —
perhaps from Paris — my 'grand tour' has been planned on a
north-to-south basis, but of course the converse is possible.
The road maps needed are Michelin nos. 61, 65 and 69.

The route has been selected by identifying twelve of the
most attractive towns and cities; five of the most beautiful
châteaux and castles, five of the most interesting 'ecclesiastic'
cathedrals and abbeys, and the most famous winegrowing
areas. Travellers interested in the many major museums will
find them in the selected towns and cities. Those interested in
archaeological sites should read the introductory chapter for
each of the four départements. Some market days and
regional specialities have been noted, and towns and places in
bold type have hotels/restaurants which offer good value for
money. Each town mentioned on the grand tour has a fuller
report in a later chapter.

Sens (pop. 28,000) is rightly called 'the gateway to Burgundy'.
Through its cathedral of St Étienne it has a historical link with
England. There are many sights to see, and a good pedestrian
shopping precinct near the river Yonne.

Two pretty towns, both bordering the Yonne, are on the N6 to
Auxerre (51 km.) — **Villeneuve-sur-Yonne** (pop. 5,000) and
Joigny (pop. 12,000). Both are well worth a visit.

Auxerre (pop. 45,000) is a medieval city perched up on a hill
overlooking the river Yonne. There are many major historic
buildings and other sights to be seen. It is essential to stay here
for one or even two nights. The famous winegrowing area of
Chablis, the lonely church of Pontigny (to which every British

traveller should make a pilgrimage), the Anglo-Scottish battlefield of Cravant, the sparkling Crémant wine caves and the grottoes of Arcy-sur-Cure are all located within half an hour's drive.

The journey from Auxerre to **Nevers** (pop. 50,000), capital of Nièvre, needs careful planning, since **Avallon** (pop. 9,000), St-Père-sous-Vézelay, **Vézelay** (pop. 600) itself, **Clamecy** (pop. 6,000), Varzy, **La Charité-sur-Loire** (pop. 6,500) and **Pouilly-sur-Loire** (pop. 2,000) are all attractive temptations en route. There is an interesting wine circuit around Pouilly for wine-lovers. Although the Auxerre-Nevers travelling distance is but 150 km., allowing for detours, the traveller is advised to take at least two days. Vézelay alone merits a stop of three hours or more. Nevers itself warrants a stay of at least a day. The tomb of St Bernadette of Lourdes makes it one of the major pilgrimage centres in France. The Ducal Palace and its convenient location for many minor excursions make it a focal point. La Charité and Pouilly-sur-Loire can be conveniently visited from here.

Autun (pop. 23,000) is 100 km. due east of Nevers. A stop should be made on the way at **Château-Chinon** (pop. 3,000), which is the centre for several interesting excursions and is at the south end of the Morvan National Park. The traveller should consider staying at Autun, where in addition to the superb cathedral and interesting Musée Rolin, there are many Roman buildings, including gateways and an amphitheatre. The major châteaux of Sully and Nolay are each half an hour's drive from Autun.

From Autun head due north-east to Arnay-le-Duc (pop. 2,500), and then north-west to **Saulieu** (pop. 3,000), which has a *réputation gastronomique*. Either stay here — and there is a wide choice of hotels — or continue to **Semur-en-Auxois** (pop. 5,500), which in my opinion is almost the prettiest medieval town in Burgundy. A stop here is strongly advised, but the small hotels are popular and often full up. Semur is another focal point from which key visits can be made to Fontenay Abbey, the château of Bussy-Rabutin, the Roman battlefields of Alesia, and pretty little Flavigny-sur-Ozerain.

From Semur head south-east to **Dijon** (pop. 160,000), about 70 km. away. This, the capital city of the Côte d'Or, has so much to offer that the traveller should allow at least two days' stay. Excursions should include the château of Talmay, Bèze for its views, lakes and caves, the rosé wine co-operative of Marsannay-la-Côte, and the sad remains of once famous Cîteaux.

From Dijon, head due south on the Wine Route N74 (*not* the autoroute), towards Beaune (38 km.), stopping at any of the famous vineyards on the way, such as Gevrey-Chambertin, and at the château of Vougeot and **Nuits-St-Georges** (pop. 5,000). **Beaune** (pop. 20,000) is one of the major sights of Burgundy. Plan to stay a minimum of a day. Local excursions include St-Romain, Santenay and Pierre-de-Bresse, and there are well-known vineyards everywhere.

From Beaune drive south towards **Mâcon** (70 km.) stopping off at Meursault, Puligny-Montrachet and staying at **Chalon-sur-Saône** (pop. 61,000) or at **Tournus** (pop. 8,000) or at both. Chalon is an industrial and trading town, but is close to the vineyards of Mercurey, Givry, Montagny, Rully and many others. It borders the river Saône, and has two excellent museums. Tournus is another small Burgundian gem. The Abbey of St Philibert on the hill overlooking the Saône, as well as the old Quarter, should be seen. Excursions from Tournus include Brancion, a feudal fortress, Cormartin château, Taizé, the interdenominational church centre, and the subterranean caves of Azé.

From Tournus drive 30 km. due south to **Mâcon** (pop. 41,000) which is also on the river Saône. Mâcon is the centre of the wine co-operatives in the Saône-et-Loire. Although not as beautiful as Beaune, Mâcon perhaps has the culinary edge. Plan to spend at least a full day here. Solutré has a famous prehistoric site, as well as a wine co-operative; Berzé-le-Châtel is a feudal castle, and of course the famous Benedictine Abbey of Cluny must be seen (25 km. due west on the N79).

Further west from Cluny, 35 km. via Charolles, well known for its white cattle breeding, is **Paray-le-Monial** (pop. 12,000),

13

which is a centre for pilgrims. From Paray-le-Monial one can visit half a dozen well-preserved Romanesque churches at Montceau, Anzy-le-Duc, Semur-en-Brionnais and others.

The grand tour ends here. You need several more weeks to see the region as it deserves. If the wines have been too mellifluous and the fine foods too rich, the spa of Vichy, with its mineral-water baths, would welcome you 70 km. southwest.

Alternative holidays

There are many ways in which to enjoy a holiday in Burgundy. It is hoped that the following suggestions, given along with some further addresses and other information, will be of use.

Art, archaeological and historical tours

Ace Study Tours, Babraham, Cambridge CB2 4AP (0223 835055).

Francophiles (Discover France), 66 Great Brockeridge, Bristol BS9 3UA (0272 621975).

Special Tours, 2 Chester Row, London SW1 9JH (01–730 2297).

Swan Hellenic Art Treasures Tours, see coach tours.

Autorail tours

Les Autorails de Bourgogne, Franche Comté, 37 rue Lamartine, 21000 Dijon (80.46.38.65).

Ballooning holidays

Abercrombie & Kent Travel, Sloane Square House, Holbein Place, London SW1 8NS (01–730 9600).

For other information on seeing Burgundy by balloon, and reservations, apply to Centre Aérostatique de Bourgogne (M. Pierre Bonnet), Résidence du Lac, Les Hetres, 21200 Beaune (80.22.62.25).

Bicycling holidays

Susi Madron's Holidays with a Bicycle, 244 Deansgate Court, Deansgate, Manchester (061–834 6800).

Boating holidays

The main address for information is the Association Régionale de Défense et de Promotion des Voies Navigables de Bourgogne, Maison du Tourisme, 1–2 Quai de la République, 89000 Auxerre (86.52.26.27).

There are 1,200 km. of navigable rivers and canals in Burgundy, practically free of commercial shipping. There are about five hundred boats available for hire for use on the rivers Yonne, Saône, Seille, Loire and Seine, and the canals de Bourgogne, du Centre du Loing, de Briare and du Nivernais.

The main ports are Mâcon, Chalon-sur-Saône, St-Jean-de-Losne, Dijon, Montbard, Auxerre and Baye. Boats may be hired at Paray-le-Monial, Verdun-sur-Doubs, Seurre, Pont

Boating holidays have for some time been popular with the French. Now that this popularity has spread to British tourists, two British companies offer a wide range of cruising choices: Hoseasons Holidays Abroad Ltd., Sunway House, Lowestoft, Suffolk NR32 3LT (0502 66622) offer five possibilities.

1. Through Nivernais Cruisers, based on Cercy-la-Tour, for the Royal Nivernais Canal and the Canal Lateral à la Loire.

2. Through Tonnerre Cruisers, based on Tonnerre, for the Canal de Bourgogne.

3. Through Connoisseur Cruisers, based on Auxerre, one can cruise along the river Yonne, the Nivernais Canal or the Canal de Bourgogne.

4. Connoisseur Cruisers have another base at Gray, on the river Saône due east of Dijon, and cover the Saône and the northern Canal de L'Est.

5. Through Burgundy Cruisers in Vermenton, south-east of Auxerre, for the Canal de Nivernais.

Blakes Holidays, Wroxham, Norwich NR12 8DH (06053 2141–5) have four local bases in Burgundy.

1. Through Blue Line at Marseilles-lès-Aubigny, they cover the Canal Lateral à la Loire.

2. Through Blue Line at St-Jean-de-Losne, they cover cruises on the Saône.

3. Through Burgundy Cruisers at Vermenton, they cover the Canal du Nivernais.

4. Through Croisières de Tonnerre, at Tonnerre, one can cruise the Canal de Bourgogne.

15

Boating holidays offer the family with young children a marvellous opportunity of seeing the Burgundian countryside. The lock-keepers are friendly, and full of advice about local foods, wines and places to see.

The boat cruising season starts on 1 April and continues to mid-October. Boats are usually hired by the week, and rates in midsummer are double those in spring and autumn.

Other companies offering boating holidays in Burgundy are:

Blue Line Cruisers, Ferry View Estate, Horning, Norwich NR12 8PT (0692 630128 or 0883 40721).

Golden France, Ferrars Road, Huntingdon, Cambs. PE18 6DH (0480 50017).

Slipaway Holidays, 90 Newland Road, Worthing, Sussex BN1 11LB (0903 213751).

Travel Solutions, 79 Annandale Road, Greenwich, London SE10 0DE (01–853 1980).

Caravanning/camping holidays

Sunsites, 1 South Street, Dorking, Surrey RH4 1YZ (0306 887733).

Château tours

Châteaux en France, Bignor, Near Pulborough, West Sussex RH20 1QD (07987 366).

David Newman's French Collection, Normandy House, Old Shoreham Road, Lancing, Sussex BN15 0QS (0903 754818).

Gîtes de France, 178 Piccadilly, London W1V 0AL (01–493 3480).

Vacances en Campagne, Bignor, Near Pulborough, West Sussex RH20 1QD (07987 344).

Villages Vacances Familles, 24 Brabazon Road, Wimborne, Dorset (0202 884199).

Coach tours

It is possible to book interesting coach tours of Burgundy from leading UK firms. Thomas Cook offer a one-week tour, via Reims on the way south and via Paris on the return journey. The tour is based on Beaune, and is ideal for visits to the vineyards and wine-tasting. Guided visits to Fontenay

Abbey, Clos de Vougeot, Bussy-Rabutin and Dijon are included.

National Holidays have a one-week tour of Burgundy, based on Dijon, which covers the Côte d'Or, Beaune and Autun. A one-day trip to Neuchatel and the Swiss Lakes is included. The outward journey south is via Valenciennes and Reims and the return journey includes a night in Tourcoing, near Lille.

The following companies also offer coach tours of Burgundy:

David Walker Travel, 10b Littlegate Street, Oxford OX1 1QT (0865 728136).

Francophiles (Discover France), 66 Great Brockeridge, Bristol BS9 3UA (0272 621975).

Global of London Ltd., at all travel agents.

National Express, at all travel agents.

Sunrise Holidays, 2 North Gate Street, Great Yarmouth, Suffolk (0493 850500).

Swann Hellenic Art Treasures Tours, Canberra House, 47 Middlesex Street, London E1 7AL (01–247 0401).

Commercial visits

Many companies are prepared to show you round their factory, and some allow you to sample their products. The following form an interesting quartet in the Dijon area:

Cassis Bailly, 10 rue de Mayence, Dijon (80.71.15.83), is a distillery, a *liquoriste,* making 'Crème de Cassis'. A half-hour visit is free, and purchase possible.

Faienceries de Longchamp, near Genlis (80.37.72.52), have a one-hour visit on Monday, Wednesday and Friday mornings to see their pottery made from clay to finished product. Closed in August.

Societé Ricard, Gevrey-Chambertin, make and distil *anis* and other spirits. The visit is free, but notice is advisable (80.52.27.27).

17

Cassis Vedrenne, Père et fils, Nuits-St-Georges, have a plant in the *zone industrielle* (80.61.10.32). They, too, make and distil *cassis* and other fruit drinks. Closed in July, during the vintage.

Fishing holidays

The Nièvre — which has more waters suitable for fishing than the other three départements put together — has no less than forty-six fishing clubs, usually for white fish and *carnassiers*. Half of them have trout fishing as well. The rivers, in the methodical French way, are classified in first and second categories. The Fédération Départementale is at 7 quai de Mantoue, Nevers, tel. 86.61.18.98. In the other départements the local Syndicat d'Initiative will advise on any available fishing facilities. The Saône stocks bream, roach, tench, carp, perch and pike; the Doubs large trout; the Grosne chub, dace and gudgeon. Perch at Sercy, bream and carp at Malay. The river Arconce produces bream in summer and chub in winter. Autun is known for its trout. Local fish dishes are *Bouillabaisse d'eau doux* with *vin blanc, pochouse au vin blanc* and *goujon* (gudgeon).

Hotel holidays

Air France Holidays in Dijon, 69 Boston Manor Road, Brentford, Middlesex (01–568 6981).

Billington Travel (Beaune, Chagny), 2a White Hart Parade, Riverhead, Sevenoaks, Kent TN13 2BJ (0732 460666).

French Leave Holidays (Chalon-sur-Saône, Cluny, Dijon, Fleurville, Mâcon, Tournus), 21 Fleet Street, London EC4Y 1AA (01–583 8383).

Transalpino, 71–75 Buckingham Palace Road, London SW1 (01–834 9656). Cheap rail tickets for travellers under 26.

VFB Holidays (Autun, Crèches-sur-Saône, Quarré-les-Tombes) 1 St Margaret's Terrace, Cheltenham, Glos. (0242 526338).

Youth Hostels Association, 14 Southampton Street, London WC2 7HY (01–836 8541).

Motoring holidays

Vacances, 28 Gold Street, Saffron Walden, Essex (0799 25101).

18

Westbury Travel/Just France, Westfield House, Bratton Road, Westbury BA13 3EP (0373 826283).

Museums

Local tours by coach, car or train can be made by consulting Centre SCETA Régional, Cour de la Gare, Dijon Ville, 21000 Dijon (80.41.67.27 or 80.41.81.35). For bus tours, apply to Bourgogne Tour, 11 rue de la Liberté, 21000 Dijon (80.30.60.40).

Pilgrimages

Interchurch Travel, 45 Berkeley Street, London W1X 1FA (01–730 9842).
Mancunia Travel, 30 Brown Street, Manchester M2 2JR (061–834 4030).
Tee Mills Tours, 21 Balham High Road, London SW12 9AL (01–673 1923).

Rail travel

There is an efficient SNCF rail network which covers Burgundy with major stations at Auxerre, Dijon, Mâcon, Le Creusot and Nevers. Various discount cards are available. The *Rail Europe Family Card* costs £5. The adult holder pays full fare, but the family covered by the card (at least three travelling together) qualifies for a fifty per cent discount. The *Carte Couple* is issued free to couples travelling together, offering a fifty per cent discount to the second person. The *Carte Jeune* is available for young people between the ages of 12 and 25, and costs about 150 francs; it is valid for summer travel at a fifty per cent discount. The *Carte Jeune,* for the same age group, offers four journeys during a calendar year at a fifty per cent discount. The *Carte Vermeil* is available for senior citizens with a fifty per cent discount. *France Vacances* Rail Rover tickets are available for nine and sixteen-day holidays at special prices. SNCF, 179 Piccadilly, London W1V 0BA (01–409 1224).

Small tourist trains can be boarded in Ruffey-lès-Echirey (80.23.83.75; M. Hubert Gaugue), and for the valley of the river Ouche from 4 rue Pasumot, 21200 Beaune (80.22.86.35).

19

Son et Lumière

Office de Tourisme de Beaune (80.22.24.51). Also at
Bourg-en-Bresse, at the Église de Brou; at the Château
St-Fargeau (86.74.05.67); at Semur-en-Auxois; and at the
Château St-Hughes, Semur-en-Brionnais.

Walking and rambling holidays

The best base is the Morvan National Park, but the *Grandes
Randonnées* (the national footpaths) cross Burgundy; the GR3
alongside the Loire, the GR7 from the Plateau de Langres to
Mâcon, and the GR13 across the Morvan. A UK-based
company offering a walking holiday is:
Serenissima Travel, 21 Dorset Square, London NW1 5PG
   (01–730 9841).

Wine-tastings and vineyard visits

Consult 'La Cour aux Vins', 3 rue Jeannin, 21000 Dijon
(80.67.85.14); or L'Ambassade du Vin — Paul Cadiau at
Pernand-Vergelesses, 21420 Savigny-lès-Beaune (80.21.53.72);
or 'Comité Interprofessionnel pour les Vins AOC de Bourgogne',
rue Henri-Dunant, 21204 Beaune (80.22.21.35).

Wine tours and tasting holidays

Francophiles (Discover France), 66 Great Brockeridge, Bristol
   BS9 3UA (0272 621975).
Glenton Tours, 114 Peckham Rye, London SE15 4JE
   (01–639 9777).
David Walker Travel (Wines and Gastronomy), see Coach
   tours.
Licensed Trade Travel, 38 Store Street, London WC1E 7BZ
   (01–580 6762).
World Wine Tours, 71 North Street, London SE4 0HE
   (01–622 9317).
French Leave Holidays (Tour FMF 1443), see Hotel
   holidays.
Vintage Wine Tours, 8 Belmont, Lansdowne Road, Bath
   (0225 315834).

Other inclusive holidays to Burgundy are offered by French Leave Holidays, 21 Fleet Street, London EC4 (01–583 8383) by air (British Airways and Air France); by National Express bus; by rail (British Rail and SNCF) and by car (ferry and hotel bookings). Their hotels are based in Dijon, Tournus, Cluny, Mâcon, Fleurville, Chalon-sur-Saône and Salles-en-Beaujolais.

Some other useful addresses

Travel Trade Departments, French Government Tourist Office, 178 Piccadilly, London W1V 0AL (01–491 7622).

SNCF French Railways, 179 Piccadilly, London W2V 0BA (01–409 1224).

French Consulate General, College House, 29–31 Wrights Lane, London W8 (01–937 1202).

Gîtes de France Ltd., 178 Piccadilly, London W1V 0AL (01–493 3480).

French Embassy (Commercial Department), 21–24 Grosvenor Place, London SW1 7HV (01–235 7080).

French Chamber of Commerce, 54 Conduit Street, London W1R 9SD (01–439 1735).

Tourist information centres

In addition to the local Syndicats d'Initiative to be found in practically every town in Burgundy, there are three tourist information centres on the A6 motorway which bisects Burgundy: Aire Principale de Service d'Auxerre-Venoy (86.52.03.44); Aire Principale de Beaune-Tailly, Acceuil Information (80.22.28.09); and Antenne Touristique de Gissey-le-Vieil, Bureau de Tourisme (80.90.83.12). Each departmental Préfecture has a very helpful major tourist office in Dijon (80.43.42.12); in Nevers (86.57.80.25); in Mâcon (85.38.21.00) and in Auxerre (86.52.26.27).

Regular events

January St Vincent's Day on the 22nd, or the Saturday

21

following, is usually celebrated in all the wine-growing areas.

February In Chalon-sur-Saône the 'Foires aux Sauvagines' take place on the 27th, attracting huge crowds for the 'Foire froide'. The carnival, with music and parade of floats, takes place for a week at the end of February/beginning of March.

March-April On Palm Sunday the wines are auctioned at Nuits-St-Georges.

May-June On Whit Monday the traditional horse race, 'Fête de la Bague', takes place at Semur-en-Auxois.

June On the third Sunday is the Lighterman's Day at St-Jean-de-Losne. The summer music festival takes place at Dijon, as does the formula one car-racing Grand Prix, on the first weekend in the month. Pilgrimages at Pontigny and Paray-le-Monial.

July In many villages the 'Festival des Nuits de Bourgogne' takes place on Fridays and Saturdays. On the 14th, water jousting takes place at Clamecy (Nièvre). The 22nd is St Mary Magdalene's Day and feast at Vézelay. In the second half of the month is a music festival at Autun.

In mid-summer a festival of music takes place in several towns, as does the Burgundy Theatre Festival and Dijon Summer Festival of films, concerts, plays and ballet. Concerts are held at Vézelay. Cluny has an art exhibition. A period costume festival is held at St-Fargeau (Yonne) from 19 July to the end of August, with a cast of 600 actors, 3,000 costumes, 50 cavaliers on horseback, dancers, musicians, troubadours, etc.

August On the first Monday the International Cycling Championship is held at Château-Chinon (Nièvre). On the first Sunday of the month (alternate years) the International Folklore Fête is held at Charolles. On the 15th there is water jousting at Coulmanges-sur-Yonne (Yonne), and also the Wines Fair at Pouilly-sur-Loire (Nièvre). At the end of August is the Flower Festival at St-Honoré-les-Bains (Nièvre), and the Charollais Cattle Festival at Bouhans (Saône-et-Loire). There are concerts at Cluny on Saturdays, and in the abbey church at Tournus. In the second fortnight a Chamber Music Festival is held in Dijon. Montbard holds a Regional Fair on the 30th.

September In Dijon on the first or second weekend are held the 'Fête de la Vigne' and an international folklore fête. On the weekend closest to the 7th a pilgrimage and costume procession is held at Alise-Ste-Reine (Côte d'Or). The mystery of St Reine is played in the open air theatre 'Des Roches'. On the first Sunday the Grape Harvest Festival at Mâcon is held. At the end of the month a music festival is held in Nevers.

October The chestnut (*marrons*) fair is held at St-Léger-sous-Beuvray (Saône-et-Loire). The Sunday after the 16th the 'Fête de Ste Marguerite-Marie' is held at Paray-le-Monial. The famous International Food and Wines Fair is held at Dijon, usually in the first fortnight of November, starting on 30th October.

November On the Sunday closest to the 11th the Auxerre Wine Festival is held at St-Bris-le-Vineux (Yonne). On the third Saturday, Sunday and Monday an equally famous festival is held called 'The Three Days of Glory' at Vougeot, Beaune and Meursault, when the young wines are sold by auction. On the fourth Sunday of the month Chablis holds its 'Fête des Vins'.

Local fairs and fêtes

France, and particularly Burgundy, takes these very seriously. Even the smallest hamlet will usually have its own fête in August. Wherever you go in the summer months ask the hotel owner, or the Syndicat d'Initiative, when and where the local fête is being held. Since it would need a separate book to record all these, Auxerre is selected as an example. In May each year there is an annual Foire-Exposition, tel. 84.46.93.30. The trading markets are held on Tuesday, Friday and Saturday mornings in the place de l'Arquebuse, and on Sunday mornings in the place Degas. The monthly fair is held on the first Tuesday in the place de l'Arquebuse and boulevard Davout, and the annual 'Foire St Martin' takes place on 10 November.

Firework displays

Like most Latin countries, France and the Burgundians enjoy these spectacles enormously, and usually have them in July and August, at weekends. In the Yonne, for example, they are held at St-Julien-du-Sault, St-Père-sous-Vézelay, Tonnerre, Vermenton, Guillon, Toucy, Villiers-St-Benoît, Noyers-sur-Serein, Rogny-lès-Sept-Écluses, Merry-sur-Yonne, Villeneuve-sur-Yonne, Armeau, Coulanges-sur-Yonne, Joigny and Avallon. The fireworks nearly always start at 10.00 p.m. and are usually set over the river, lake or port. The local Syndicat will tell you the time and place.

Local crafts

The French have had a great resurgence of a 'back-to-the-countryside' range of 'manufacturing' activities. Assuming the Yonne is the first département you will visit, going from north to south, you will find nine craft workshops for work in wool, silk, straw or leather, two making marionettes or dolls, seven for objects of stone or glass, five for wood, three for metal, and no less than twenty for pottery or porcelain. The day of the hand craftsman is back again in Burgundy.

Reading matter

The Companion Guide to Burgundy, by Robert Speaight (Collins, 1975), gives an excellent technical account of the architectural splendours of Burgundy.

Burgundy, by Anthony Turner and Christopher Brown (Batsford, 1977), gives a good account of the history of Burgundy, as does **Burgundy** by Stephen Lucius Gwynn (Constable, 1934).

The Country Wines of Burgundy and Beaujolais, by Patrick Delaforce (Lennard, 1987) presents good value wines of the region and pinpoints where best to obtain them in the U.K.

The Wines of Burgundy, by H. W. Yoxall (Penguin, 1974), covers the same subject.

Guide de Tourisme de Bourgogne (Michelin, 1982, green covers) is an excellent, well-presented guide. It does not, however, cover wine, wine co-operatives, hotels, restaurants, gîtes, etc.

CHAPTER THREE:
THE WINES OF THE REGION

The wines and their vineyards described in this book are those to be found in the four adjacent départements which compose modern Burgundy. There is a separate section on the Beaujolais wines grown south of Mâcon. As early as AD 630, the dukes of Burgundy were granting lands, planted with vines, to hard-working monks. Later, St Bernard and the monks of Cîteaux created many Cistercian vineyards which exist to this day, the famous Clos Vougeot and the Clos de Bèze being but two examples. Burgundy, including Beaujolais now produces about 2.2 million hectolitres of wine each year. The main wine-growing areas, with production figures in hectolitres, are as follows:

	white wines	red and *rosé* wines
Chablis	140,000	—
Côtés de Beaune	40,000	115,000
Côte de Nuits	negligible	140,000
Côte Chalonnaise	9,300	32,000
Le Mâconnais	175,000	61,000
Beaujolais	6,000	1,265,000
Regional *appelations*	102,000	114,000
	472,300	1,727,000

The overall proportions in the whole of Burgundy are: white wines about 21.5 per cent; red and *rosé* wines about 78.5 per cent. Later in this book, within the regional chapters, there are lists of the wine villages where tasting facilities are available. It should be remembered that the word '*degustation*' embodies a commercial invitation to stop, to try a glass or two of the local wine *and* to buy a bottle or two of it. It is not an offer to the weary traveller of a free drink to help him on his way!

From the point of view of the *vigneron* (wine-grower), the best months for visits are between November and January, when outdoor work is at a minimum. Try in any case to avoid the *vendange* months of September and October, although the major wine co-operatives have a tasting facility throughout the year. For the smaller *vignerons,* Saturday is the most favoured day for visits.

The *raison d'être* for wine co-operatives is to be found in areas where small *vignerons* are unable to make and sell their wine profitably. Banded together with good management and capital deployed for purpose-built *chais* (wine stores) the end result is a reliable, honest, well-made wine, marketed successfully at a modest price. In the very well-known small vineyards of the Côte d'Or there is less necessity for co-operatives as to a certain extent the famous wines sell themselves to buyers from all over the world. But in the regions of the Côte Chalonnaise, Côte de Beaune, Côte de Mâcon and Beaujolais, efficient co-operatives thrive to everybody's profit. Many co-operatives make a small charge of 3 to 6 francs per glass for visitors, which may be waived if a purchase of bottles (usually from 16–45 francs) is later made.

A brief word about the wine classifications, which are rigorously controlled in France. The real aristocrats among vineyards are called *les grands crus,* which are so grand that they are known simply by the vineyard name without a mention of the commune on the label. But in some cases a commune has added its name to the most famous local vineyard in order to cash in on its reputation. Gevrey-Chambertin is an area commune, not a single famous vineyard. Vosne-Romanée is also the name of a commune. Wine bearing the label of a genuine *grand cru* single vineyard can be double or triple the price of wine bearing the collective name of the commune next door.

The *premier crus* are the next rank below the *grands crus*. The name of the commune now comes first, such as 'Volnay-Chevrets'. Usually the words 'Premier Cru' are on the label. The commune *appellation* applies to wines from a group of vineyards or communes, such as Santenay, Volnay, Pommard etc. The name of the vineyard must be printed in letters half the size of the commune.

Wine vintages vary from year to year depending on nature's demands. Heavy frosts, too much rain, too much sun and other permutations will affect the final vintage result. Generally speaking, the finer wines of the Côte d'Or (i.e. from Dijon to Beaune) have produced good recent vintages for their red wines in 1983, 1982 and 1978. Conversely, 1981 was an indifferent year, and 1980 and 1979 only average. For the white wines of the Côte d'Or the pattern was similar; 1983, 1982 and 1978 were excellent years, 1980 was a poor year, and 1984, 1981 and 1979 were average. Of course, within these groupings there were exceptions.

The wine-growing areas that should be visited are listed below in a roughly north-to-south order.

Chablis is due east of Auxerre. Only white wines are made in the area, in four quality categories. *Grand cru* Chablis comes only from the seven vineyards on the east side of the town across the river Serein: Blanchot, Les Clos, Valmur, Grenouilles, Vaudésir, Preuses and Bougros. Next come the *premiers crus,* some well-known vineyards being Montée de Tonnerre, Fourchaume, Les Fourneaux, Côte de Lechet, Beauroy, Vaucoupin, Vosgros, Les Lys, Vaulorent, Monts de Milieu and Montmains. The third category is Chablis, without a vineyard specification, and finally Petit Chablis, which is the lowest category for quality.

Les Côteaux d'Auxerre vineyards are just south of Auxerre. The 'Clos de la Chainette' is well known. Others are Chitry, St-Bris, Irancy and Coulanges-la-Vineuse. The first two produce Bourgogne Blanc, Aligoté and Sauvignon, and the latter two good Bourgogne reds and *rosés.*

At St-Bris-le-Vineux there is an excellent co-operative, Sicava, producing 'Crémant de Bourgogne' — white sparkling Burgundy grown under precise Champagne-quality procedures. The other three small areas are Épineuil (near Tonnerre), Joigny and Vézelay.

Further west in the département of Nièvre, there are two wine-

27

growing areas mentioned in more detail in the relevant chapter. At Pouilly-sur-Loire there are two communes on the 'Route des Vins' — Tracy and St Andelain, producing Pouilly Blanc Fumé from the Sauvignon grape, and Le Chasselas, a lighter white wine. A little further north, Cosne-Cours-sur-Loire produces a reasonable red wine.

From the Nièvre we move due east to the Côte d'Or. The first wine-growing area is the **Hautes-Côtes** de Nuits, a long, thin strip bordering on the N74 due south from Dijon. It is called the 'Route des Grands Crus', and technically ends at a village called Corgoloin. This area of about 20 km. in length and a few hundred metres in width encompasses some of the finest red wine 'names' in the world: Gevrey-Chambertin, Chambolle-Musigny, Vougeot, Vosne-Romanée, Nuits-St-Georges and others.

On this golden wine route the first port of call is **Gevrey-Chambertin**. Amongst the 400 hectares of vineyards are no less than eight legendary *grands crus* — more than any other commune in Burgundy. The two 'Kings of Kings' are Chambertin itself and Chambertin Close de Bèze. The six lesser 'Kings' have 'Chambertin' added after the vineyard name — Charmes, Ruchottes, Griotte, Mazoyres, Latricières, Mazis — all famous red wines. Hilaire Belloc produced the classic phrase 'I forget the name of the place, I forget the name of the girl, but the wine was Chambertin.' Next come the commune of **Morey-St-Denis**, which has five *grands crus* — Clos-St-Denis, Clos de la Roche, Clos de Tart, Clos de Lambrays and Bonnes Mares.

Chambolle-Musigny follows, which has two *grands crus* — Musigny and Les Bonnes Mares. It also has a dozen *premier crus* which are considered on a par with most *grands crus,* including Les Charmes and Les Amoureuses. Next comes **Vougeot,** which is a large walled commune, all under the 'Grand Cru' cognomen. Then **Vosne-Romanée,** which produces the most expensive wines in the world — the *grands crus* Romanée Conti, La Tâche and Richebourg. Next door is the commune of Échézeaux with two *grands crus* — Les Échézeaux and Grands Échézeaux.

28

The **Nuits-St-Georges** commune is the largest in the département of the Côte d'Or. There are no *grands crus* but many *premiers crus*, including Les St Georges, Pruliers, Cailles, Poirets and Vaucrains.

Continuing on the N74 to Beaune and still further south are the **Côtes de Beaune** and the **Hautes-Côtes de Beaune**, with more famous names — Aloxe-Corton, Pommard, Volnay, Santenay, Chassagne-Montrachet, and the famous white wine of Meursault.

Aloxe-Corton is a few kilometres north of Beaune. It has the *grands crus* Le Corton, Corton-Charlemagne (white) and Charlemagne. It also has seven *premiers crus*. Savigny-lès-Beaune borders on Beaune itself with many *premiers crus*. Pommard is a large commune, but has no single well-known vineyard apart from Les Rugiens. There are no *grands crus* in Beaune, but Volnay, a small commune south-west of Pommard, has some excellent *premiers crus*.

From Volnay via Monthélie, to neighbouring Meursault, Puligny-Montrachet and Chassagne-Montrachet, all three communes straggling south from Beaune towards Mâcon. All three have superlative white wines. The *grands crus* are Montrachet, Chevalier-Montrachet, Bâtard, Les Croits and Bienvenues. The little village of **Blagny** is the melting-pot between and including the Meursault and Montrachets.

Halfway between Beaune and Mâcon are the **Mercurey** or Chalonnais and Mâconnais regions, where the wine co-operatives come into their own in the département of Saône-et-Loire. The main vineyards in the Mercurey area are at Chagny, Rully, Mercurey itself, Givry and Montagny on the D981, still heading due south. Rully and Montagny wines are mainly white; Mercurey and Givry mainly red. Besides Bourgogne Aligoté, a fruity, lively white wine, there is the aptly named Bourgogne Passe-Tout-Grains red. Leading wine experts in the UK rate the Chardonnay grape white wines of Montagny, and the Pinot Noir grape red wines of Mercurey, Rully and Givry (and the white from the same areas) as the best-value wines from Burgundy appearing on the English wine market.

29

In the Mâconnais area, Pouilly-Fuissé Blanc is well known. Nearby are the wine co-operatives of Solutré, Prissé, Viré and Chaintré, which produce mainly good, honest white wines. But the majority of Mâcon production is plain, red wines — Mâcon Rouge is not as good value as Mâcon Blanc. Indeed, the village *appellations* of Mâcon-Viré, Mâcon-Lugny, Pouilly-Vinzelles, Pouilly-Loché and, of course, Pouilly-Fuissé, offer consistently good value.

Some 50 km. due east of Mâcon the area round **Bourg-en-Bresse**, famous for its poultry, produces some good-value, honest wines. Examples are the white Roussette de Vireu and Roussette de Seyssel, the red Mondeuse and Château Laman, and the Cerdon Rosé.

Wine type/production

Santenay 8,000 hl, 98 per cent red (Pinot Noir).

Bourgogne Hautes-Côtes de Beaune 1,000 hl red and *rosé* (Pinot Noir).

Côtes de Beaune-Villages 4,000 hl red (Pinot Noir) and white (Pinot Chardonnay).

Bourgogne Blanc 15,000 hl (Pinot Blanc and Chardonnay).

Bourgogne Rouge 40,000 hl Pinot Noir.

Bourgogne Aligoté 45,000 hl Aligoté, occasionally with Pinot-Chardonnay.

Rully 3–5,000 hl, 50 per cent red (Pinot Noir) and 50 per cent white (Pinot-Chardonnay).

Bourgogne Passe-Tout-Grains 18–20,000 hl mixed two-thirds Gamay Noir (*white juice*) with one-third Pinot.

Mercurey 18–20,000 hl red (Pinot Noir) and a little white (Pinot-Chardonnay).

Givry 5,000 hl red (Pinot Noir) and a little white (Pinot-Chardonnay).

Montagny 4,000 hl Bourgogne Blanc (Pinot-Chardonnay).

Mâcon Blanc 10,000 hl Pinot Blanc and Chardonnay.

Mâcon Blanc Villages 100,000 hl white wines.

Mâcon Rouge 55,000 hl Gamay Noir *à jus blanc.*

Mâcon Rosé 25,000 hl Gamay Noir *à jus blanc*: special vinification.

Pouilly-Fuissé blanc. 40,000 hl Pinot Blanc and Chardonnay.

St-Vérand 20,000 hl white (Pinot Blanc and Chardonnay).

Pouilly-Vinzelles and Pouilly-Loché 4,000 hl Pinot-Chardonnay.

Hl = hectolitre

Beaujolais

In the very south of the Saône-et-Loire département and in the northern sector of the Rhône département is the wine-growing area of Beaujolais. Villefranche-sur-Saône is the regional capital; Beaujeu and Belleville are two small wine towns. The best-quality areas are north of Villefranche. A total of 1,265,000 hectolitres of wine is made each year, mainly from the Gamay grape.

Production of white wine is only about 6,000 hectolitres. There are three categories of quality: Beaujolais, Beaujolais Supérieur (or Villages) and the *grands crus*. One of the differences between the first two is alcoholic strength: the former has a minimum strength of 9 degrees for red and 9.5 degrees for white, and the latter 10 degrees for red and 10.5 degrees for white. Beaujolais Villages wines are grown on a 22,000 hectare area, of which the 'Appellation Contrôlé' *crus* are limited to 40 hectolitres of wine per hectare, compared to 50 hectolitres for the lesser qualities.

The area of Beaujolais is concentrated into a rectangle roughly 55 km. from north to south, and 15 km. in width. The traveller from the north should pass through St-Amour (260 hectares and 16,000 hectolitres), Juliénas (560 ha. and 33,000 hl.), Chénas (240 ha. and 14,000 hl.), Moulin-à-Vent (640 ha. and 38,000 hl.), Fleurie (800 ha. and 50,000 hl.), Chiroubles (320 ha. and 19,000 hl.), Morgon (1,050 ha. and 60,000 hl.), Côte-de-Brouilly (290 ha. and 19,000 hl.), Brouilly (1,200 ha. and 75,000 hl.), Beaujolais Villages (6,300 ha. and 380,000 hl.) and finally Beaujolais (9,100 ha. and 550,000 hl.). There are between 9,000 and 13,000 vines of Gamay Noir planted per hectare. The vintage is usually in mid-September and lasts two or three weeks. The fermentation lasts five to seven days. After the grapes have had the main pressing, the remains of grapes, skins and pips are distilled to make Marc or Eau de Vie de Bourgogne.

There are 2,500 small family-owned vineyards from one to four hectares, and 1,400 between four and seven hectares. Very few vineyards are over seven hectares in size. The most popular storage container is a wooden cask (la pièce) of 216 litres, which is the basic sale unit. Smaller containers are la feuillette of 110 litres, le quartant of 50–55 litres, le demi-muid of 6 hectolitres. The main storage casks of wood or of cement are usually of 50 hectolitres.

The price differentials are interesting. The standard cask of 216 litres of Beaujolais averages about 1,900 francs, Beaujolais Villages 2,100 francs, Brouilly 2,600 francs, Chénas 2,400 francs, Chiroubles between 3,000 and 4,000 francs, Côte-de-Brouilly 2,600 francs, Fleurie 3,200 francs, Juliénas 3,000 francs, Morgon 2,700 francs, Moulin-à-Vent 3,500 francs and St-Amour 3,100 francs. In 1978–79 prices were about 25 per cent higher for the named crus than they are now. Prices are naturally more stable for the larger amounts of Beaujolais and Beaujolais Supérieur made each year.

The hypermarchés (super-supermarkets) in France now account for 50 per cent of domestic sales of Beaujolais. Switzerland is the largest export market, followed by USA and West Germany, with the UK in fourth place with 83,000 hectolitres on average each year.

Beaujolais Nouveau or Primeur is a very young, light and fruity red wine which is eagerly awaited each year from about 15 November, not only in France — especially Paris — but in other European capitals, including London. The race is to the swiftest, but perhaps it is better to journey than to arrive? Beaujolais Nouveau now accounts for nearly 55 per cent of all sales.

Monsieur Berger is the president, and M. Canard is the secretary of the 'Fédération des Co-opératives Vinicoles du Rhône'. 210 boulevard Vermorel, 69400 Villefranche-sur-Saône, tel. 74.65.39.32. There are eighteen co-operatives and two 'Groupements de Producteurs' in Beaujolais. Several villages in the Saône-et-Loire make AC Beaujolais wines — St Vérand, Chaintré, Chânes and St-Amour. Many AOC areas overlap each other.

Le Bois-d'Oingt, tel. 74.70.62.81, has a tasting *caveau*, 'Terrasse des Pierres Dorées', open at weekends only. A few km. south-west of Villefranche, created in 1959, this co-op has 128 *vignerons* farming 210 hectares and producing 13,000 hectolitres each year.

Bully, tel. 74.01.27.77, has a *caveau* open on weekends and holidays. The members farm 476 hectares, of which 50 per cent is made as Beaujolais Nouveau.

Chénas, tel. 74.04.11.91, is at the Château de Chénas, founded in 1934, and has 270 *vigneron* members on 250 hectares producing 15,000 hectolitres.

Chiroubles, tel.74.04.20.47. Tasting either at the *caveau* of the co-op or at the 'Chalet de Dégustation de la Terrasse'. It was founded in 1929 and has a 'museum' of 2,000 varieties of vines at the Domaine de Tempéré.

Corcelles-en-Beaujolais. 'Éventail de Vignerons Producteurs' tel. 74.66.03.89. This group of forty *domaines/vignerons* is based on an attractive manor house or wine château stocking *crus* of Beaujolais and of the Mâconnais. Tasting at the château daily.

Fleurie. 'Cave co-op des Grands Vins', tel. 74.04.11.70. Tasting either at the co-op or at 'Le Caveau', open all the year round. Founded in 1927, it has 305 members farming 373 hectares producing 17,000 hectolitres.

Gleizé. The 'Co-operative Vinicole', tel. 74.65.39.49, is a couple of km. south-west of Villefranche. The *caveau* is open every day. Founded in 1932. Its members farm 230 hectares.

Juliénas. The 'Cave Co-op des Grands Vins', tel. 74.04.42.61 is sited in a handsome manor house, the Château du Bois de la Salle. Alternatively, taste their AOC Juliénas in the 'Cellier de la Vieille Église'. Founded in 1960, the members farm 300 hectares.

Lachassagne, tel. 74.67.01.43, is 8 km. due south of Villefranche. Tasting at weekends only. Founded in 1954. The 123 *vignerons* farm 208 hectares.

Létra. 'Cave Co-op Beaujolaise', tel. 74.70.30.52. Tasting on Sundays and holidays. Founded in 1956. The 175 members farm 400 hectares.

Liergues. 'Cave Co-op Vinicole', tel. 74.68.07.94. Tasting on Sundays and holidays. Liergues is a few km. south-west of Villefranche, on the same road as Gleizé. Founded in 1929. The members farm 250 hectares and produce 12,000 hectolitres.

Le Perréon. 'Cave Co-op Beaujolaise', tel. 74.03.22.83. Tastings every day except Tuesday. Founded in 1958. The members farm 250 hectares and produce 12,000 hectolitres.

Quincié-en-Beaujolais. 'Producteurs, Distributeurs des Vins du Beaujolais' is at Le Pont des Samsons, tel. 74.04.30.35. Created in 1928, the *cave* has capacity for 68,000 hectolitres.

St-Bel. 'Cave Co-op des Coteaux du Lyonnais', tel. 74.01.11.33. Founded in 1956. The 230 members farm 180 hectares.

St-Étienne-des-Oullières. 'Cave Co-op de St Étienne', tel. 74.03.43.69. Tasting at the 'Caveau de St-Étienne' every day except Friday. 8 km. north-west of Villefranche. Founded in 1958. The members farm 388 hectares.

St-Jean-d'Ardières. 'Cave Co-op Bel-Air', tel. 74.66.13.92. Tastings at 'Caveau Vivier Daniel' at Les Rochons, or 'Domaine de Ruty', or 'Maison des Beaujolais' on RN6 — all open every day. Founded in 1930. The 300 members farm 425 hectares.

St-Laurent d'Oingt. 'Cave Co-op Beaujolaise', tel. 74.70.20.51. This is a modern purpose-built *chai* where the usual Beaujolais AOC red can be bought in bottles, *bonbonnes* or *cubitainers*. Tasting at the 'Belvedere des Pierres Dorées' every day except Sunday and holidays. Founded in 1960. The members farm 260 hectares.

St-Vérand. 'Cave Co-op Beaujolaise', tel. 74.70.73.19. Tastings only on weekends or holidays. This is the northern-most AOC Beaujolais wine. Founded in 1959. The members farm 320 hectares.

Theizé. 'Cave Beaujolaise de Beauvallon', tel. 74.70.75.97. Tastings at the *chais* on weekends and holidays and at 'Caveau Delacolonge' every day. Founded in 1959. The 173 members farm 332 hectares. The village is about 11 km. south-west of Villefranche.

Other villages offering tastings are Beaujeu, Châtillon-d'Azergues, Chazay d'Azergues, Cogny, Jullié, Jacenas, Lucenay, Odenas, Pommier, Regnié-Durette, St-Jean-des-Vignes, St-Lager, Salles, Vaux-en-Beaujolais and Villié-Morgon. Many of the smaller co-operatives stock their wines in small oak casks, rarely aged beyond three or four years.

The eighteen *caves co-opératives* account for 43 per cent of the sales of Beaujolais Nouveau (75 per cent of which is Beaujolais and 25 per cent Beaujolais Villages). They are responsible for 4,000 *vignerons* farming 5,400 hectares of vines and producing each year about 300,000 hectolitres, out of the grand total of 2.2 million hectolitres from the whole of the region.

Now for a look at the individual areas.

AOC Brouilly covers the communes of Odenas, St-Lager, Cercié, Quincié and Charentay. At Odenas is the beautiful Château de la Chaize, built in 1676 — a historic monument. The Marquis de Roussy de Sales has won many *Médailles d'Or* at Paris for his AOC Brouilly. The Château is the longest storage cave in Beaujolais — 108 metres in length! The Brouilly wine is fruity but soft, with a well-developed bouquet but drink it young. The small villages of St-Étienne-

Ia-Varenne and St-Lager are also in the Brouilly region.

AOC Chénas was once an area covered by *chênes* (oak trees), hence the name. Now it is known for its vineyards and its windmills. Moulin-à-Vent is a well-known name for the vineyards to the east and south of Chénas. The wine is generous, fruity and *bouqueté*, but lighter than Moulin-à-Vent. Communes include La Chapelle de Guinchay (in the Saône-et-Loire) and Chénas itself.

AOC Chiroubles produces a fruity, tender, charming wine which needs to be drunk young and fresh. Besides the commune of Chiroubles there is Villié-Morgon.

AOC Côte-de-Brouilly is the name given to the vineyards along the hills of Brouilly which are shared with Cercié, Odenas, Quincié-en-Beaujolais and St-Lager. The wine is a dark purple colour, of high alcoholic strength, fruity and *bouqueté* — one of the best in Beaujolais.

AOC Fleurie is a light, perfumed wine 'evoking spring-time flowers', again to be drunk young and fresh in order to taste the grapy flavour. Villages include Chiroubles (again), Emeringes, Fleurie itself, Lancié and Romanèche-Thorins (in the Saône-et-Loire). Try the 'Bon Cru' restaurant, route de Romanèche, in Fleury.

AOC Juliénas has a very long history of making wines when the rest of Beaujolais was still wooded. Juliénas is a fresh and fruity wine, but darker and fuller bodied than neighbouring St-Amour. It should be drunk young, like most Beaujolais. Villages include La Chapelle de Guinchay (in the Saône-et-Loire), Jullié, and Juliénas itself, where at the restaurant 'Chez la Rose', tel. 74.04.41.21., you can taste *coq au vin maison, andouillettes* or *escargots,* and drink the proprietor's own wine. The Château de Juliénas and Château des Capitans have working *vignerons* and vineyards.

AOC Morgon is a rather different wine — more of a Burgundy than a true Beaujolais. It has a strong, dark colour (like granite, they say locally) with a perfume of redcurrants and kirsch, and a robust, fruity base which allows it to mature for better drinking. Communes include Chiroubles, Lancié, Lantignié and Villié-Morgon. Two of the local *ferme-manoirs* are called Château Bellvue and Château Grange-Clochard.

AOC Moulin-à-Vent is the name for the commune of Romanèche-Thorins and La Chapelle de Guinchay, both villages being in the Saône-et-Loire département. It is a coarser wine of deep ruby colour, and is claimed to be the best Beaujolais! Some older Moulin-à-Vent, aged in bottles, produces a body, bouquet and class almost that of the Côte d'Or red wines. Both villages have a population of 2,000 with many small local châteaux and, of course, ancient windmills.

AOC St-Amour covers part of La Chapelle de Guinchay, Leynes and St-Amour-Bellevue (all three villages in the Saône-et-Loire) and part of Juliénas. In a village with this name, what more appropriate than to try AOC St-Amour with the local regional specialities at a meal at the 'Auberge du Paradis' in the village, tel. 85.37.10.26. But Paradise is closed on Thursdays!

Finally, **AOC Beaujolais-Villages** is claimed by certain *vignerons* at Beaujeu, Blacé, Charentay, Denicé, Jarnious, Jullié, Lancié, Lantignié, Montmelas, Le Perréon, Quincié-en-Beaujolais, Regnié-Durette, St-Etienne-des-Oullières, St-Étienne-la-Varenne, St-Lager, Salles-Arbuissonnas, Vaux and Villié-Morgon.

Harper's *Wine and Spirit Magazine* sponsors an annual tasting at the end of November in London of the wide range of Beaujolais Villages Nouveau (usually about nine entries) and Beaujolais Nouveau (usually about forty entries). In 1986 Georges Duboeuf, imported by Berkmann Wine Cellars, won the first category and Louis Jeanniard, imported by Knightsbridge Wines, won the second category. It should be noted that Jaffelin Beaujolais Nouveau, imported by Jackman, Surtees & Dale has been in the first three for three consecutive years. Also in the 1986 tasting, Charles Vienot wine was in the first three in both categories.

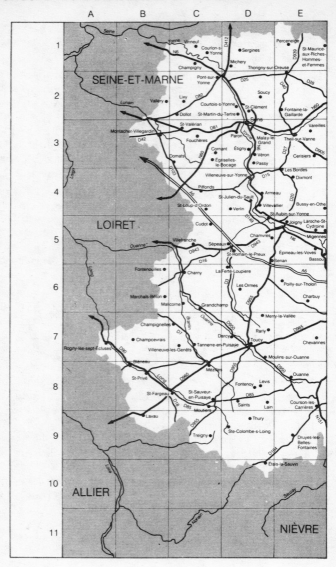

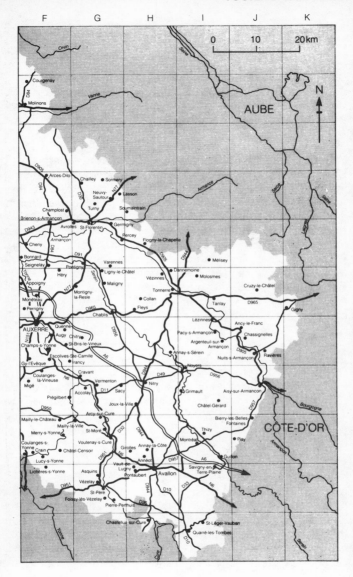

CHAPTER FOUR :
TOURING THE YONNE

The département of the Yonne is the north-western part of Burgundy, likely to be first visited by the traveller coming from either Paris or the Champagne country. It takes its name from the beautiful, placid river on which the major towns — Sens, Joigny and Auxerre — are to be found. The Yonne has a population of 300,000, spaced over an area of 7,500 square kilometres. The truly essential places to visit are Auxerre, Avallon and Vézelay, with side-trips to Chablis, for its world-famous white wine, and Pontigny, for its historical links with England. Visit, too, the marvellous châteaux of Tanlay and Ancy-le-Franc — among the finest in Burgundy. The two major towns in the Yonne on which to base regional tours are Sens and Auxerre. A third possibility is Avallon.

Sens

In Sens the Syndicat d'Initiative has devised a circular tour, or *circuit touristique,* of the city which can be done easily on foot. The Syndicat is in the place Jean-Jaurès, on the main road coming from Paris, tel. 86.65.19.49. There are thirty-three points of call.

- **North-west tour**
  A suggested north-west regional tour from Sens follows a route initially due west to Villeroy, St-Valérien, and either north to Dollot or west to Cheroy, then north to Valléry, Villethierry, Champigny-sur-Yonne, Chaumont, Courlon and then south-east to Serbonnes, Pont-sur-Yonne, Villenavotte, Nailly, St-Martin-du-Tertre and back to Sens. This tour is called 'Le Gatinais' and covers the northern valley of the river

Yonne. Look at the châteaux of Nailly, Valléry and Chaumont.

- **South-west tour**

The south-west tour is via Paron, Gron, Collemiers, Cornant, Egrisselles-le-Bocage, Chaumont, Piffonds, St-Martin-d'Ordon, Verlin, east to St-Julien and Villevallier, and north to Armeau and Le'Grand Palteau. Linger in Villeneuve-sur-Yonne, and return via Rousson, Marsangy and Étigny to Sens. Look at the châteaux of Marsangy, Chaumont and Piffonds and the church at Étigny.

- **North-east tour**

The north-east tour wanders through the minor roads to St-Clément, Soucy, north-west to La Chapelle and Fleurigny, east to Thorigny-sur-Oreuse, north to Grange and Sognes, south-east to St-Maurice, Courgenay and Vauluisant, Villeneuve l'Archevêque, west to Foissy, Saligny, and back to Sens. This tour is called 'La Champagne Sénonaise et la forêt de Lancy'. Look at the châteaux of Fleurigny, standing proudly surrounded by a moat; Thorigny, the manor house de la Houssaye (6 km. east of Sens, near Malay-le-Grand) and the churches of Soucy, Sognes and Villeneuve l'Archevêque (and the old windmills there).

- **South-east tour**

The south-east tour, known as the 'Circuit de la forêt et du pays d'Othe', runs via Maillot, Malay-le-Grand, Le Close de Noe, Theil, Vaumort, Cerisiers, Villechetive, south to Bussy-en-Othe, north through the forest of Othe to Dixmont, Les Bordes, Grange au Doyen, west to Passy, north to Sens, via Veron and Rosoy. Look at the château of Passy, the churches of Dixmont, Cerisiers and Maillot, the cider apple orchards of the Othe, and the lakes of St-Ange.

Auxerre

In Auxerre the main Syndicat d'Initiative is at 1–2 quai de la République, overlooking the River Yonne, tel. 86.52.26.27 and 86.52.06.19. They recommend a tour of the city taking in seventeen places, including the cathedral of St-Étienne, the préfecture, the abbey of St Germain, the clock tower, the

41

town hall and the church of St Pierre.

- **North-west tour**

The north-west regional tour leads due north to Joigny via Appoigny and Migennes, west on the N443 to Béon, Sépeaux and Charny, south-east on the N450 via Grandchamp and Villiers-St-Benoît to Toucy, and back due east to Auxerre on the N965. Look out for the fortified village and church of Appoigny and the church at Laroche-St-Cydroine, between Migennes and Joigny. You can then spend half a day happily looking at the attractive medieval town of Joigny and the château at Grandchamp.

- **Southern tour**

The southern circuit starts due south through the vineyards of Irancy and St-Bris-le-Vineux, Escolives and Coulanges, then due west through the Puisaye countryside to Druyes-les-Belles-Fontaines, Treigny, the château of Ratilly, north to the château of St-Fargeau, and back via Mezilles and Toucy to Auxerre. You may get lost between Coulanges-sur-Yonne and St-Fargeau on the minor roads! This is a delightful circuit embracing the Auxois vineyards, several very fine châteaux and the churches of Treigny and Toucy.

- **North-east tour**

The Auxerre circuit going north-east and east must be one of the most interesting in Burgundy. Drive north-east on the N77 to Pontigny, continue across the Armançon to St-Florentin, south-east via Flogny to Tonnerre, east to Tanlay, south to Ancy-le-Franc and cross country to Chablis; again you may get temporarily lost on these minor roads. After you have looked at Chablis, tasted the delicious wines at 'La Chablisienne' (and perhaps purchased some bottles), return due west on the D965 to Auxerre. This tour is perhaps too much for one day if you wish to stop at the major points — the magnificent abbey of Pontigny, the St-Florentin church, the finest châteaux in Burgundy at Tanlay and Ancy-le-Franc — and then go on to sample the dry, delicate white wines of Chablis.

● **South-east tour**

The south-eastern tour from Auxerre aims for the pretty medieval town of Noyers via Chablis and south on the D956. There are then two possibilities. Either continue east via Censy, Pasilly, Étivey and Aisy-sur-Armançon before heading south-west via Vassy, Santigny and Montréal to Avallon, or take the shorter route to Avallon following the river Serein.

Avallon

The Syndicat, which is located at 24 place Vauban, tel. 86.34.14.19, in one of the most attractive medieval houses in the town, recommends a twenty-eight-point visit taking in the collegiate church of St-Lazare, the Tower of the Elected, the town hall, the porte and bastion, the Gaujard Tower, law courts and museum, plus strolls along the ramparts.

Glorious **Vézelay** is half an hour's drive west from Avallon via Pontaubert and St-Père. You will need half a day to explore the basilica and the medieval village. Then either return direct to Avallon, or travel due north to Auxerre on the D951 via Blannay, Arcy-sur-Cure (where you should stop and look at the incredible grottoes), Vermenton (Romanesque-Gothic church), and Cravant (scene of the terrible Anglo-Scots battle) on the N6.

Highlights

Below is a selection of recommended places for visitors to see during their regional tour.

Annay-sur-Serein (H–7). Local craftsmen make carpets by hand, and there is a pottery. The nearby town of Perrigny has stone statues of St Germanus (Germain) and the English St Edmund Rich of Abingdon (Edmé).

Appoigny (F–6) was owned by St Germanus (Germain) of Auxerre and his family, and became the residence of successive bishops of Auxerre.

Arces-Dilo (F–4). St Thomas à Becket lived at Dilo, where he consecrated the church in 1168.

43

Arcy-sur-Cure (G–9) has a series of eighteen large natural grottoes situated along the line of the river Cure. Thousands of years ago these served as shelters for hunters of game, which included bears. A guided tour of 'la Grande Grotte', which takes nearly an hour, costs about twenty francs and covers one of the two and a half kilometres of grottoes. Well worth a visit. Open March to December.

Armeau (D–4). The Château de Palteau was owned by M. de Saint-Mars, the 'Man in the Iron Mask', who was banned from the Paris Court in 1698 for conspiracy. In the pretty village there is an old wine press of the type *à cage d'écureuil* (squirrel-cage).

Asquins (G–10) was for centuries a departure point for those making the great pilgrimage through France to north-west Spain to St James (Jacques) of Compostella. The annual fête of St Jacques is on the last Sunday of July.

Auxerre (F–7) is the préfecture and capital of the département and is twinned with Redditch in England. It knew commercial prosperity and peace under the Emperor Agrippa as the *chemin de Lyon,* and was a major route from the south to the northern sea harbours. But in the third century it was destroyed by the invading Alamans and Francs. The citizens then built a considerable *castrum* in quadrilateral shape, with a high wall, 1100 metres in perimeter, overlooking the river Yonne. Much of it — with some imagination — can be seen today between the rues Sous-Murs, des Boucheries and 4 Septembre. Auxerre became a bastion of Christianity in the fourth century. The old church of St Pèlerin stands on the site where the early Christian pilgrims came to the city. St Germanus (Germain) was the most celebrated Bishop of Auxerre in the period AD 418–448, and his fame spread throughout Europe. The first monastery in Auxerre, founded by him, attracted to it St Cosmé and St Damien. St Patrick, the evangeliser of the Irish, lived here for some time while studying under St Germanus. In 1424 King Henry VI ceded Auxerre to Duke Philip the Good of Burgundy, and it reverted to the French crown in 1477. The English occupation lasted for twenty years. At the time of the French Revolution there were twenty-seven churches in the town.

Auxerre perches on a hill overlooking the river. It is a most attractive town, with many sites of interest that should be visited. In the city centre is the old medieval quarter with a beautiful clock tower, town hall, episcopal palace, Roman gallery and ramparts. The cathedral of St Étienne, a Gothic edifice of the thirteenth century, has a very interesting and well-restored Romanesque crypt. The abbey of St Germain has famous Carolingian crypts, the 'Saintes-Grottes', claimed to be the most beautiful pre-Romanesque site in all France, with ninth-century frescoes. Two more churches which are worth a visit are St Pierre and St Eusèbe. In addition there are three interesting museums.

Avallon (H–10) was on Emperor Agrippa's road from Lyon to Boulogne and is part of Arthurian legend. In the seventeenth century new religious orders were installed there — the 'minimes' in 1607, the Capucins in 1653 and the 'visitandines' in 1660: the latter were nuns of the Order of the Visitation of the Virgin to St Elizabeth. Avallon is a picturesque town with extensive ramparts, six circular towers, bastions and a famous clock tower dating from 1456. There is a notable salt-store and also the collegiate church of St Lazare dating from the twelfth century. Well worth a visit.

Bassou (E–5) is a small village where, in the middle of the eighteenth century, the snails *(escargots)* of the Burgundian vines were discovered to be a gastronomic pleasure!

Bierry-les-Belles-Fontaines (J–9). In 1738 King Louis XV created the barony of Anstrude in favour of the Scottish family then called Anstrutter, Seigneurs of Bierry, who came to France centuries earlier to serve King Francis I. The Château d'Anstrude was built in the early eighteenth century and can be seen today.

Bléneau (B–8). The château and town were besieged by the English in 1359 at the start of the Hundred Years War. Both were owned for centuries by the powerful Courtenay family.

Bonnard (F–5). This little port on the river Yonne was built in 1672 in order to send the wines of Chablis and Tonnerre to the thirsty citizens of Paris.

45

Brienon-sur-Armançon (F–5) was owned for centuries by the archbishops of Sens until 1789. It was a fortified town in the fourteenth century, and was visited in 1429 by Joan of Arc. The little port is now a canal cruising centre, but was important for the transport of wood to Paris in the nineteenth century. This is a picturesque small town with avenues of lime trees, old houses with wine cellars, an old forge granary, and an oval stone washing tank dating from the seventeenth century. The sixteenth century collegiate church of St Loup is where on the first Sunday in September the saint's heart is shown at the *fête patronale.*

Chablis (G–6) was founded by the monks of St Martin de Tours who took refuge from the Norman invaders there in AD 867 with their holy relics, and set up a monastery under the protection of King Charles the Bald. In June 1940 the centre of the town was destroyed by German bombardments. Chablis is world famous for its white wines, and a visit to the wine co-operative is recommended. The 'Foire aux Vins' is held on the fourth Sunday in November. Chablis is well worth a visit. Look at the old grape press, the cellar of the monks of Pontigny, the 'L'Obédienceries' and the residence of the monks of St Martins of Tours. Above all, however, taste the famous white wine.

Champcevrais (B–7). In 1851 the inhabitants took part in the Rebellion de la Puisaye and many were transported as convicts to Algeria.

Champigny (C–1). At the harbour of Port Fouquet, local wines were shipped on the river Yonne to yet more thirsty citizens in Paris.

Champlost (F–4). In 1358 the château was captured by the English army commanded by Philbert de Vaudré, governor of Auxerrois for the Duke of Burgundy.

Champs-sur-Yonne (F–7). The wines of St-Bris were stored here before shipment to Paris on the river Yonne.

Charny (C–6) was occupied by the English in the fifteenth century.

Chastellux-sur-Cure (H–11). The feudal château of

Chastellux with eight towers dominates from its granite crags the valley of the river Cure. Marshal de Beauvoir, the conqueror at the battle of Cravant in 1423, lived here.

Châtel-Censoir (F–9) was owned by the bishops of Auxerre. Tradition has it that the church of St Potentien with its eleventh century Romanesque choir, was built on a pagan site. The grottoes 'des Fées' and the rock 'la Pierre qui Tourne' make it an interesting village to visit. The cult of St Potentien, the relics and miraculous spring, made Châtel-Censoir an important pilgrimage place up to the Revolution.

Châtel-Gérard (I–8) was the old hunting rendevous of the dukes of Burgundy.

Cravant (G–8), a bustling village, was the site of the bloody encounter between the Anglo-Burgundian army and the French-Scots army in 1423.

Cudot (C–5). A shepherdess named Alpais, born here in 1155, contracted leprosy at the age of twenty and was healed miraculously as the result of the appearance of the Virgin Mary. She survived for forty years living only on the Communion food, and performed miracles of healing. She discovered a miraculous spring which cured skin maladies. Alpais had many revelations, transcribed by the monks of Echarlis, in which she described the Solar System three hundred years before Copernicus and Galileo. She was canonized in 1874 and her tomb is in the church of Notre Dame in Cudot. The St Alpais fountain still produces clear drinking water for the village.

Dollot (C–2). The château was taken in 1426 after eight days of siege by the Earl of Warwick and his English troops.

Domats (C–3) has the miraculous fountain of St Clair.

Dracy (D–7). Joan of Arc stayed at the Château de la Bruyère in 1429.

Druyes-les-Belles-Fontaines (E–9). This little fortified village with noteworthy town gates and ruined château overlooks the twelfth-century church of St Romain and the grottoes of the 'Cave aux Fées' and of St Roman. Worth a visit to see castle, church and grottoes.

47

Escolives-Ste-Camille (F–7) is a major archaeological site with early Neolithic baths, gymnasium, covered swimming pool and small baths on pillars. Open during the summer.

Foissy-lès-Vézelay (G–10) has an important archaeological site, 'les Fontaines-Salées'.

Fontenoy (D–8), near Auxerre, was the scene of the bloody battle on 25 June 841 which divided Charlemagne's empire. There were far-reaching consequences for the rest of Europe, which the Treaty of Verdun two years later confirmed, and the Kingdom of France was then separated from the German Empire.

Grimault (I–8) has prehistoric grottoes called 'Grandes Gueules'.

Guillon (I–9). King Edward III of England signed a treaty here in 1360 with Philippe de Rouvres, Duke of Burgundy — to the latter's disadvantage!

Irancy (F–7). King Charles the Bald issued a diploma in AD 861 for the red wines of this pretty village with its vaulted wine cellars.

Joigny (E–5). This attractive town overlooks the river Yonne. It is well known for its wines of St Jacques, its medieval timbered houses, paved streets and covered passageways. The river was bridged before 1330 and the inhabitants are still proud of having beaten off the English troops in 1429. Joigny is known either as the *Porte de la Bourgogne* by those travelling south or *Clé de la Champagne* by those travelling north. The inhabitants became known as the *Maillotins* after they had murdered the Comte de Joigny with mallets!

Lain (D–8). Joan of Arc stayed at the Château de Test-Milon, which was owned by her companion Aymar de Prie, on her way to the coronation at Reims.

Lixy (C–2) has a set of ancient troglodyte habitations in the nearby hamlet of Fontanelles.

Malicorne (C–6). The old château served as a base for the military forays of the English *routiers* of Sir Robert Knollys in 1358.

Maligny (G–6). Sieur Gilles de Maligny defended his château here vigorously and successfully against the attacks of King Edward III in the fourteenth century.

Migé (F–8). The English troops occupied the château in 1356.

Migennes (E–5). Julius Caesar and his legions met those of his lieutenant Labienus here in 52 BC. The monks of Citeaux founded an early monastery in Migennes.

Montacher-Villegardin (B–3) was partly destroyed by German bombardment on 15 June 1940: the damage to the church of St Éloi has been repaired.

Montréal (I–9) is a medieval village perched on a hill where lived the sixth-century Queen Brunhaut and her grandson Thierry. King Edward III occupied the château here in 1360. The ancient collegiate church of Notre Dame is worth a visit. Built in the twelfth century, it was later restored by Viollet-le-Duc.

Moûtiers (C–8). A hospice for pilgrims, dedicated to St Peter, was founded here in AD 690. A monk Raoul Glaber, who lived c. 1000 at the priory, wrote of his encounters with the Devil. A miraculous fountain of St George is nearby.

Noyers (I–8). A medieval village with narrow vaulted lanes where the protestant Huguenots sheltered, until in 1568 Catherine of Medici's army captured it. The church of Notre Dame, aracades, law courts and museum merit a visit.

Paron (D–3). A penitent named Bond in the eleventh century founded a hermitage on the hill overlooking the village, later transformed into a priory. The old harbour on the river Yonne is called Port St Bond.

Pierre-Perthuis (G–10) was captured by English troops in 1360.

Pont-sur-Yonne (C–2). The walled town was captured by the English troops in 1420. Several centuries later Napoleon stayed here on his return from captivity on Elba.

Pontigny (G–5). The lonely, dignified abbey of Notre Dame and St Edmund (Edmé) of Pontigny merit a visit. The twelfth century Cistercian pile harboured three persecuted English archbishops — Thomas à Becket, Stephen Langton and Edmund Rich, who was buried there in 1240. As a consequence it became an important pilgrimage site.

Quarré-les-Tombes (I–11) was the site of battles long ago between the Normans and the Saracens. The eighth century sarcophagi can still be seen grouped around the church dedicated to St George, the patron saint of soldiers as well as of England. Of the original two thousand tombs, 112 are now on view from the ill-fated 'Quadrata Villa', the fortified quadrilateral camp where the slaughter took place.

St-Bris-le-Vineux (F–7) takes its name from the Christian martyred here in the fifth century. The church of St Prix et St Cot dates from the thirteenth century, and nestles amongst the picturesque dovecots and gabled old houses, many with vaulted wine cellars. The nearby wine caves of Bailly in the old stone quarries are also well worth a visit.

St-Clément (D–2). A young Spanish Christian, Colombe, was martyred north of Sens and her body abandoned near the fountain of Azon. King Clotaire II founded an abbey called Ste-Colombe-de-Sens in AD 620 and a chapel was built in St-Clément to honour the martyr. A pilgrimage takes place each year on Easter Friday.

St-Fargeau (C–8) has the interesting château of the same name and the church of St Ferréol, dating from the thirteenth century.

St-Florentin (G–5). Crocus, leader of the Vandals, martyred two young Christians, Florentin and his disciple Hilaire, here in AD 406. The relics were kept and a Benedictine abbey was built to house them. The town is also well known for Joan of Arc's visit in 1429 and more recently for its excellent local cheeses, St Florentin and Soumaintrain. This ancient hillside town, with its picturesque narrow streets, old houses, fortifications, ramparts, towers, grain market and church with exceptional stained glass windows and rood loft, is well worth a visit.

St-Léger-Vauban (I–11) is now more celebrated for being the birthplace of Marshal de Vauban, France's greatest military engineer, who was born here in 1633, than for the early Christian saint martyred a thousand years before.

St-Maurice-aux-Riches-Hommes-et-Femmes (E–1) has perhaps the most curious name in all Burgundy. Moreover, until 1793 it was also known as 'Maurice-les-Sans-Culottes' (breechless)!

St-Moré (G–9) is a tiny hamlet with no less than twenty-two prehistoric grottoes, near the river Cure. Nermont, Blaireau, L'Homme et Mammouth are the best known.

St-Père (G–10) is near Vézelay and has an important archaeological site called 'Les Fontaines Salées', ruins of Gallo-Roman thermal baths and mineral springs. A regional museum displays prehistoric objects, sculptures and coins. The village was occupied by the English in 1360.

Sainte-en-Puisaye (D–8). Priscus (St Prix, who became St Bris) and his companions, French-Roman soldiers converted to Christianity, were martyred here for their faith in the second century. St Germanus (Germain) of Auxerre built a monastery for them in the fifth century.

Seignelay (F–5). Charles de Savoisy, favourite of King Charles V, built in 1410 a magnificent château with thirteen towers in honour of Jesus Christ and the twelve apostles. Sadly it was demolished during the Revolution.

Sens (D–3) was a Christian city in the third century, converted by the saints Savinien and Potentien. Sens became the religious centre of a huge area including the bishoprics of Chartres, Auxerre, Paris, Orléans, Troyes and later Meaux and Nevers. Until 1622 the Archbishop of Sens was also titled Primate 'des Gaules'. Now it is a large, bustling city with the Gothic synodal Palace (restored by Viollet-le-Duc), the cathedral of St Étienne (with its famous treasury), several museums and many old timbered buildings. Well worth a visit.

Soucy (D–2) was destroyed by the English troops in the fourteenth century. The painter Jean Cousin (sixteenth century) and the poet d'Assoucy (seventeeth century) were born and lived here.

Tanlay (I–6) was famous for its Huguenot traditions of the seventeenth century, whose leaders lived in the marvellous château of the same name.

Tannerre-en-Puisaye (C–7) was captured by Sir Robert Knollys, the English *routier* in 1360.

Thorigny-sur-Oreuse (E–2) was taken by the English troops in 1425. The family of Le Jay lived in neighbouring Fleurigny and accompanied King John the Good into exile and captivity in London. Another member of the family perished at the battle of Cravant in 1423 and Fleurigny was taken by the Anglo-Burgundians.

Tonnerre (H–6) was the original crossroads of the main routes from Sens to Alesia and from Auxerre to Langres. It remained a fortified town in the Middle Ages. King Edward III took the town in 1359 but failed to take the château. Unhappily in the Second World War it suffered two bombardments which damaged the centre and the church of Notre Dame. The notorious Chevalier d'Eon, famous transvestite and Louis XV's secret agent, was born here in 1728. There are local sweets called 'Chevaliers d'Eon' — such is fame. La Fosse Dionne is a beautiful fountain-basin surrounded by a gallery and recently renovated. The town is well worth a visit.

Toucy (D–7). In 1423 the Anglo-Burgundians burned the village and church, and six years later Joan of Arc passed through it. Pierre Larousse (1817–75), author of the *Grand Dictionnaire* which bears his name, was born here. The town was badly damaged by a German bombardment in 1944. Outside the church of St Pierre is a feudal-age moat. The old timbered houses and narrow streets make Toucy worth a visit.

Valléry (B–2) has the church of St Thomas de Canterbury, built in 1612 by Henry II, Prince de Condé, in honour of our 'turbulent priest'.

Varennes (G–5) is a small village but was an important French military munitions establishment destroyed by the retreating Germans in 1944.

Vermenton (G–8) was seized in 1358 by the ubiquitous Sir

Robert Knollys, the English commander, who refortified it and held it for the English until 1371. In the next century it returned to Anglo-Burgundian control. This wine-growing area was made even more prosperous by the industry of floating timber on the river Cure towards Paris from the sixteenth century.

Vézelay (G–10). The famous abbey of the Madeleine is one of the wonders of the world, perched upon a hill overlooking the valleys and river Cure. On no account to be missed.

Vézinnes (H–6). The château was built by John Stuart in 1540. He was Captain of the Scottish Guard to King Francis I.

Villeneuve-sur-Yonne (D–4). King Louis VII fortified this town as a *bastide* in 1163 against the Champagne war lords. It was the royal residence of the French kings Philip Augustus and Saint-Louis. The English troops occupied it in 1420. The strong bridge over the river Yonne was built in the thirteenth century. The medieval city is worth a visit.

Castles and châteaux

It is a miracle that any châteaux remain standing in Burgundy after the ravages of the Hundred Years War, the Wars of Religion, the whims of several French kings, the Imperial troops in 1640, the French Revolution, and the wars of 1870, 1914–18 and 1939–45. Nevertheless, there are many hundreds of châteaux in this department.

The Yonne has fewer classified châteaux than the other départements of Burgundy. Being the northernmost region, it almost certainly suffered more intense damage from invaders from the north — including the UK — than the southern departments. Nevertheless it has some absolute treasures, at Ancy-le-Franc, Tanlay and St-Fargeau. Two strongholds from the Middle Ages — Courgenay and Drues-les-Belles-Fontaines — are also worth a visit.

I have included only exceptional buildings, classified as MH *(Monument Historique)* or IMH *(Inscrit à l'Inventaire des Monuments Historiques)*. Would-be visitors are advised to check opening times either with the nearest tourist information office or with the Comité Départemental du Tourisme, 1/2 quai de la République, 89000 Auxerre, tel. 86.52.26.27.

Ancy-le-Franc (J–7) is a magnificent sixteenth century Renaissance château, with an elegant courtyard and sumptuously decorated inner apartments. The quadrilateral courtyard has four corner pavilions. Open 23 March to 1 November. Entrance 20 francs — and well worth it, as this is one of Burgundy's proudest possessions.

Arcy-sur-Cure (G–9). The manor house of Chastenay was originally owned by Knights Templars and Alchemists. Pilgrims on the route to Compostella called here. Closed Sunday mornings. Entrance about 22 francs. The medieval village beside the famous grottoes has the eighteenth-century Château d'Arcy.

Auxerre (F–7). The Préfecture was an episcopal palace, and has a superb Roman gallery. See also the Château de Sparre and the old château of the Counts of Auxerre near the Hôtel de Ville.

Chastellux-sur-Cure (H–11) has a magnificent, eight-towered feudal castle on a granite hill overlooking the river Cure, but the interior is closed.

Cruzy-le-Châtel (J–6). The Château de Maulne is a sixteenth century Renaissance building in pentagonal shape on five levels, with corner towers.

Druyes-les-Belles-Fontaines (E–9) was at the end of the twelfth century a stronghold of the Counts of Auxerre and Nevers, and was a prototype for many other medieval forts. It is situated on a hill overlooking the village. Open in mid-summer only. Entrance 10 francs. Exhibitions and concerts in season.

Fleurigny (D–2), near Thorigny, has a fourteenth century façade and chapel, and an elegant Renaissance courtyard. Open April to mid-September. Entrance 15 francs.

Grandchamp (C–6) has a sixteenth century château with towers and a dovecot, erected by a descendant of Luca della Robbia.

Lichères-sur-Yonne (F–10) has the seigneurial manor house of Faulin, built in the fifteenth and sixteenth century, with towers, interesting windows and staircase.

Maligny (G–6) has a keep, partly restored in the eighteenth century.

Nuits-sur-Armançon (J–7) has a sixteenth century Renaissance château in an attractive park. Open mid-May to mid-October. Entrance 10 francs.

Les Ormes (D–6) has the Château de Bontin, built in the seventeenth century.

Passy (D–3) has a château set in grounds with formal gardens and moats.

Piffonds (C–4) has a 1472 dovecot, postern house, gatehouse drawbridge and round towers.

Pisy (J–9). The old feudal château dominates the valley of the Serein. It has an octagonal tower, an eighteenth century chapel, guardroom and windmills.

Ratilly-Treigny (C–9), one of the Burgundian splendours, is near St-Fargeau. It is a thirteenth century red stone castle with a main courtyard flanked by six round towers. Seventeenth century keep. Inside is a pottery studio and a permanent Puisaye ceramic exhibition. Open all year round. Entrance 8 francs.

St-Fargeau (C–8) is well worth a visit. It is a twelfth century pentagon of rose-coloured bricks, with six pepper-pot towers. The courtyard was constructed by Le Vau. Open end March to end October. Entrance 20 francs. St Hubert Park is nearby.

St-Loup-d'Ordon (C–4) was built in the reign of Louis XIII and restored in the nineteenth century, but has Roman vaulted cellars, dovecot and park.

Sens (D–3) has a thirteenth century Gothic synodal palace, restored in the nineteenth century by Viollet-le-Duc. The old prison still has thirteenth century graffiti on the walls.

Tanlay (I–6). One of Burgundy's outstanding sights, the Renaissance château is sited in a wood, is moated and has a vast quadrilateral courtyard flanked by towers. The 1610 entrance is known as 'Le Petit Château'. The Tour de la Ligue houses Admiral Coligny's collection of 'provocative frescoes'. Closed in mid-winter. Entrance 20 francs.

Thizy (I–9) has an old stronghold, repaired in the fifteenth century with many towers of all shapes and sizes, Gothic dungeons and thirteenth century keep.

Tonnerre (H–6) has the 'Vieil Hôpital' of the thirteenth century, with immense vaulted rooms. The tomb called 'Belle Mise' is a fifteenth century scupltural masterpiece. Closed Tuesdays. Entrance 8 francs.

Valléry (B–2) has the Renaissance Château de Condé, with ramparts dating from the Middle Ages; it was formerly the medieval fortress of the Seigneur de Valléry. Open March to mid-November. Entrance 10 francs.

Cathedrals, abbeys and splendid churches

This département has much of the finest religious classic architecture in France. The crypt in St Germain d'Auxerre is a rare example of Carolingian architecture. The basilica of Vézelay represents Romanesque Burgundian architecture, and the cathedrals of Sens and Auxerre were the first of the great Gothic cathedrals in France. Renaissance buildings of note include Appoigny, the façade of St Pierre in Auxerre, St Jean de Joigny and the church of St Florentin. The twelfth century Abbey of Pontigny is also exceptional.

The French government has graded all churches in the country. Since every town and village has a church, the decision which to include has been difficult. Just one example of this difficulty is provided by the small village of Aisy-sur-Armançon (J–8), which has a population of 350 people. Its thirteenth century church is entirely vaulted, with a unique nave, a side chapel with a seventeenth century tabernacle, a wooden statuette of St Catherine and two stone tombs dated 1521 and 1527. Interesting? Well, along with hundreds of others it has necessarily been omitted. The seventy churches classed as MH *(Monument Historique)* should have been included but on appeal to the experts in the Yonne, I have concentrated on a selection of about thirty and simply listed the remainder alphabetically.

Remember that small entry fees are charged for visiting unusual crypts, viewing displays of treasures, etc.

Appoigny (F–6). The thirteenth century church of St Pierre and St Paul was an ancient collegiate church. See above.

Auxerre (F–7). Abbey church of St Germain. Of all the vestiges of pre-Romanesque Burgundy, the crypts (the 'Saintes Grottes') of St Germanus (Germain) are the most precious. The central nave of the crypts is the sanctuary, dedicated to St Maurice d'Agaune, built by St Germanus at the beginning of the fifth century. The two aisles were built by Queen Clotilde between 493 and 545. The ninth-century chapels have retained part of their original painted decorations, including the fresco representing the martyrdom of St. Étienne (St Stephen). Nineteenth century demolitions separated the thirteenth century church, built over the crypt, from the fine Romanesque bell-tower surmounted by a tall, eight-sided stone spire. Behind the walls of the Renaissance cloister, next to the Gothic church, several twelfth century blind arcades have recently been discovered.

Cathedral of St Étienne (St Stephen). Of the Romanesque cathedral, which was destroyed early in the thirteenth century and replaced by a new Gothic construction, there remain some very fine eleventh century crypts with a triple central nave of six groined, vaulted bays with massive pillars. These are separated by the very thick walls of the aisles communicating with a semi-domed chapel, the arched ceiling decorated with the famous eleventh century fresco of Christ on horseback.

The church of St Eusèbe has a very fine Romanesque tower surmounted by an octagonal stone spire built in the fifteenth century.

The church of St Pierre is in the Renaissance style.

Avallon (H–10). The twelfth century collegiate church of St Lazare is famous for its two beautiful doorways in Romanesque-Burgundian style as well as its tenth century crypt.

Chablis (G–6). The Gothic church of St Martin and the thirteenth century church of St Pierre are both of interest.

Châtel-Censior (F–9). The church of St Potentien was an eleventh century Romanesque collegiate church. The Romanesque choir, the chancel carvings and the crypt should be seen.

Cravant (G–8). The church of St Pierre and St Paul has a thirteenth century nave, a huge Renaissance choir, vaulted roofs and windows.

Dixmont (E–4). The church of St Gervais and St Protais has a thirteenth century bell tower, main doors and colonnades.

Druyes-les-Belles-Fontaines (E–9). The perfect fortified twelfth century Romanesque church of St Romain has a handsome, semicircular main doorway, barrel-vaulted nave and domed apsidal chapel.

Escolives-St-Camille (F–7). The Romanesque church of St Pierre and St Paul contains the magnificent twelfth century tomb of St Magnance, who escorted St Germanus's body from Ravenna to Auxerre.

Joigny (E–5). The church of St André was, until the fifteenth century, the priory of Notre Dame. Part of the nave is twelfth century; the main door is Renaissance.

The church of St Jean was built during the Renaissance and reconstructed in the sixteenth century. The church of St Thibault, mentioned in a document of 1080, has since been reconstructed.

La Ferté Loupière (D–6). The twelfth century church of St Germain has a triple nave, vaulted in wood. Among the paintings on the walls is a *danse macabre* with three dead and three live people!

Laroche-St-Cydroine (E–5) is one of the most important Romanesque buildings in the département, built in the eleventh century under the jurisdiction of the Benedictine Abbey of La Charité-sur-Loire. The choir is shaped, most unusually, into a Greek cross. The octagonal two-tier church tower rises above the transept.

Ligny-le-Châtel (G–6). The church of St Pierre and St Paul has a Romanesque timbered nave with six traverses and transept; a bell tower of the twelfth century and a vast Renaissance choir with lateral chapels, surmounted by a square tower.

Mailly-le-Château (F–9). The church of St Adrien is a thirteenth century Gothic building with a triple nave of four traverses.

Montréal (I–9) has a twelfth century collegiate church of Notre Dame, restored by Viollet-le-Duc, built on a terrace over-looking the valley of the Serein. The furnishings are noteworthy.

Moûtiers (C–8). The church of St Pierre and St Paul has a wooden vaulted twelfth century nave and choir, fifteenth century sanctuary and twelfth century porch.

Neuvy-Sautour (G–4). The church of St Symphorien of Autun was in ruins in the nineteenth century but was then restored. The three naves with four traverses date from the fifteenth century, the clock tower from the sixteenth-seventeenth centuries. The doorways of the sixteenth century transepts are in the form of a triumphal arch.

Noyers (I–8). The Notre Dame church of the fifteenth century is described as being of 'flamboyant Gothic style'.

Pontaubert (H–10). The church of the Nativity of Notre Dame is in the twelfth century Romanesque-Burgundian style. It formerly belonged to the Knights Hospitallers. The two upper tiers of the tower and the main doorways are of the Gothic style of the thirteenth century.

Pont-sur-Yonne (C–2). The church of the Assumption is twelfth century; the main door, tower and triple nave are of Gothic style.

Pontigny (G–5). The magnificent (but unloved) abbey of Notre Dame and St Edmé of Pontigny was built in 1114 by the monks from Citeaux and is one of the most important remaining examples of Cistercian architecture. It is set back 200 metres from the village road. The tomb of the English St Edmé (Edmund) was the site of an important pilgrimage.

59

Compared to the sad vestiges of Cîteaux and the few remaining glories of Cluny, it is remarkable that Pontigny still survives in solitary splendour.

St-Bris-le-Vineux (F–7). The church of St Prix and St Cot was built in the thirteenth century and restored in the nineteenth. The vaulted nave and clock tower are original.

St-Fargeau (C–8). The church of St Ferréol has a thirteenth century façade and triple nave.

St-Florentin (G–5) dates mainly from the sixteenth and seventeenth centuries. The sixteenth century glass windows are remarkable.

St-Julien-du-Sault (D–4). The church of St Pierre was a thirteenth century collegiate church and has beautiful glass windows. The Chapel of St Julien is to be found within the remains of the Château de Vauguillain.

St-Léger-Vauban (I–11) has three sites — the church of St Léger (partly fifteenth century), the monastery of Ste-Marie-de-la-Pierre-qui-Vire, where one can assist with the offices of the Benedictine monks (tel. 86.32.21.23) and the neo-Gothic abbey of Ste Marie.

St-Père-sous-Vézelay (G–10) has a thirteenth century church of Notre Dame and a fifteenth century presbytery, which is now a museum.

Sens (D–3). The Gothic cathedral of St Étienne (Stephen) was commenced in 1140. Its stone tower is 78 m. high. It has a huge nave and is noteworthy in many respects. The treasury contains vestments of St Thomas à Becket and of the other English saint, Edmé (Edmund). One of the windows shows the life of St Thomas à Becket (two-thirds of the way up the nave on the north side). The eleventh century Romanesque church of St Savinien has a crypt with eighth-ninth century inscriptions relating to the martyrdom of the saint. The abbey of St Jean, in the Gothic style of the thirteenth century, is now the hospital chapel.

Vermenton (G–8). The church of Notre Dame is both Romanesque and Gothic, but is mainly of the twelfth century.

Nearby is the old abbey of Reigny, with a scriptorium and thirteenth century refectory.

Vézelay (G–10) has the basilica of St Madeleine. The nave, built between 1120 and 1140, when the crowds of pilgrims coming to pray near the relics of the 'Madeleine' became too great to be contained in the earlier building, is 62 metres long and 12 metres wide; its height of 18 metres is amazing and surprisingly the area is full of light. It has ten two-storey bays, semicircular arches with tall windows above, the first nine groined, the tenth an ogival arch. Sturdy arch bands in sʼone of alternating brown and ochre accentuate the rhythm of the cruciform pillars flanked by four columns topped with ingeniously carved capitals. Friezes of palm leaves, rosettes and ribbons run along the wall-ribs, the string course between the storeys, the curve of the recessed arches and the arch-bands, underlining the strong architectural features. The narthex, built a few years later, has a central nave and two lateral three-bay groin vaulted naves with tribunes above. It opens on to the nave through three admirable sculptured doorways. These sculptures, particularly the one over the central door known as the 'Tympanum of Pentecost', are among the major works of art of the western world. The early Gothic choir and the transept were built between 1185 and 1215 and their shimmering white columns offer a striking contrast to the golden colours of the nave.

Villeneuve-sur-Yonne (D–4). The church of Notre Dame dates mainly from the thirteenth century with additions by Jean Chéveau and Jean Cousin.

Other MH-grade churches are to be found at **Anneot** (H–9), **Argenteuil-sur-Armançon** (I–7), **Brienon-sur-Armançon** (F–5) **Bussy-en-Othe** (E–4), **Charbuy** (E–6), **Chassignelles** (J–7), **Chevannes** (E–7), **Chitry** (G–7), **Collan** (H–6), **Coulanges-la-Vineuse** (F–8), **Courlon-sur-Yonne** (C–1), **Dannemoine** (H–1) **Fleys** (H–6), **Germigny** (G–5), **Gigny** (K–6), **Gy-L'Evêque** (F–7), **Irancy** (F–7), **Joux-la-Ville** (H–8), **Lasson** (G–4), **Lucy-sur-Yonne** (F–9), **Melisey** (I–5), **Michery** (D–1), **Molosmes** (I–6), **Parly** (D–7), **Poilly-sur-Tholon** (E–6), **Prégilbert** (F–8), **Ravières** (J–7), **Sacy** (G–8), **St-Aubin-sur-Yonne** (D–5), **St-**

Privé (B–8), **Ste-Colombe-sur-Loing** (D–9), **Savigny-en-Terre-Plaine** (I–10), **Seignelay** (F–5), **Senan** (D–5), **Thury** (D–9), **Tonnerre** (H–6), **Treigny** (C–9), **Turny** (G–4) and **Vault-de-Lugny** (H–10).

Museums

The Yonne has a wonderful collection of museums, particularly at Auxerre and Sens.

Arcy-sur-Cure (G–9). In the town hall is a display of objects from the Gallo-Roman and Merovingian eras and collections of flint implements and bones representative of the Paleolithic fauna.

Auxerre (F–7) has the Conservatoire de la Nature Paul-Bert, 5 boulevard Vauban, tel. 86.51.51.64. Open all year. The Musée d'Art et d'Histoire is at 3 place Coche d'Eau, tel. 86.51.09.74. The Chapelle des Visitandines, 98 rue de Paris, tel. 86.51.09.74, has a collection of gemstones and polychrome sculptures. Closed Tuesdays and holidays. For the Musée Géoligique, apply first to M. J.-P. Bardin, 27 chemin privé du Carré-Patissier, tel. 86.51.29.79.

Avallon (H–10) has the Musée de l'Avallonais, place de la Collegeial, tel. 86.34.03.19. Open all year. Small entrance fee.

Escolives-Ste-Camille (F–7). For the Association des Amis d'Escolives, contact M. Daniel Prost, Le Moulin, 9 rue Raymond-Kapps.

Joigny (E–5). The Musée du Pasteur-Vincent and Petit Musée du Protestantisme are at the municipal library, place Valet, tel. 86.62.05.62, ext. 62.

Merry-sur-Yonne (F–9) has a small museum at the Grotte de la Roche-au-Loup, chemin de la Ferme de Ravereau. Open August to mid-September.

Noyers-sur-Serein (I–8) has a small museum, open in summer, which has assembled collections from excavations and archaeological surveys in the region. Contact the Mairie.

Pourrain-les-Vernes (E–7) has a Musée de la Guerre 1939–45. Contact M. Johannes Sontrop, Atelier Sontrop, tel. 86.41.13.27. Open all year.

St-Fargeau (C–8) has a Musée de Cheval at the château. Entrance 12 francs.

St-Léger-Vauban (I–11) has the Musée Vauban at the Mairie. Marshal Vauban (1633–1707) was a soldier, architect, town-builder, economist, politician and philosopher. Open all year. Entrance 8 francs.

St-Père-sous-Vézelay (G–10) has a museum on the archaeological site, tel. 86.33.23.14. Open March to December Entrance 10 francs.

Sens (D–3). The new museum, 5 rue Rigault, tel. 86.64.15.27, groups together all the collections of Sens. This is now a major collection ranging from the prehistoric collection of Auguste Hure to the time of Napoleon. Well worth a visit. The cathedral treasure is unique.

Vézelay (G–10) has a collection, *La sculpture oubliée de Vézelay,* in the old monks' dormitory. Consult the Mairie, tel. 86.33.24.62. Open mid-June to mid-September. Entrance 10 francs.

Villeneuve-sur-Yonne (D–4). There are relics of the local Acheulean stone industry here, and of the iron mines in the forest of Othe; furnishings originating from the sepulchre of the 'Colombine' (a necropolis of the Bronze Age); a Hallstattian torque; Gallic ceramics; furnishings of a villa and the pottery from Gallo-Roman workshops at Bussy-le-Repos. Visit on request at the town hall, tel. 86.87.07.45.

Viliers-St-Benoit (C–7) has a Musée d'Art Regional, tel. 86.45.73.05. Closed mid-December to mid-January. Entrance 6 francs.

Wine co-operative and local wines

There are two major wine-growing areas in the Yonne: Chablis and the Coteaux de l'Auxerrois. Small vineyards are to be found at Tonnerre/Béru, Épineuil, Joigny and Vézelay.

• Chablis

Chablis consists of twenty communes grouped about 15 km. east of Auxerre along the valley of the river Serein. The world-famous dry white wine is made of the Pinot Chardonnay grape, producing *grands crus*, twenty-two *premier crus*, Chablis and Petit Chablis.

Beines, 5 km. west of Chablis, has nine *vignerons*, of whom six offer tasting facilities. The *premier cru* Troemes is produced here, as well as Chablis and Petit Chablis.

Chablis itself has thirty-six *vignerons*, including the important Cave Co-opérative de Chablis, 'La Chablisienne', which is described in more detail below.

La-Chapelle-Vaupelteigne, 4 km. north-west of Chablis, has five *vignerons*.

Chemilly-sur-Serein, 7 km. south-east of Chablis, has four *vignerons*.

Chichée, 4 km. south-east of Chablis, has seven *vignerons*.

Courgis, 5 km. south-west of Chablis, has five *vignerons*; two offer tastings.

Fleys, 7 km. east of Chablis, has eleven *vignerons*, including three *premiers crus*.

Fontenay-près-Chablis, 6 km. north of Chablis, has four *vignerons*.

Lignorelles, 10 km. north-west of Chablis, has seven *vignerons*.

Maligny, 12 km. north-west of Chablis, has eight *vignerons*; one offers tastings.

Milly has nine *vignerons*.

Poinchy has seven *vignerons*.

Villy has three *vignerons*.

Other communes include Béru, Ligny-le-Château, Pouilly-sur-Serein, St-Cyr-les-Colas and Viviers.

There are 1500 hectares of land devoted to wine production in the Chablis area, usually producing about 65,000 hectolitres per annum; in 1979 exceptionally 100,000 hectolitres were produced. Chablis *grands crus* cover only 90 hectares, *premiers crus* about 450, Chablis about 800, and Petit Chablis the balance of 160. All Chablis can be drunk young but the two superior qualities will keep well for a number of years. The best vineyards in the *grands crus* are Blanchot, Les Clos, Valmur, Grenouilles, Vaudésir, Les Preuses and Bougros — the 'Magificent Seven', all on the east side of the town.

The best known of the *premiers crus* are Fourchaume, Montée de Tonnerre, Mont de Milieu and Vaucoupin on the east side of the river Serein, and Butteaux, Forêts, Montmain, Vaillons, Les Lys and Côte de Léchet on the west side. There are twenty-two vineyards altogether denominated *'premier crus'*. Le Petit Chablis, usually grown on a chalky soil at Beines, Lignorelles, Maligny and Villy, is excellent when drunk very young and mildly chilled.

The wine festivals are the 'St Vincent Tournant' in February, the 'St Pierre' in July, the 'Fête de la Vigne' in the second fortnight of August and the 'Fête des Vins' on the last Sunday of November. At all these perform 'La Confrérie des Piliers Chablisiens' and their folk-singing group 'Le Regain de Chablis'.

M. Jean-Michel Tucki is the genial director of the Cave Co-opérative de Chablis, 'La Chablisienne', 8 boulevard Pasteur, 89800 Chablis, tel. 86.42.11.24. The co-operative was founded in 1923, has 250 members and produces more Chablis than anybody else. The stock of 60,000 hectolitres is held in 1300 hectolitre steel containers. At each vintage seven large lorries are kept busy collecting the grape juice from the members of the co-operative, who receive a set price per litre depending specifically on the designation of their vineyard. All the bottling is done at the co-operative. The *grands crus* are kept for five years — these are usually Grenouilles and Les Preuses. 1983 was a good year and 1985, despite frost in January and April, will be of good quality. The co-operative also stocks Bourgogne Aligoté and Bourgogne Méthode Champenoise, a sparkling white wine. The Aligoté was recently priced at 23 francs, the Petit Chablis at 33 francs, the Chablis 1983 at 42 francs and the 1984 at 38 francs, and Chablis *premiers crus*, depending on the vintage, at 56, 55 and 51 francs per 75 centilitre bottle. The *grands crus* were 74 and 80 francs per bottle. The co-operative is definitely worth an extensive visit. It welcomes tasters who are also prepared to buy a bottle or two.

● Les Coteaux de L'Auxerois

This is the generic name given to the sensible wines grown just south of Auxerre. They are reputed to have a delicate bouquet of violets and raspberries.

Chitry has twenty-six *vignerons*, of whom nineteen offer tasting facilities of their white wines — Bourgogne Blanc, Bourgogne Aligoté and Sauvignon de St-Bris.

Coulanges-la-Vineuse has twelve *vignerons*, all with tasting and buying facilities for their red wines.

Irancy is famous for a charter from King Charles the Bald in AD 861 with a diploma for what is now known as AOC Bourgogne-Irancy (red wine) and VDQS Sauvignon de St-Bris (white). Irancy has twenty-five *vignerons*, all with stocks of reds and *rosés* with tasting facilities.

St-Bris-le-Vineux (a well-deserved name) has twenty-one *vignerons* producing white, red and rosé wines. The 'Fête de Sauvignon' takes place there on 11 November, when the 'Chevaliers des Trois Ceps' take part in the festivities and *'joyeuses manifestations'*.

Vincelottes has AOC Bourgogne Pinot Noir and Aligoté. Clos de la Chainette is the best known of the Auxerre wines.

● Other wine-growing areas

Épineuil is just north of Tonnerre, about 28 km. east of Auxerre. Once upon a time the wines of Tonnerre were famous — more so than those of Auxerre or Chablis, until the Phylloxera blight devastated the vineyards. Now fifty hectares of Pinot Noir vines are in production at Béru, by three *vignerons*, and at Épineuil — a *'village vert'* — where the wines are now AOC Bourgogne-Épineuil. At Molosmes, the

'Fête des Vignerons' of St Vincent is on 22 January.

Joigny, which is halfway between Sens and Auxerre, has the wines of the Côte St Jacques, which have a good local reputation. There you can taste the delicious *vin gris*, their Bourgogne *rosé*, grown on the four hectares of vineyards overlooking the town and the river Yonne.

Vézelay is 12 km. west of Avallon. At St-Père you find the vineyard of Clodu, short for '*clos au duc*', the original wines of the old dukes of Burgundy. The grapes are Chardonnay, Pinot Noir and Auxerrois.

Other small wine and agricultural co-operatives are to be found at Tonnerre, Ancy-le-Franc, Cheny and St-Florentin — mainly for *vins ordinaires*.

- **Recommended visit**

'Sicava Bailly' is the wine co-operative at the Caves de Bailly, 89530 St-Bris-le-Vineux, tel. 86.53.34.00, 10 km. south of Auxerre. M. Alain Cornelissens is the efficient young director of this well-organised co-operative which specializes in Crémant de Bourgogne, a white or *rosé* sparkling wine made by the Champagne method. The brand name 'Meurgis' is the local word for the small heaps of stones raked or taken from the vineyard surface to improve the soil.

The co-operative society was formed in 1972. Eighty *vigneron* members in the area south of Auxerre, at St-Bris-le-Vineux, Chitry-le-Fort, Irancy and Coulanges-la-Vineuse own 300 hectares of vines. In the first category are Pinot Noir, Pinot Gris, Pinot Blanc Chardonnay; in the second category are Gamay Noir *à jus blanc*, Aligoté, Melon and Sacy. The end result is an 85 per cent production of sparkling white wine using the genuine Champagne method, and 15 per cent sparkling *rosé*.

Sicava sparkling wines are excellent and should be tasted. Visitors should telephone in advance to make an appointment. Amongst the UK buyers are Fox and Co., Young and Co. and Majestic Wine Warehouses.

CHAPTER FIVE:FOOD AND BOARD IN THE YONNE

The Yonne is one of the richest agricultural départements in France. Cows, pigs and poultry are to be found in the farms near every village. Mushroom, *cèpes* and *girolles* are grown in seventeen villages. Bee-keeping — and the resulting honey — are to be found in a score or more of villages. Fruit trees and particularly cherry orchards, are to be found at Augy (F–7), Escolives-Ste-Camille (F–7), Irancy (F–7), Migé (F–8) and Quenne (F–7).

Truffles — getting rarer these days and commanding incredible prices — are noted at Arcy-sur-Cure (G–9) and Châtel-Gerard (I–8). Fish are bred at Augy (F–7), Chamvres (D–5), Marchais Beton (B–6), Prégilbert (F–8), Avrolles (G–5), St-Romain-le-Preux (D–5), Sépeaux (D–5), Verlin (D–4), Villefranche (C–5), Villeneuve-sur-Yonne (D–4) and Voutenay-sur-Cure (G–9). Roe deer and wild boar (*sangliers*) are raised at Annay-la-Côte (H–9), Girolles (H–9), Lucy-sur-Yonne (F–9) and Vareilles (E–3); pheasants at Merry-la-Vallée (D–7), Moulins-sur-Ouanne (D–7) and Villefranche (C–5); waterfowl (*gibiers d'eau*) at Lavau (B–9) and quail at Chailley (G–4).

Cheeses are made at twenty or more villages from both cows' and goats' milk. Soumaintrain (H–4) is well known. Aisy-sur-Armançon (J–8) produces *fromage le cendre*, ash grey in colour. Appoigny (F–6) is known for its gherkins (*cornichons*), spices and vinegar.

Biscuits are made at Chablis (G–6) and Augy (F–7); *pain beurré* is made at Crain (F–9); and biscuits and meringues at St-Bris-le-Vineux (F–7). Tonnerre (H–6) produces cheese brioches (*gougères*) and sweets called 'Marguerites de Bourgogne' and 'Chevaliers d'Eon'. Mailly-la-Ville (G–9) produces chocolate. But the prize for variety must go to Mézilles (C–8), well known for its fruit trees (cherries, apples and pears), its breeding of rabbits (for eating) and its beagle dogs and horses (not for eating).

Modest hotels and restaurants

Auxerre (pop. 45,000) is the préfecture and capital town of the Yonne. There are five hotel-restaurants shown in the summary, where it is possible to stay comfortably and just within the budget. The Seignelay, 2 rue du Pont, tel. 86.52.03.48, with 24 rooms, is recommended (2 star). Mme Rafestin has six double rooms priced at 80 francs, but these can be noisy, being on the street side.

There are plenty of restaurants in Auxerre offering a *prix fixe* menu below or near 50 francs. They include; Le Saint Hubert, quai de la République; Le Vaulabelle, 36 boulevard Vaulabelle; L'Ancien Chai, 12 rue de la Fraternité; Le Buffet de la Gare, place de la Gare; Le Grill Saint Pierre, 33 rue du Pont; Le Petit Bourguignon, 34 rue Joubert and various *crêperies*.

Auxerre is famous for its gastronomic delights. Try garlic sausage baked in brioches; genuine *escargots de Bourgogne* in Chablis wine; trout from the river Yonne stuffed with herbs; chocolate snails filled with almond praline and chocolate truffles with rum-soaked grapes.

Sens (pop. 28,000) is the second largest town in the Yonne. There are five good-value hotels in the summary. The Hotel des Deux Ponts, as the name suggests, overlooks the river Yonne, on the west side of the town. It has 14 rooms priced from 70–95 francs, at 22–24 avenue Lucien-Cornet, tel. 86.65.26.81. Pension terms start from a 3-day stay. Breakfast 18 francs. Restaurant closed Sundays. Parking facilities.

Sens has several local restaurants with low *prix fixé* menus, including the Brasserie, Le Senonais, 99 rue de la République and La Potinière, 51 rue Cécile-de-Marsangy, overlooking the river.

Joigny (pop. 12,000) is the third largest town. It is pretty, overlooking the wide river Yonne. The Hôtel le Lion d'Or, with 22 rooms, at 5 rue Roger-Varrey, tel. 86.62.17.00 is good value. The rooms are priced at 65–80 francs, breakfast at 16 francs, and *prix fixé* menus range upwards from 50 francs. Closed August.

Avallon (pop. 9,000) is the fourth largest town. A good value hotel-restaurant is Au Bon Accueil, 4 rue de l'Hôpital, tel. 86.34.09.33, with 14 rooms at 80–90 francs each. Breakfast 12–15 francs. It is twenty metres from the huge main square of Avallon, where parking is easy.

Villneuve-sur-Yonne (pop. 5,000). The Hostellerie du Dauphin has rooms from 75 francs and a *prix fixé* menu at 70 francs.

Vézelay (pop. 600) is no more than a village but as its abbey and basilica attract travellers from all over the world there are a number of hotel-restaurants. At the foot of the hill by the main square with easy parking, is the Hôtel du Cheval Blanc with rooms at 88–134 francs, breakfast at 18.50 and a *prix fixé* menu at 60 francs. On the other side of the main road is the Relais du Morvan, with a *prix fixé* menu of 66 francs but the rooms are expensive.

Map ref.	Town	Hotel	No. of rooms	Tel. (prefix 86)
J—7	Ancy-le-Franc 89160	du Centre	13	75.15.11
G—9	Arcy-sur-Cure 89270	des Grottes, RN6	7	40.91.47 closed Wed. and 10/1–31/1
F—7	Auxerre 89000	de la Poste, 9 rue d'Orbandelle	24	52.12.02 closed Fri. and 15/11–15/12
		de Seignelay, 2 rue du Pont	24	52.03.48 closed Mon. and 10/1–10/2
		du Commerce, 5 rue René-Schaeffer	20	52.03.16 closed 15/12–1/1
		le Sainte Nitasse, route de Chablis	31	46.95.07 closed 24/12–2/1

		de la Renommée, 27 rue d'Eglény	23	52.03.53
H–10	Avallon 89200	du Parc, 3 place de la Gare	27	34.17.00 closed Sun. and 15/12–15/1
		au Bon Accueil, 4 rue de l'Hôpital	14	34.09.33 closed Sun.
B—8	Bléneau 89220	de France, 17 rue d'Orléans	14	74.92.63
G—6	Chablis 89800	de l'Étoile, 4 rue des Moulins	15	42.10.50 closed Mon. pm.
C—6	Charny 89120	de la Gare, 30 avenue de la Gare	12	63.61.59 closed Mon. pm. and 15/12/–15/1
		du Cheval Blanc, 4 rue des Ponts	9	63.60.66 closed Tue. pm. and Fri. pm.
F—8	Coulanges-la-Vineuse 89480	des Vendanges, 12 rue A. Vildieu	5	42.21.91 closed Sun., Mon. and Jan.
F—9	Coulanges-sur-Yonne 89480	du Lion d'Or, place Hôtel de Ville	14	29.71.72 closed 22/12–10/1 and 6/10–23/10
E—9	Druyes-les-Belles-Fontaines 89560	des Sources, place Jean-Bertin	12	41.55.14 closed Mon. and Feb.
E—5	Épineau-les-Voves 89400 Chambéry	le Porcelet, 10 route de	7	91.25.31 closed Sun. and Fri.
H—5	Flogny-la-Chapelle 89360	de la Poste, 30 RN	40	75.42.33
F—6	Héry-les-Baudières 89550	le Soleil Levant, 1 rue d'Auxerre	8	40.11.51 closed Mon. and Nov.
E—5	Joigny 89300	le Lion d'Or, 5 rue Roger-Varrey	22	62.17.00
		la Poste, 44 avenue Gambetta	10	62.40.52

71

I–7	Lézinnes 89160	de la Gare, 4 rue de la Gare	10	75.66.14
G—9	Mailly-la-Ville 89730	de l'Étoile, route d'Avallon	12	40.40.55 closed Fri. and 15/3–30/3
E—5	Migennes 89400	l'Escale et la Gare, place Eugene Laporte	12	80.20.99
F—6	Monéteau 89470	le Lido, 4/29 rue de l'Yonne	10	40.61.92 closed Fri. pm.
G—6	Montigny-la-Resle 89230	le Soleil d'Or, RN77	11	41.81.21 closed Mon. and Dec.
G—5	Percey 89360	des Pêcheurs	16	35.01.55 closed Sun.
H–10	Pontaubert 89200	au Soleil d'Or, route de Vézelay	15	34.15.74
C—2	Pont-sur-Yonne 89140	aux Trois Rois, 9 avenue Résistance	13	67.01.05 closed Sun.
G—5	St Florentin 89600	de l'Est, 7/9 Faubourg St Martin	28	35.10.35 closed Sat.
G—10	St Père-sous-Vézelay 89450	à la Renommée, Route Nationale	9	33.21.34
C—3	St-Valérien	la Réunion (15 km. west of Sens on D81)	15	88.62.07 closed Sun.
F—5	Seignelay 89250	du Commerce, 3 rue Gatelot	19	47.71.21 closed Sun. and Mon.
D—5	Senan 89710	de la Place, 15 route de Joigny	9	63.42.26 closed Fri. and Sept.
D—3	Sens 89100	de la Gare, 35 place de la Gare	18	65.12.77 closed 25/8–25/9
		le Saint-Pregts, 89 rue Gén. de Gaulle	18	65.19.63 closed Fri. and Sat.
		du Centre, 4 place de la République	15	65.15.92 closed Fri. and and Sun. and

				15/9–15/10
		des Deux Ponts, 22–24 avenue Lucien-Cornet	14	65.26.81 closed Sun.
		le Bourgogne, 51 rue Thénard	12	64.52.61 closed Fri.
H—6	Tonnerre 89700	du Centre, 63 rue de l'Hôpital	30	55.10.56 closed Jan.
G–10	Vézelay 89450	du Cheval Blanc, place du Champ de Foire	8	33.12.12 closed Thu. and Fri.
		de la Terrasse, place Cathédral	6	
		Relais du Morvan, place du Champ de Foire	9	33.25.33
D—4	Villeneuve-sur-Yonne 89500	la Pergola (12 km. south on N6)	15	87.16.41
		Hostellerie du Dauphin, 12 rue Carnot	8	87.18.55
D—4	Villevallier 89127	le Pavillon bleu (20 km. south of Sens on RN6)	25	63.12.22

Camp sites

The camp sites are usually owned and well run by the local municipality. The number of *placements* varies from 20 to 220. Rates for a *placement* range from 3 to 6.50 francs, per car from 3 to 5 francs and per person from 4 to 9 francs per day. The majority of camp sites have a restaurant in or near the site. The majority (but not all) have caravan facilities. In all cases a telephone reservation is advised, with questions on current rates and facilities required or hoped for (fishing, swimming, tennis, sailing, etc.). A letter of confirmation should follow.

Two examples: a car plus caravan plus two people at Asquins would cost 15.60 francs per day and at Auxerre 19.00 francs.

Some of the telephone numbers are those of the local

Mairie, which co-ordinates bookings for the local camp site. Some sites are open throughout the year. Opening dates vary enormously — many open at Easter and close in late autumn.

Map ref.	Town		
G—8	Accolay 89460 Cravant.	Camping municipal 'du Moulin-Jacquot'. M. Gagnepain,	tel. 86.53.54.47
G—9	Arcy-sur-Cure 89270 Vermenton.	Cam. 'de l'isle-St-Jean'. Mairie	tel. 86.40.91.69
G–10	Asquins 89450 Vézelay.	Cam. 'Le Pâtis', (Tue. and Fri. only)	tel. 86.33.20.14
F—7	Auxerre 89000	Cam. mun., 8 route de Vaux,	tel. 86.52.11.15
H–10	Avallon 89200	Cam. mun. 'de Sous-Roche',	tel. 86.34.10.39
B—8	Bléneau 89220	Cam. mun. 'de la Pépinière',	tel. 86.74.93.73
F—5	Bonnard 89400	Cam. mun. 'Le Pâtis'. Mairie,	tel. 86.73.25.55
F—5	Brienon-sur-Armançon 89210	Cam. 'Les Graviers', C–D 84. M. Mathieu,	tel. 86.56.11.79
D—3	Cerisiers 89320	Cam. mun.,	tel. 86.88.21.88
C—7	Champignelles 89350	Cam. 'Le Petit Villars'. M. Guillaume,	tel. 86.45.10.40
G—6	Charny 89120	Cam. mun. 'Le Pâtis', route de la Mothe,	tel. 86.63.63.56
F—9	Châtel-Censoir 89660	Cam. mun. 'du Petit-Port'. Mairie,	tel. 86.29.51.03
F—5	Cheny 89400 Migennes.	Cam. mun. Mairie,	tel. 86.80.16.88
F—9	Coulanges-sur-Yonne 89480	Cam. mun. 'Les Six-Arpents',	tel. 86.29.51.03
F—2	Courgenay 89190 Villeneuve-Archevêque.	Cam. mun. M. Vermet,	tel. 86.86.80.26
G—8	Cravant 89460	Cam.'Au Vieux-Moulin',	
E—2	Fontaine-la-Gaillarde 89100 Sens.	Le Haut-du-Colombier. Mme Sarrazin,	tel. 86.65.61.02
G—5	Germigny 89600 St-Florentin	Cam. mun. 'l'Armançon', route de Cheu. M. Peyronnon,	tel. 86.35.02.46
E—5	Joigny 89300	Cam. mun. 'd'Épizy',	tel. 86.62.07.55

I—7	Lézinnes 89160 Ancy-le-Franc.	Cam. mun. 'La Gravière- tel. 86.75.60.50 Moulin', Mme Munier,
F—9	Mailly-le-Château 89660 Chatel-Censoir Bouchets,	Cam. mun. 'Le Pré-du- tel. 86.40.44.85 Roi', le Pertuis des
F—9	Merry-sur-Yonne 89660 Chatel-Censoir.	Cam. 'Les Tilleuls', tel. 86.29.50.53
E—5	Migennes 89400	Cam.mun. 'Léo-Lagrange'. tel.86.80.17.63 Mairie,
F—6	Moneteau 89470	Cam. mun. 2 rue de tel. 86.40.63.93 Gué-de-l'Épine. Mairie,
I—7	Pacy-sur-Armançon 89160 Ancy-le-Franc.	Cam. mun. 'La Motte'. tel.86.75.63.74 Mme Terillon,
D—3	Paron 89100 Sens.	Cam. mun., chemin de tel. 86.65.03.44 Contre-Halage,
C—2	Pont-sur-Yonne 89140	Cam. mun. de l'île tel. 86.67.03.62 d'Amour,
A—7	Rogny-les-sept-Écluses 89220 Bléneau.	Cam. mun. 'Les Lancières'. tel. 86.74.60.79 M. Chambaud,
D—5	St-Aubin-sur-Yonne 89300 Joigny.	Cam. 'Le Site Joli'
C—8	St-Fargeau 89170	Cam. mun. 'La Calanque'. tel. 86.74.04.55 M. Bordier,
G—5	St-Florentin 89600	Cam. 'de la Plage', tel. 86.35.08.13
D—4	St-Julien-du-Sault 89330	Cam. mun., route de tel. 86.63.22.58 Villevallier,
G—9	St-Moré 89270 Vermenton.	Cam. mun. tel. 86.35.08.13 Mme Chevalier,
G—10	St-Père-sous-Vézelay 89450	Cam. mun., tel. 86.33.26.62
D—3	Sens 89100	Cam. mun. 'Entre-deux- tel. 86.65.64.71 Vannes', route de Lyon,
D—1	Sergines 89410	Cam. mun. 'Les tel. 86.66.30.97 Champs-Blancs'.
H—6	Tonnerre 89700	Cam. mun. 'de la tel. 86.55.15.44 Cascade', avenue A-Briand
D—7	Toucy 89130	Cam. 'Le Pâtis', tel. 86.44.13.84
G—8	Vermenton 89270	Cam. mun. 'Les tel. 86.53.50.01 Coulemières',
G—10	Vézelay 89450	Cam. mun. 'de l'Ermitage', tel. 86.33.24.18
C—7	Villeneuve-les-Genêts 89350 Champignelles	Cam. 'Le Bois- tel. 86.45.45.41 Guillaume'. M. Marois,
D—4	Villeneuve-sur-Yonne 89500	Cam. 'du Saucil', tel. 86.87.00.69

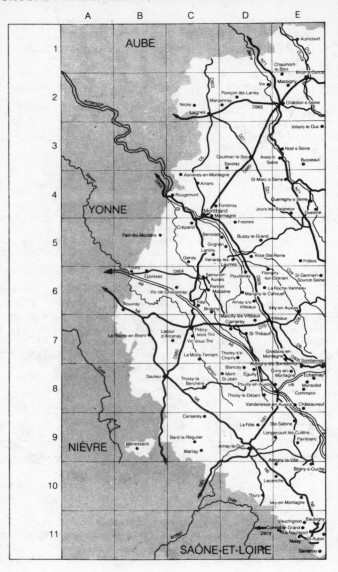

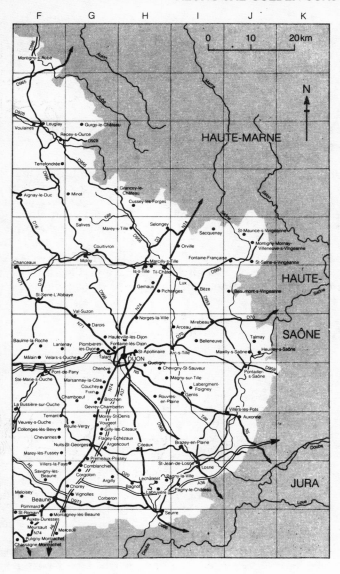

CHAPTER SIX:
ALONG THE GOLDEN COAST

The Côte d'Or — the Golden Coast' — is an unusual name for a French département, since bureaucracy decreed that all départements should be named after the major river flowing through them. The name calls to mind the golden glories of the Valois dukes of Dijon and the golden slopes of the famous vineyards of the **Côte de Beaune** and the **Côte de Nuit.** The perfect Cistercian abbey of Fontenay in the north-west, the medieval city of Semur-en-Auxois and the fascinating archaeological and architectural sites of Alésia, Saulieu and Flavigny should not be missed.

Tribal roots

The original tribes in this département were the Eduens, the Mandubiens, the Sequanes and the Lingons. They fought valiantly against Julius Caesar's legions at the great battle of Alésia (Alise-Ste-Reine), where Vercingetorix, their leader, was finally beaten in 52 BC. He — poor devil — was taken to Rome as a captive, and was strangled there six years later. The Roman occupation brought prosperity to the area until the barbarians — Vandals, Suèves and Alains — mounted their great invasions.

At the end of the ninth century AD the first Duchy of Burgundy was created. Robert the first, son of Robert le Pieux, King of France, became Duke of Burgundy in AD 1031. For three more centuries the Capetian dukes of Burgundy grew increasingly powerful until the last duke, Phillipe de Rouvres, died and the Duchy returned for a short time to the French crown. From 1363, when the King, Jean the Good, passed the

Duchy to his son, Philip the Bold, the power and the independence returned — helped by their English allies. After him came John the Fearless, Philip the Good and Charles the Rash — the four Grand Dukes of Burgundy, who turned the provinces into a state which rivalled France itself. The death of the last duke in 1477 brought their grandeur to an end. The French kingdom included the Duchy thereafter. The Burgundian prosperity has never faltered, with the Côte d'Or usually the most affluent of the four départements.

Regional tours

There are six natural divisions to this beautiful département:

1. The valley of the river Ouche, which runs parallel with the Canal de Bourgogne until they both join the river Saône near St-Jean-de-Losne. This is an area to the south-east of Dijon.

2. The Morvan National Park.

3. The Auxois, with Semur as its chief town, north-west of Dijon.

4. The valley of the river Saône, which is to the east of Dijon, including Auxonne.

5. The Châtillonais, which is a large area north and north-west of Dijon.

6. La Côte Vineuse and Les Hautes-Côtes, covering the wine-growing areas south of Dijon, with Beaune as the chief town.

The four attractive focal points for the Côte d'Or circuits are Dijon, Beaune, Semur-en-Auxois and Châtillon-sur-Seine.

Dijon

Dijon has its Tourist Office in the place Darcy, tel. 80.43.42.12 and an Information Bureau at 34 rue des Forges. Since Dijon is a city with an immense cultural background, it is suggested that a whole day should be spent looking at its seven museums: the famous Beaux-Arts in the east wing of the Palais

79

des Ducs; the Rude Museum, rue Vaillant; the Magnin Museum at 4 rue de Bons Enfants (near the place de la Libération); the Archaeological Museum in the rue Dr Maret, north of the cathedral; the Natural History Museum at avenue Albert I, near the Jardin de l'Arquebuse; the Sacred Art Museum, 15 rue Ste-Anne, and finally the Burgundian Traditions and Way of Life Museum, 17 rue Ste-Anne.

The guided tours of the town on foot depart each day at 4.00 p.m. from the Tourist Office in the place Darcy. There are eighteen points of interest, including the churches of Notre Dame and St-Michel, the Palace of the Dukes with the Bar Tower, the Tower of Philippe le Bon, Salle des États, the Court of Justice, the church of St-Philibert and the cathedral of St-Benigne.

A little further out of the centre is the Chartreuse de Champmol, now a hospital, with two superb works by the sculptor Claus Sluter. The Sacré Coeur church in north Dijon is a masterpiece of modern art with mosaics, crypt and notable stained glass windows.

Since Dijon is a gastronomic centre, you can visit mustard and condiment factories, manufacturers of *cassis* and bottlers/ canners of snails, blackcurrant sweets, ham specialities, etc. Alternatively, visit Dijon when the International Gastronomic Fair is in progress!

● **South-east tour**

A Dijon-based tour to the south-east could take the D968 to Brazey-en-Plaine to St-Jean-de-Losne, a fortified town with a fifteenth century (MH) church, then north-east by the D24 to **Auxonne**, which has an interesting old quarter, arsenal, château, church of Notre Dame and Bonaparte museum. From Auxonne drive west of the N5 to Villers-les-Pots to see the elegant Gothic chapel of La Levée, adopted by the young Napoleon, north to Poncey-lès-Athée on the D976 and on to Pontailler-sur-Saône — a Gallo-Roman 'city' on an island. Try to make a detour on the D976 north to see the superb château of Talmay. Then north-east to **Mirebeau** on the D959, the old Roman legionnaires' town — well worth looking at — and a thirteenth century Romanesque church. Next, drive north-west to **Bèze** to see the remains of the seventh century abbey and the thirteenth century houses in the village square. The view of the Bèze from the tree-lined river esplanade is worth stopping for. Then go north-east to **Fontaine Française,** which has a distinguished eighteenth century château. Next, travel west to **Selongey** on the D27: the two châteaux on the north side of the road at Chazeuil and Sacquenay are worth a detour. Selongey, with its protohistoric camp at Montfourose is a 'must' for archaeologists and there is a thirteenth century Romanesque church and the sixteenth century chapel of Ste-Gertrude. From Selogney, head due south on the D3 back to Dijon via Is-sur-Tille.

● **Beaune wine route**

The famous wine route from Dijon to Beaune is full of temptations. The D122 and later the N74 not only have irresistible wine villages whose names are world-famous, but a line of attractive châteaux at Marsannay-la-Côte, Brochon, Gevrey-Chambertin (several), Vougeot, Pernand-Vergelesses, and Aloxe-Corton. There are several wine museums and ancient *pressoirs* en route. Since all the eighteen wine villages between Dijon and Beaune have something of interest in addition to the *vignobles* ask the Tourist Office in Dijon for their brochure No. 4 of the Côte d'Or, 'Le Vignoble' (written in French).

● **North-west tour**

A short north-west tour from Dijon would start by the N71 to **Ste-Seine-l'Abbaye** to see the Gothic abbey and the Samaritaine fountain. Keep on the same road, passing the source of the river Seine on your left, to **Poncey-sur-l'Ignon** to see the château and church. Here also is the source of the river Ignon, which links with the Tille and later joins the Saône. Then drive via Chanceaux (Thenissey, on your left, has two châteaux) to **Baigneux-les-Juifs**, which takes its name from the medieval colony of Jews who lived there. The Gothic church and Hermitage, which is a place of pilgrimage, and several fifteenth century houses are worth a visit. North-west on the D21 are two more châteaux at Jours-lès-Baigneux and Villaines-en-Duesmois. The D954 and N454 north and east take you to **Aignay-le-Duc**, a medieval village with the Menhir of Pierre Fiche, the tumulus of Grands Champs, several pretty old houses and thirteenth century church. Return to Dijon via Étalante, Moloy, Saussy and Messigny on the D16 and D996.

Châtillon-sur-Seine

Châtillon-sur-Seine is in the far north of the département and is very well worth a visit for its châteaux, Romanesque churches and museums. It is in every way a *'ville pittoresque'* and is a most satisfactory focal point for a regional tour.

- **North-east tour**

To the north-east from the D965 are the villages of Mosson (château), Brion-sur-Ource (church), Courban (church), and north on the D996 is **Montigny-sur-Aube**, where the Rennaissance château, with its own sixteenth century chapel and series of old bridges over the river Aube, is noteworthy. Try going cross-country, north-west a few kilometres, to see the castle and church at **Autricourt**, aiming for Noiron-sur-Seine, and back on the N71 to Châtillon — first calling in at Pothières (castle) and Mont Lassois.

- **Westward route**

To the west of Châtillon, off the D965, is the château at Larrey, lovely lakes, and Romanesque churches at Marcenay, Laignes and Griselles, Gallic *oppidum* at Vertault, and celebrated monastery at Molesmes — the last three all on the D953, northbound.

- **Southern route**

South of Châtillon are chateaux at Villaines-en-Duesmois, Rochefort, Essarois, Villiers-le-Duc, and churches of interest at St-Marc-sur-Seine and St-Germain-le-Rocheux. Aisey-sur-Seine has a tumulus, a sarcophagus and a grotto.

Semur-en-Auxois

Semur-en-Auxois is on the western border of the département and is another pretty and interesting centre for a regional tour. The Office de Tourisme is on the place Gaveau, tel.

80.97.05.96. The town itself has everything a tourist could wish for — hotel-restaurants, medieval cobbled streets, old houses, thirteenth century *château-fort* with *donjon*, many town mansions of note, a classic thirteenth century church of Notre Dame, ramparts, towers, river view and museums — all very photogenic.

From Semur there are half a dozen essential sites to explore: to the west the fine fourteenth century château of Époisses, archives and local cheeses; to the south a château at Précy-sous-Thil, and at Saulieu the Basilica of St-Andoche; to the south-east the thirteenth century church at St-Thibault, and the picturesque little town of Vitteaux with its many medieval mansions and twelfth century Romanesque church. Posanges, just north of Vitteaux, has an excellent fifteenth century château. Flavigny-sur-Ozerain, with its medieval paved streets, gates and tower, is one of the prettiest villages in Burgundy.

The real gems of the Semur circuit are still to come. **Fontenay Abbey** is on the outskirts of the small village of Marmagne. Not only has it an early English history, but it is in incomparable condition. **Alise-Ste-Reine** is Burgundy's most famous archaeological site. Do a little homework first to find out where Caesar's legions were encamped and how they managed to surround the wretched Gauls, and have some sympathy for the gallant Vercingetorix defending his country against the invader, and finally submitting to a humiliating end in Rome. See the châteaux of **Frolois** and **Bussy-le-Grand** — home of the saucy, provocative Comte de Bussy-Rabutin. Again, to get the full flavour of the satirical paintings inside the château, a little homework beforehand will be beneficial. Another nearby Renaissance château is Jours-lès-Baigneux. Finally, due north, is **Montbard**, which has Buffon's park, Gothic mansions, the Tower of Aubespin and notable museums.

To sum up, Semur could be the base for nearly a week of joyful visits. The only thing missing in all these beautiful sites are the vineyards.

Beaune

Beaune is the final selected focal point for tours in the Côte d'Or. The Tourist Office, tel. 80.22.24.51, is in the place Carnot, appropriately in one of the medieval houses. The visitor will need to time the visit carefully to the Hôtel Dieu and its famous Polyptyque, since the guided tours are infrequent. The Basilica of Notre Dame and tapestries, and the two museums — of wine, at the 'Hôtel' des Ducs de Bourgogne, and the Beaux-Arts — are both worth visiting. To the north-east of Beaune is the famous abbey of **Citeaux** in the village of St-Nicolas on the D966: here you can pay homage to the founders of the Cistercian order which swept the western world for more than five centuries.

- **South-west tour**

To the south and south-west of Beaune begins another roll-call of famous wine villages, but interlaced with châteaux of repute at Pommard, Meursault and Santenay. **La Rochepot**, near picturesque Nolay, is perhaps the best preserved, and is certainly worth a detour. The villages with Romanesque churches include Pommard, Volnay, Monthélie, Auxey-Duresses, Meursault, Puligny-Montrachet and Santenay. A tour via the N73, then the N6 and back to Beaune via the N74, will take between four hours and four days, depending on resistance to the temptations encountered en route.

- **Eastern route**

To the east lies the town of **Seurre**, a 'port' on the river Saône, and known not only for the prelate Bossuet, but also for mustard, vinegar and fish dishes! Nearby are the châteaux of Auvillars-sur-Saône and Brion, and the sixteenth century chapel in the château of Pagny-le-Château.

- **North-west tour**

Finally, to the north-west of Beaune, are **Savigny-lès-Beaune**, with château, church of St-Cassien and museum; Cussey-la-Colonne with its Roman remains; Arnay-le-Duc, a fortified small town with château and fifteenth century church; and the châteaux of Châteauneuf and, above all, **Commarin**.

The Morvan National Park

On 16 October 1970 the French government created this huge natural park in the centre of Burgundy. It was formed out of sixty-four communes almost equally from the four départements — Côte d'Or, Saône-et-Loire, Nièvre and Yonne. It has only 31,000 inhabitants in its area of 173,615 hectares. It consists of a narrow rectangle 25 km. across in the south and 35 km. in the north, and 60 km. from north to south. The towns which are technically in the area are Saulieu, Vézelay and Château-Chinon. There are woods, covering one-third of the area and harbouring wild game, and river tributaries of the Yonne, Cure, Arroux, Ternin, Chalaux, Cousin, and many others, teeming with freshwater fish. There are many *lacs* (natural lakes) and *étangs* (man-made ponds) which stock delicious freshwater white fish. No less than 60,000 *pêcheurs* fish there each year. The main lakes are Des Settons (360 hectares), De Pannecière (520 hectares), De Chamboux (75 hectares), St-Agnan (142 hectares), Chaumeçon (135 hectares) and Du Crescent (165 hectares).

- **Facilities**

For those who like an open-air holiday, the Morvan is ideal — perfect walks and rambles, horse or pony riding, swimming canoeing, sailing and regattas, nature studies, bicycling, looking at the waterfalls, water mills, the wild fowl and wild animal life such as roe and fallow deer, and wild boar (*sangliers*). The beech and oak forests, bracken and broom, and in the spring wild orchids, purple foxgloves, bilberries, etc. are spectacular. Visit and talk to the many craftsmen and watch their work on pottery, woodwork or slating roofs. The northern half of the Morvan is relatively flat, but south of Montsauche you come to the Haut-Morvan, with the mountains of Beuvray (821 m.), Preneley (855 m.) and the Bois du Roi or Haut Folin (901 m.), where you can ski.

- **Circular route for motorists**

A recommended circular route for visiting the area by car is as follows:

1. Start at Autun and head west to St-Honoré-les-Bains. The

80 km. route takes about three hours via the D978 to St-Léger-sous-Beuvray and Larochemilay.

2. North to Château-Chinon via Moulins-Engilbert.

3. North via Charmard and Ouroux to Montsauche.

4. North-east to St-Brisson, where the Maison du Parc is the focal headquarters of the Morvan Park.

5. North-west to Vézelay via Quarré-lès-Tombes, Chastellux-sur-Cure and St-Père.

6. East to Avallon and south-east to Rouvray.

7. South-east to Saulieu.

8. South back to Autun (45 km.) via Chissey-en-Morvan and Lucenay l'Évêque.

Morvan is no place for people in a hurry. The pace of life is very leisurely. The roads are good but wind enticingly around the countryside. The small *auberges, gîtes* and camp sites are peaceful and welcoming. The little restaurants serve delicious low-cost meals, and the local wine could come from any of the four départements of which Morvan is a part. Try *jambons de Morvan, soupe à choux, canard à chataignes,* and the trout.

To sum up, this is an ideal place for a family holiday. The places you should visit are Autun, Avallon, Saulieu, Vézelay, Château-Chinon and the spa town of St-Honoré-les-Bains.

Further information from the Maison du Parc, St-Brisson, 58230 Montsauche, tel. 86.78.70.16.

Points of interest

Alise Ste-Reine (D–5) is famous in Burgundian annals for the desperate siege and battle in 52 BC between the Roman legions of Julius Caesar and the reunited Gaulish tribes under Vercingetorix. Inevitably, the well-trained legions stormed the Gaulish stronghold, and their leader was taken from the battlefield of Alesia to Rome as a captive where he was subsequently put to death. A vast bronze monument to Vercingetorix was built by Millet in the nineteenth century on the hills overlooking the battlefield. Excavations have revealed the Roman battle lines, a theatre, a forum and a Merovingian church.

In AD 252 a 16-year-old Christian martyr, called Reine, was beheaded at Les Trois-Ormeaux for refusing to change her faith and marry a Roman centurion. She was later canonized and pilgrims came from all over France to worship at her shrine. In 1659, under the patronage of St Vincent de Paul, a hospital was built for the use of the sick pilgrims. The hospital, chapel and museum should be visited.

Arnay-le-Duc (D–9) is an ancient fortified town with ramparts, gatehouses, towers, a circular keep *(donjon)*, old stronghold château of the Princes of Condé and the 'Tour de la Motte-Forte'. On 13 June 1570 Henri of Navarre at the age of 16 (before he became King) won a notable victory here over the Catholic army of Marshal Cossé-Brissac. Well worth a visit.

Aubigny-lès-Sombernon (E–8) is a tiny hamlet rated by the Burgundian authorities as a *'village remarquable, placé parmi les premiers de la region'* — a rare honour.

Auxey-Duresses (F–11). This pretty wine village with gastronomic specialities has a lovely view over the valleys and vineyards. The 'Fête des Vignerons' is on 24 August.

Auxonne (J–9) is a town on the banks of the river Saône and fishermen were at work here in the ninth century. Rather later, between 1786 and 1791, Napoleon made several visits. The old town has much to commend it — a fortified château, many guard towers, seventeenth century arsenal, thirteenth century church of Notre Dame and the Bonaparte museum. Definitely worth a visit.

Beaune (F–10) is one of the show-pieces of Burgundy. It was evangelized in the fifth century by St Martin of Tours. It was originally called 'Belena', then 'Belno-Castrum' and was the site of an ancient pre-Roman Gaulish pilgrimage. Later the dukes of Burgundy made Beaune one of their chief residences. Nicolas Rolin, Chancellor to the Duchy in 1443–51, and his wife were responsible for the building of the Hotel Dieu and the Hospice de la Charité, for which the world will remain forever grateful. The guided tour is essential to see the famous polychrome roof, hospital, etc. The bell tower, Romanesque collegiate church of Notre Dame with its Flemish tapestries, thirteenth century church of St Nicolas, Museum of Fine Arts, museums of the 'Vins de Bourgogne', and the museum of the 'Hotel-Dieu' are quite incomparable. Be prepared to spend a minimum of a day in Beaune, and preferably much longer. The annual sale of the wines of the 'Hospices de Beaune' takes place over three days at the end of November, when fine wines, mainly red, from superb vineyards are auctioned in new oak casks, each of 270-bottle capacity.

Belleneuve (I–7) is a village officially classified as the '*village que j'aime*'. The Fête of the Forest and the 'Noces de Muguet' (lily of the valley) is held at the beginning of May, accompanied by the folklore group the 'Compagnons de l'Albane'.

Benoisey (D–5). This small hamlet has an annual fête. 'Quasimodo', held on Low Sunday.

Bèze (I–6) is a pretty village overlooking the river of the same name, with two thirteenth century houses in the square, several towers, and tree-lined avenues and promenades.

Brianny (C–6). The warlocks and witches (*sorciers*) of La Martole meet on the 'champ de Fâ' in this small hamlet.

Brion-sur-Ource (E–2). Before their uneasy alliance the English troops fought and beat the Burgundians here in 1359.

Bussy-le-Grand (D–5) should be visited to see the famous château where the exiled Count of that name amused himself (and posterity) by his savage and cynical paintings of the personalities at the court of Louis XIV.

Châtillon-sur-Seine (E–2). Aldon, who founded the Augustine Abbey of Notre Dame here in the twelfth century, was a friend of the great St Bernard. Châtillon, with its strategic situation, was regarded as one of the key fortresses to the Burgundian duchy. In 1870 Garibaldi's troops audaciously set fire to the town. In 1940 the town was 65 per cent destroyed by German aerial bombardment. On 9 September 1944 the two French divisions of Generals de Lattre and Leclerc met here before the final attack on Paris. Napoleon's Marshal Marmont was born here, as were the writers M. Désiré and Charles Nisard. There are many places worth a visit, including the ruins of the château of the dukes of Burgundy, the Maison Philandrier, the church of St Vorles, with its tenth century walls, the Cistercian church of St Nicolas and the archaeological museum with the famous Treasure of Vix.

Chenôve (G–8). In 'La Cuverie' can be seen the two huge wine presses which made the table wine for the dukes of Burgundy.

Comblanchien (G–10). On 21 August 1944 this small village was mainly destroyed by the fleeing Germans, who shot their French hostages. A monument records the French names.

Crépand (C–5). This small village was the site of a battle on 8 January 1870 between Garibaldi's troops and the Prussians. A monument to Garibaldi is in the main square.

Dijon (H–7). For four centuries, the fifth to the ninth, Dijon was the See of the bishops of Langres. Later, under the Grand Dukes of Valois, it knew unprecedented fame and wealth. In 1513 it was attacked by thirty thousand Swiss and German troops. In 1870, despite strong resistance, the German armies took Dijon. Among its famous citizens have been the engineer Eiffel, the musician Rameau, the poet Crébillon, the prelate de Bossuet and the sculptors Dubois and Rude. The visitor will need at least a day, and preferably more, to explore the glories of the Hôtel de Ville, the ancient Ducal palace, the Préfecture, the Palais de Justice, the many handsome and distinguished churches and museums, including the cathedral of St Bénigne, the abbeys of St Bénigne, St Philibert, St Michel and the Musée des Beaux Arts. The ancient splendours of the Ducal buildings are matched by the richness of the arts displayed in the many museums and the gastronomic pleasures. Try the several small restaurants clustered round the main covered market place. There are two Tourist Offices in the centre which will supply a free, detailed guide leaflet of this lovely city.

Fain-lès-Moutiers (B–5). Catherine Labouré (1806–76), a nun of La Charité, lived here and was canonized in 1947. A chapel and statue, both named after her, are to be found in the village.

89

Fixin (G–8). Claude Noisot, an officer in Napoleon's Imperial Guard, retired to this village and commissioned a bronze monument to the Emperor by the Dijon sculptor Rude. The Noisot park reproduces many Napoleonic memories — the fortifications of Elba, a statue entitles the 'Dreams of Napoleon', and a Napoleonic museum. From the fort-shaped belvedere one has views over the vineyards and plains leading to Dijon.

Flavigny-sur-Ozerain (D–6). Julius Caesar's camp can be seen here. The village was occupied by English troups in 1359. In 1848 Lacordaire founded an order of Dominican monks here. It is a medieval village with narrow paved streets and Gothic and Renaissance houses; the main town gates, the Carolingian crypt of Ste-Reine in the old Benedictine abbey and the church of St Genet make pretty Flavigny worth a visit. It is known locally for its *anis* liqueur.

Fontaine-lès-Dijon (G–7) was the birthplace in 1091 of St Bernard, founder of the abbey of Clairvaux. A convent and chapel still commemorate him here.

Genay (C–5). Here on 3 August 1944 a battle was fought by the Allies against the retreating Germans.

Grignon (D–5). St Reine, before her martyrdom in AD 252 by the Romans, was held in prison at the château Grignon.

Grosbois-en-Montagne (E–7). This tiny village harbours an eighteenth century library with over 40,000 volumes and manuscripts dating from the fourteenth century.

Leuglay (F–3). In the eighteenth century the village parson had a vision and subsequently discovered hidden under the altar in his church the bodies of Christians martyred by the Vandals fourteen hundred years before. The relics are now honoured under the name 'des Bons Saints'.

Magny-sur-Tille (H–8). On 22 April each year a pilgrimage takes place here in memory of St Françoise Sauvestre, to whom were attributed many miracles. She lived and died in this village.

Manlay (C–9). In 1944 the German troops and the *maquis* of Morvan fought a savage battle which completely destroyed the village. Chancellor Adenauer and the Archbishop of

Cologne helped to finance the repair and restoration.

Massingy (E–2). The warlocks and sorcerers hold their sabbaths here under 'Les Jumeaux de Massingy' and 'la Chassaigne' — two massive twin boulders facing each other.

Merceuil (F–11). The modern Archéodrome de Beaune has reconstructed in great detail the life and times of the local inhabitants from the Neolithic to the Gallo-Romans. Worth a visit.

Mirebeau (I–7). Remains of the huge Roman camp of Caesar's Eighth Legion can be seen at the site called 'Epée de la Tène'.

Mont-St-Jean (D–8). In the fifth century, Raoul de Mont St Jean brought back the holy relics of St Pélagie, a martyred Christian virgin from Palestine. In this picturesque feudal village the château, ramparts, keep, ancient hospital and Romanesque church (which contains the relics of the saint) are worth a visit. Charollais cattle munch peacefully in the fields of the valley of the river Serein.

Montbard (C–4). This town contains museums celebrating the famous local naturalists François Buffon and Daubenton. The remains of the old stronghold and particularly the tower of Aubespin and the orangery in the Parc de Buffon are worth a visit.

Montigny-Mornay-Villeneuve-sur-Vingeanne (J–5) has the longest name of any village in France.

Montoillot (E–8). During the war of 1870 Menotti Garibaldi made his campaign headquarters in this tiny hamlet.

Nod-sur-Seine (E–3). On 12 September 1944 this village was the meeting place of the two liberation armies. The First French army from Provence in the south met Leclerc's army from Normandy.

Nuits-St-Georges (G–9). Besides being famous as a wine-growing region, this was the site on 18 December 1870 of a bloody battle between the French troops under General Crémer and the Bavarian division of General Glumer. There is a notable Gallo-Roman site called 'Les Bollards', the grotto of

Trou-Leger, a bell tower, the château and churches which are all worth visiting.

La Rochepot (E-11). In addition to its beautiful château, the grotto called 'Le Trou du Père Guste' and the dolmen called 'La Pierre qui Vire' are worth a visit.

St-Aubin (E–11). The cult of this saint was introduced in Burgundy in the ninth century by the son of the provost of the abbey of St Aubin of Angers. It is a pretty little wine village with narrow, winding, cobbled streets and old stone houses with large courtyards.

St-Germain-Source-Seine (E–6) is the site of a Gallo-Roman temple dedicated to the goddess Sequana. The land round the source of the great river Seine belongs to the city of Paris.

St-Romain (F–11). The grottoes of Perthuis and Grenier here were used as natural forts in Gallo-Roman times. The archaeological collection is open during the summer months.

Saulieu (B–8). This, the ancient town of Sidolocus, was evangelized in the third century by St Andoche and St Thyrse on their way from Autun to Alesia by Agrippa's Roman road. The English took the town in 1359. Now it is a bustling place on a major crossroads, with a choice of a dozen hotels.

Semur-en-Auxois (C–6). Legend has it that this town was founded by Hercules on his return from Spain. Originally a Gallo-Roman *castrum*, it became a fortress of the dukes of Burgundy. It is one of the most attractive small towns in Burgundy and necessitates a visit to see the fortress (Le donjon), the Porte Sauvigny, and the magnificent church of Notre Dame. Semur is nearly surrounded by the river Armançon, and its ramparts on a rose-coloured granite spur show what a natural stronghold it has been over the centuries.

Talant (G–7) is a picturesque town near Dijon with the remains of a château owned by the Burgundian dukes. It has many fifteenth, sixteenth, and seventeenth century houses, an old armoury, a tower and cellars.

Velars-sur-Ouche (G–7). The chapel of Notre-Dame-de-l'Étang with its twelfth century statue of the black Virgin, has been a pilgrimage centre for five hundred years. St François de Sales, St Jeanne de Chantal, Bishop Bossuet, King Louis XIV and the Grand Condé came here to pray on 2 July and 8 September.

Villers-les-Pots (J–9). Napoleon Bonaparte, when a young soldier serving at Auxonne, often came here to pray at the chapel of Notre Dame-de-la-Levée.

Villiers-le-Duc (E–3). Eudes III, Duke of Burgundy, founded a Cistercian abbey here in 1193 which subsequently became a favourite hunting rendezvous of the Burgundian dukes. On 10 June 1944, thirty-seven members of the French *maquis* were killed here by German troops.

Vitteaux (D–7) is a picturesque village. The thirteenth century Maison Bélime, convent and Halles are worth a visit. The Hospital chapel serves as a small museum.

Vix (D–2). The Treasure of Vix was discovered in 1953 in a prince's sepulchre in this tiny hamlet at the foot of Mount Lassois. The jewels, ceramics, chariots, amphorae and bronze bowls have been moved to the museum at Châtillon-sur-Seine. The huge sixth century funeral urn is perhaps the most famous relic of them all.

Castles and châteaux

This department has a rich selection of castles and châteaux. Among them are the ruins of Thil, Chaudenay, Vergy, Mont-St-Jean and Montbard, the strongholds of Châteauneuf, Corcelles-les-Arts and Posanges, and the Renaissance châteaux of the seventeenth century — Commarin, Bussy-Rabutin, Époisses, Chailly-sur-Armançon and Jours-lès-Baigneux — which were châteaux built for comfort rather than castles built for defence. Finally there is the group of eighteenth century châteaux erected for the nobility, which often escaped the egalitarian destruction of the Revolutionary mob: Arcelot at Arceau, Beaumont-sur-Vingeanne, Bressey-sur-Tille, Grancey, Lantenay, Vantoux at Messigny-et-Vantoux, and Fontaine-Française. I have included only exceptional buildings, classified as MH (*Monument Historique*) or IMH (*Inscrit à l'Inventaire*

93

des Monuments Historiques). Would-be visitors are advised to check opening times either with the nearest tourist information officer or with the Association Départementale du Tourisme, Hôtel du Département, BP 1601–21305 Dijon, tel. 80.73.81.81.

Arceau (I–7). The eighteenth century Château d'Arcelot has an interesting Italianate salon, fine staircases, tapestries, chapel and mausoleum set in a pretty park.

Arnay-le-Duc (D–9) has the sixteenth century château of the Princes of Condé, with towers, old kitchen and chimneys, and crenellated chapel.

Asnières-en-Montagne (C–4) has the remains of the fifteenth century Château de Rochefort, with its several towers, chimneys and castle chapel.

Beaumont-sur-Vingeanne (J–6) was built in 1724 by Claude Jolyot, an abbot and chaplain to Louis XV, on the slope of a vineyard, set in an attractive park. It is considered to be an eighteenth century folly. Open mid-summer and September.

Beaune (F–10). The Hôtel-Dieu is not, strictly speaking, either a château or a 'religious' building. The fifteenth century hospital and museum are set round a substantial, paved, quadrilateral courtyard. Most of the buildings have the well-known unique polychrome tiled roofs. All the rooms, including dormitory, chapel, *cour d'honneur*, apothecary and gallery, and the old wells, are in excellent repair. The altarpiece of The Last Judgement by Rogier van der Weyden (1450) is large, detailed, colourful and exquisite. Just look at the individual faces of the damned, and those who, doubtless for excellent reasons, have been spared! One of the most interesting sites in Burgundy. Guided tour only. Closed April. Entrance 15 francs.

Brochon (G–8) has a neo-Renaissance château built in the late nineteenth century, now the Stephen Liegard school. The fountains and water garden are of interest.

Bussy-le-Grand (D–5) has a very pretty and interesting mainly seventeenth century château, in excellent state, set in formal gardens with a moat. The satirical portraits inside are well worth seeing, and include several English personalities of the age. The Count of Bussy-Rabutin was' exiled from court by Louis XIV, and took his revenge: it is said that he painted the hundred or so cynical and amusing portraits himself; he certainly wrote the scurrilous epigrams on each. Guided tour only. Open all year. Entrance 12 francs.

Châteauneuf (E–8) has a stronghold *château-fort*, the best of its kind in Burgundy, with a twelfth century keep, octagonal towers and interesting chapel. Open all year. Guided tour. Entrance 9 francs.

Chorey (G–10) and **Clamerey** (D–7) also have listed châteaux.

Collonges-lès-Bévy (F–9) is near Gevrey-Chambertin. The château was built in 1660 by Prosper Bauyn, a Dijon councillor in the Chamber of Accounts. Interesting interiors, and relics of General Cassendi and Gaspard Monge. Open summer. Entrance 12 francs.

Commarin (E–8) was originally a fifteenth century castle with fortified courtyard and round towers. It is very elegant, and is situated in a large wooded park. It is well worth a visit. Closed winter. Entrance 22 francs.

Corgoloin (G–10) has the Château de Cussigny, an L-shaped castle, rebuilt in 1743 by the Seigneur des Barres with *cour d'honneur*, dovecot, chapel and chimneys, set in a park.

Courtivron (G–5) is a classic *château-fort* built in the nineteenth century, now dominated by a huge keep, surrounded by a moat. Open summer only. Entrance free.

Dijon (H–7). The Hôtel de Ville is the old palace of the dukes of Bourgogne, built in the fourteenth century with later additions. Visits can be made only to the Fine Arts Museum, the Chapel of the Elect (*Élus*), and the Tower of Philippe 'Le Bon'. Open all year. Entrance 8 francs. Preferably buy a 'carte unique' for 12 francs, valid for one year, which enables the visitor to see all seven of the town's museums.

Époisses (B–6) has a château that was a royal residence in the eleventh century, Merovingian times. Within the walls are a church and various shelters for the village population. Inside are magnificent furniture, Beauvais tapestry, paintings, and archives with letters of Madame de Sévigny. Despite the ravages of the Revolution, well worth a visit. Interior can be visited only July to November. Entrance 15 francs.

Fontaine-Française (J–5). Henry IV paid two visits to this fortress in the sixteenth century. It was made into a private dwelling in the eighteenth century. There is rich and varied furniture and tapestries, and a watermill, fountains, and formal park. Worth a visit. Open summer only. Entrance 18 francs.

Frolois (E–5). The castle was built in the fourteenth century and repaired in the sixteenth. It is a rectangular building on a rocky spur dominating the valley of the river Vau. The furniture, painted tapestries and classic façade all make it worth seeing. Closed mid-winter. Entrance 13 francs.

Gevrey-Chambertin (G–8). The Abbey of Cluny owned this castle in the early eleventh century. It was rebuilt at the end of the thirteenth century in order to house and stock the Abbot's wine. The keep stands defended by a fortified gate. Open all year. Entrance free.

Grignon (D–5) was a tenth century *castrum*, and became a home of the dukes of Burgundy. Open all year. Entrance 16 francs.

Jours-lès-Baigneux (E–4) is a Renaissance château rebuilt in the sixteenth century. It has an arcaded façade, the Joyeuse Tower of 1578, and a noteworthy staircase. Open March, April, July and August. Entrance 13 francs.

Lantenay (F–7) has the seventtenth century Château des Bouhier with two stone staircases of note. Open April to Mid-September. Entrance 6 francs.

Lantilly (C–5). The château was reconstructed in 1709, and has not been repaired since. Apart from its one hundred windows it has tapestries and portraits. It is set in a park. Open April to end October. Entrance 16 francs.

Lux (I–6) was built in the twelfth century and restored in the sixteenth. The original home of the governors of Burgundy. Open June to end September. Entrance 13 francs.

Marigny-le-Cahouet (D–6) was built in the thirteenth century and later repaired. It has four corner towers, a gate tower, drawbridge over the moat, Renaissance gallery and castle chapel. Open June to end September. Entrance free.

Ménessaire (B–9) was built in the twelfth century and rebuilt in the fifteenth. It has four towers at each corner, and polychrome tiled roofs. The 'grand salon' is noteworthy. Open July to mid-September. Entrance 12 francs.

Meursault (F–11). The château contains an interesting collection of wine utensils and pictures. Open February to end November.

Pommard (F–10). The château, founded in 1098 by the Duke of Burgundy, stands in 20 hectares of vines. Open April to November. Entrance 18 francs.

Quemigny-sur-Seine (E–4). The château was built in the fourteenth century and the original crenellated keep and circular towers still exist. The salons, staircases, vaulted kitchen and terraced park all make it worth a visit.

La Rochepot (E–11) is one of the most photogenic châteaux in Burgundy. 'La Roche' is self-evident. Regnier Pot, Chamberlain of Philip the Bold, reconstructed the château in the fifteenth century, and it was entirely restored in the nineteenth. Closed November and December. Entrance 13 francs.

St-Seine-sur-Vingeanne (J–5) has the *château-fort* of Rosières, which has a massive keep, gatehouse, etc. Open all year. Entrance free.

Savigny-lès-Beaune (F–10) has three sites worth seeing. The fourteenth century château is rectangular with circular towers, magnificent dungeons, staircase, and park planted with vines. The car exhibition is housed within the château. Open all year. Entrance 12 francs. Also Le Petit Château of the seventeenth century; and the Manor House of Nicolay of the same period — the formal French gardens are highly rated.

Semur-en-Auxois (C–6). The *château-fort*, Le Donjon, was rebuilt in the thirteenth century. Built in quadrilateral shape, it

97

has four named circular corner towers. The town gatehouse, 'Porte Sauvigny', is also worth seeing, and the town ramparts. Open summer months only. Entrance 11 francs.

Talmay (J–7) has a château of the eighteenth century dominated by a thirteenth century high crenellated keep surmounted by a pepper-pot roof. Inside, the furniture, tapestries and grand staircase are worth seeing. Open summer only. Entrance 16 francs.

Thoisy-la-Berchère (C–8). The fifteenth century château has later restorations. The main hall is flanked by a large circular tower and two polygonal towers. There is a guardhouse, Renaissance furniture, tapestries and paintings by Boucher, Lebrun and Largillière.

Vic-de-Chassenay (C–6) has the fourteenth century Château de Bourbilly, reconstructed in the nineteenth century. Open April to end September. Entrance 15 francs.

Vic-sous-Thil (C–7) has the ruins of the ancient oval château of Thil on the top of a hill overlooking the Auxois. A high, narrow, square tower stands near the Gothic collegiate church of the fourteenth century. The two together are worth a visit. Open for the first seven months of the year. Entrance 13 francs.

Vougeot (G–9). Château Clos-Vougeot was built in 1551 by Dom Loisier, Abbot of Citeaux. It is most decorative, standing proudly amongst the vineyards. It has four twelfth century wine grape *pressoirs* and cellars. Open all year. Entrance 12 francs.

Cathedrals, abbeys and splendid churches

Pre-Romaneque architecture in this département is best illustrated by the crypts of St Bénigne at Dijon and at Flavigny-sur-Ozerain. There are many examples of fine Romanesque architecture, and St Vorles at Châtillon is but one showing a Lombard influence. The Cistercian art from Citeaux can be seen at Fontenay, St-Pierre and St Nicolas at Châtillon. The magnificence of Cluniac art can be seen at Saulieu and Beaune. Thirteenth century Gothic architecture is best seen at

Notre Dame in Semur-en-Auxois, Notre Dame and St Bénigne at Dijon, St-Seine-l'Abbaye and St-Genest at Flavigny. Later one finds Renaissance art on the façade of St Michael's church in Dijon and the façade of the chapel in Pagny-le-Château; and seventeenth and eighteenth century art is found at the convents and other religious buildings at Dijon, and the chapel of the Oratory in Beaune.

Agencourt (G–9) has a thirteenth century church with a rare clock tower arcade.

Aignay-le-Duc (F–4) has a thirteenth century church with a polychrome sixteenth century stone high altar.

Alise-Ste-Reine (D–5). The parish church of St Léger was built from the seventh to the eleventh century, and has a notable statue of the saint, scene of a pilgrimage, hospital chapel and two crosses, the Piroir and one at the crossroads, both of the sixteenth century.

Autricourt (E–1) has a fifteenth century church.

Auxonne (J–9) has the thirteenth century church of Notre Dame with a notable Virgin and Child — she is the *'Vierge au raisin'.*

Bagnot (H–10). A twelfth century Romanesque church with paintings on the walls — 'Les diables de Bagnot' — representing the Last Judgement.

Bard-le-Régulier (C–9). The twelfth century church of St Jean l'Évangéliste has superb fourteenth century choir stalls and an octagonal twelfth century tower.

Beaune (F–10). Notre Dame is a twelfth century Romanesque collegiate church of Cluniac architecture, and has a black Virgin, Flemish tapestries, etc. The church of St Nicolas has a castellated clock tower and a thirteenth century sculptured tympanun showing the life of St Nicholas. The eighteenth century oratory chapel, Carmelite chapel and Jacobite chapel are of note.

La Bussière-sur-Ouche (F–8) has a twelfth century Romanesque abbey of Notre Dame in the Cistercian style. There are twelfth century stone tombs with recumbent figures. Guided visits are possible (tel. 80.33.02.29).

Bussy-le-Grand (D–5) has a twelfth century Romanesque church, housing paintings by Poussin, Murillo and Andrea del Sarto.

Châtillon-sur-Seine (E–2). The church of St Vorles is very old and was repaired in the tenth century. It has a remarkable sepulchre and the subterranean chapel of St Bernard. The twelfth century church of St Nicolas is built to a Cistercian plan, and has sixteenth century stained-glass windows and a polygonal tower. The twelfth century church of St Pierre was rebuilt to a Cistercian plan.

Cîteaux (St Nicolas-lès-Cîteaux) (H–9) is probably the saddest site in Burgundy. The once glorious abbey, which founded more than a thousand others throughout the world, is now a pale shadow — the ravages of the imperial forces under Gallas in 1636 and the frenzy of the Revolution proved too much. There remain the twelfth century chapel, the fifteenth century library, a seventeenth century dormitory, and very little else. *Sic transit gloria mundi.*

Coulmier-le-Sec (D–3). The Renaissance Maison des Templiers and the thirteenth century church built to a cruciform plan, are both *sites classés.*

Cussey-lès-Forges (H–4), built in the twelfth century, has a Romanesque clock tower and fortified walls for archers.

Dijon (H–7). The cathedral of St Bénigne is of thirteenth century Burgundian Gothic style. The saint was a third century evangelist, and the original basilica was built in AD 535. It was restored by St Mayoul, Abbot of Cluny, between 1002 and 1018. Only the octagonal crypt remains of the original basilica; after the Revolutionary ravages took their toll, the whole church was restored in the nineteenth century. The spire is nearly 100 metres high. The small chapel of Ste Marie dates from the ninth century and the Benedictine dormitory next door from the thirteenth. The gardens and cellars are of note.

The thirteenth century church of Notre Dame is a masterpiece of Burgundian Gothic art. It has a unique façade with gargoyles and a Flemish mechanical clock of the fourteenth century. In a small apse is a twelfth century black wooden Virgin, which is greatly venerated.

The sixteenth century church of St Michel, with its handsome Renaissance façade, statues, and mausoleum; the twelfth century Romanesque-Burgundian church of St Philibert (now an exhibition hall); the fifteenth century church of St Étienne; the fifteenth century flamboyant Gothic church of St Jean; the Chapel of Ste Croix de Jerusalem and the seventeenth century Carmelite chapel are all *Monuments Historiques* and well worth visiting. Dijon is a haven for fine Romanesque, Gothic and Renaissance churches.

Flavigny-sur-Ozerain (D–6). This small medieval village of under 400 inhabitants boasts not only the thirteenth century church of St Genest, with its famous triptych, 'The Angel of the Annunciation', but also the eighth century abbey of Ste Reine, with a hexagonal Carolingian crypt, 'Notre Dame des Pilliers', recently uncovered.

Fontenay (Marmagne) (C–4). The abbey was founded in 1118 by St Bernard, but perfected, finished and funded by the English St Edmund (Edmé). This is one of the major ecclesiastical sites in France. Church, cloister, chapter room, dormitory, heated rest room, writing room, gateway-lodge, bakery, infirmary, workshops, gardens, fish-breeding tank, and a small prison for delinquent monks — all are in perfect condition. The old Minster of Notre Dame is a perfect example of the austere, formal style of the Cistercians, in contrast to the magnificent, opulent Cluny style. Should be seen by every visitor to Burgundy. Open all year, with guided tours. Entrance 20 francs.

Gurgy-le-Château (G–3) has a thirteenth century Gothic church, an ancient chapel in a Templar château.

Laignes (C–2) has a thirteenth century Gothic church.

Malain (F–7) has a seventeenth century church with noteworthy crosses.

Marcilly-lès-Vitteaux (D–7) has a sixteenth century stone Calvary in the church square, and two more Calvaries of note, in Dracy and on the road to Velogny.

Meursault (F–11) has a fifteenth century Gothic church with a castellated octagonal Gothic clock tower and a twelfth century stone Virgin.

Minot (G–4) has a thirteenth century church.

Mirebeau (I–7) has a thirteenth century Romanesque church, with notable statues, altar, chandeliers and bell tower.

Montigny-sur-Aube (F–1) has a sixteenth century chapel in the château, with Italianate Renaissance interior décor.

Nicey (C–2) has a thirteenth century church, with sculptures, tympanum and evangelist symbols.

Nuits-St-Georges (G–9) has the thirteenth century church of St Symphorien, with an unusual clock tower.

Pagny-le-Château (I–10) has a sixteenth century brick chapel in the old château, and fifteenth century tombs with effigies.

Pichanges (H–6) has a fortified church with a twelfth century Romanesque choir and clock tower.

Plombières-lès-Dijon (G–7) has a thirteenth century church with a choir and an octagonal clock tower.

Pouilly-en-Auxois (E–8) has the fourteenth century chapel of Notre Dame Trouvée with richly decorated furnishings, sixteenth century *pietà*, statues and black Virgin, and the Calvary dates from the fifteenth century. All are noteworthy.

La Rochepot (E–11) has a twelfth century Romanesque church.

Rougemont (C–4) has a thirteenth century abbey.

Rouvres-en-Plaine (H–8) has a thirteenth century Cistercian church built on a cruciform plan, with noteworthy stone tombs, and statues of St John the Baptist.

Sacquenay (I–5) has a thirteenth century church which was fortified in the fifteenth century.

St-Jean-de-Losne (I–10) has a fifteenth century church built of brick and stone, with a curious clock tower.

St-Maurice-sur-Vingeanne (J–5) has a thirteenth century church.

St-Seine-l'Abbaye (F–6) has a twelfth century Gothic abbey; the wall paintings are of note.

St Seine-sur-Vingeanne (J–5) has a fourteenth century church with a high clock tower and a church door with tympanum.

St-Thibault (D–7) has a thirteenth century church with architectural influence from the Champagne country; the choir is narrow and very tall. The north door and the rich furnishings have merit.

Ste-Sabine (E–9) has a thirteenth century Gothic church; the cemetery cross and statuary are worth a look.

Santenay (E–11) has the thirteenth century Gothic church of St Jean de Narosse, with wooden porch, rounded tympanum, and three fifteenth century wood polychromes.

Saulieu (B–8). The basilica of St Andoche was first erected in AD 306, then destroyed by the Saracens. Charlemagne rebuilt it and presented the abbot with his altar-book and the famous vineyard 'Clos de Corton Charlemagne'. The nave is traditional Cluniac architecture. Famous for the sculptured cornices — look for the 'Flight into Egypt', the 'Hanging of Judas', and the 'False Prophet Balaam and his Ass'.

Savigny-lès-Beaune (F–10). The church of St Cassien has a twelfth century Romanesque transept and a clock tower of merit.

Selongey (H–5) has a thirteenth century church and the chapel of Ste Gertrude, a place of pilgrimage. Both worth visiting.

Semur-en-Auxois (C–6). The thirteenth century church of Notre Dame was restored by Viollet-le-Duc in the nineteenth century. The glass windows, ciborium and fine fifteenth century tombs are of note.

Talant (G–7) has a thirteenth century church with good statuary and tombs.

Thoisy-le-Désert (D–8) has a thirteenth century church with *pietà*, statuary, Virgin and Child and clock tower arcade.

Til-Châtel (H–6) has a twelfth century Romanesque church, with tympanum, thirteenth century transept and a doorway with five arches.

103

Vic-sous-Thil (C–7) has a Romanesque collegiate church, with some fourteenth century Gothic additions. It has a unique nave and a high, fortified clock tower. This is a superb Burgundian site perched on a historic hillside close to the equally famous château. It is a small village with 200 inhabitants, but is definitely worth a detour.

Villiers-le-Duc (E–3). The ancient abbey of Val des Coues has a Renaissance façade and its own grotto and water mill.

Vix (D–2) has the church of St Marcel, with a twelfth century nave.

Museums

Alise-Ste-Reine (D–5) has the Musée d'Alésia, tel. 80.96.10.95, displaying Gallo-Roman finds.

Arnay-le-Duc (D–9) has a Maison Régionale des Arts at the Hospice St-Pierre, 15 rue St-Jacques, tel. 80.90.11.59.

Auxonne (J–9) has a Musée Bonaparte at the Château Prost, tel. Mairie, 80.31.10.65, which covers local archaeology and regional folklore in addition to memorabilia of the great man's visits to the town.

Beaune (F–10) has an important Musée des Beaux-Arts in the Hôtel de Ville, tel. 80.22.22.80. The Musée du Vin de Bourgogne, rue d'Enfer, tel. 80.22.08.19, covers the history of the vine and Burgundian wines. The Musée de l'Hôtel-Dieu is visited as part of the grand tour of the Hôtel-Dieu.

Châtillon-sur-Seine (E–2) houses the famous Treasure of Vix in the Musée Archéologique, rue du Bourg, tel. 80.91.24.67; the Musée Marmont, place Marmont, contains memorabilia of Bonaparte's famous Marshal.

Dijon (H–7) has many excellent museums. The Musée des Beaux Arts, place de la Sainte-Chapelle, tel. 80.30.31.11, is rated as the second most important in France, and houses the great tombs of Philip the Bold and John the Fearless. There is an archaeological museum at 5 rue du Dr Maret, tel. 80.30.88.54. The Musée Magnin, 4 rue des Bons Enfants, tel. 80.67.11.10, contains paintings by Bosch, Poussin, Fragonard and Vouet, among others. The Musée Rude, 8 rue Vaillant, tel.80.30.31.11, has many sculptures by Rude; the Musée de la Vie Bourguignonne, 17 rue Ste-Anne, tel. 80.30.65.91, the Musée d'Histoire Naturelle, avenue Albert 1er, Jardin de l'Arquebuse, the Musée des Hospices Civils and the Musée d'Art Sacré, 15 rue Ste-Anne, tel. 80.30.06.44, are all self-explanatory.

Fixin (G–8) has the Musée Noisot of Napoleon, Parc Noisot, tel. 80.52.45.52.

Flavigny-sur-Ozerain (D–6) has a Musée Lapidaire, with gemstones and sculptures from the Gallo-Roman era.

Montbard (C–4) has the Musée d'Archéologie in the Château in the Parc Buffon; and the Musée Buffon, also in the Parc Buffon, has exhibits relating to the life and work of the naturalist Comte Buffon. The Musée Daubenton is in the rue Daubenton, and the Musée des Beaux-Arts is in the Chapelle, rue Piron, tel. 80.92.01.34.

Nuits-St-Georges (G–9) has an archaeological museum, rue Camille-Rodier, tel. 80.61.12.54, displaying the Gallo-Roman finds from Bollards and Merovingian burial stones from Argilly.

Puligny-Montrachet (F–11) has a Napoleonic museum at the Château.

Reulle-Vergy (G–9) has a museum of arts and crafts, open in summer only.

Saulieu (B–8) has the Musée François Pompon, Parvis de la Basilique, tel. 80.64.09.22, with regional archaeological finds.

Savigny-lès-Beaune (F–10) has a car exhibition, the Musée de la Moto, at the Château, tel. 80.21.55.03.

Semur-en-Auxois (C–6) has a museum-cum-library in the old Jacobin convent, rue Jean-Jacques Collenot, tel.80.97.05.96, with medieval sculptures as well as manuscripts and 30,000 volumes.

Seurre (H–11) has the Écomusée de la Saône, rue Bossuet, tel. 80.21.15.92, open in summer only.

105

CHAPTER SEVEN:
A GOURMET'S PARADISE

If you enjoy good food and wine you'll find it difficult to go far wrong in the Côte d'Or. The wines are world famous, the food delicious and I've tracked down a number of hotels and restaurants which are well within the budget.

To begin this chapter I've summarised the flavour of the region's cooking by listing its gastronomic specialities. I then look at the local wines, the wine co-operatives, and give you some addresses to help with your planning. The rest of the chapter is devoted to finding a roof over your head. I've listed modest hotels and restaurants as well as camp sites, stating the address, telephone number and map reference.

Gastronomic specialities

Specialities from the region include *jambon persillé,* snails, *oeufs en meurette, pochouse* (fish stew), *coq au Chambertin, poulet Gaston-Gérard,* cheeses from Citeaux and Époisses and *anis* made at Flavigny (D–6). Dijon is world famous for its mustard, *cassis* and *pain d'épice.*

Snails come from Chenôve (G–8) and Duesme (E–4). Fish are bred at Aisey-sur-Seine (E–3), Châtillon-sur-Seine (E–2), Corgoloin (G–10), Époisses (B–6), Flagey-Échézaux (G–9), Marmagne (C–4) and St-Maurice-sur-Vingeanne (J–5), where there is also game breeding. There is a wild boar game park at Ternant (F–9). Bèze has an annual *Fête aux andouilles et comichons* on 15 August.

bitter are made at St-Marc-sur-Seine (E–4), and goat cheese comes from Fresnes (D–5), La Bussière-sur-Ouche (F–8), Chassagne-Montrachet (F–11), Labergement (I–8), Époisses (B–6), Poinçon-lès-Larrey (D–2), Puligny-Montrachet (F–11), Villy-en-Auxois (E–6), Venarey (D–5) and La Roche-Vanneau (D–6).

Mushrooms are grown at many small villages in the area, and bees are kept at Baubigny (E–11), Busseau (E–3), Châtillon-sur-Seine (E–2), Chaumont-le-Bois (E–2), Lantenay (F–7) and Savoisy (D–3). Mustard is made at Couchey (G–8), condiments at Velars (G–7) and vinegar mustard at Seurre (H–1), which is also known for its *pochouse*. Confectionery and *pâtes de fruits* are produced at Gevrey-Chambertin (G–8), biscuits at Labruyère (H–10) and sweets at Semur (C–6).

Cassis is made at Argilly (G–10), Baulme-la-Rouche (f–7), Collonges-lès-Bévy (F–9), Gemeaux (H–6), Hauteville-lès-Dijon (G–7), Malain (F–7), Marey-lès-Fussey (F–9), Marsannay-la-Côte (G–8), Morey-St-Denis (G–9), Nuits-St-Georges (G–9) and Villers-la-Faye (G–10). There are distilleries at Chevannes (F–9), Cormot-le-Grand (E–11), Gevrey-Chambertin (G–8), Gilly-lès-Citeaux (G–9), Thury (D–10), Vougeot (G–9), Nuits-St-Georges (G–9), Recey-sur-Ource (F–3), St-Jean-de-Losne (I–10), Mirebeau (I–7) and Merceuil (F–11). There are *malteries* at Brazy-en-Plaine (I–9).

Local wines

The two main wine-growing areas of the Côte d'Or — the Côte de Nuits in the north and the Côtes de Beaune in the south — produce some of the finest wines in the world.

• The Côte de Nuits

Gevrey-Chambertin, Morey-St-Denis, Chambolle Musigny, Flagey-Échézeaux, Vosne-Romanée and Nuits-St-Georges are the most famous communes of the Côte de Nuits. They produce top quality red wines — deep, rich and long-lasting, and, because of the marlstone soil, the *grands crus* and *premier crus* are just about the noblest red wines in the world. Only one grape may be used to make these famous red wines — the Pinot Noir. It is hard to grow, being a delicate vine which needs loving care.

To travel south from Dijon on the **'Route des Grands Crus'**, the D122, is a memorable experience. Every *amateur de vin* visiting Burgundy should take this route. You set off through Chenôve, a large suburb of Dijon, and the first port of call is at Marsannay-la-Côte. The small wine co-operative to be found there is unique in that it specializes in *vin rosé* — AOC Bourgogne — Marsannay.

The same wine, made of Pinot Noir grapes at 12/12.5 degrees, is grown in the neighbouring village of Couchey by ten *vignerons*. (Couchey also has a mustard factory and two châteaux — that of Jean de la Coste of the eighteenth century, and that of Bauffremont of the fifteenth and sixteenth centuries). The 'Cave Co-opérative des Grands Vins Rosés' is at 21 rue de Mazy, tel. 80.52.15.14. It was founded in 1929 and has eighteen members owning 50 hectares. The main building is on the 'Route des Grands Crus'.

There are twenty-four *vignerons* at Marsannay-la-Côte, most of whom offer tasting facilities from their *caves*. Mme Humblin is the co-operative's secretary at 27 rue Vignes, tel.80.30.08.38.

The highest-class Côte de Nuits vineyards, known at *têtes de cuvées*, start at the village of Fixin.

Fixin has no less than six *crus classés*: Clos du Chapitre, Les Herrelets, Les Arvelets, Aux Cheusots, Les Meix-Bas and Clos de la Perrière. Of thirty-four local *vignerons*, twenty-two have *caves* for tasting. Fixin has the well-known Napoleonic Museum Claude Noisot.

Gevrey-Chambertin has the AOC *grands crus* of Chambertin, Chambertin Clos de Bèze, Ruchottes-Chambertin, Chapelle-Chambertin, Mazeyères-Chambertin, Griotte-Chambertin, Mazis-Chambertin, Latricière-Chambertin, Charmes-Chambertin, Clos St-Jacques, Vareilles, Fouchère, Étournelles and Cazetiers. Le Chambertin and Clos de Bèze are known as the 'King of Wines' and 'the Wine of Kings' respectively. M. Lucien Dupont runs the local co-operative. Of 109 *vignerons,* ten offer tastings.

Morey-St-Denis has AOC *grands crus* Clos de la Roche, Clos-St-Denis, Clos de Tart, Bonnes Mares and Clos des Lambreys. The local co-operatives are 'Des Vins Fins', run by M. Hubert Lignier, tel. 80.34.31.79, and the 'Co-op Union de Propriétaires', run by M. Marcel Jeanniard, rue de la Bidaude, tel.80.34.32.12. They produce AOC Village and Morey-St-Denis. There are sixty-five local *vignerons* but only three have *caves* and tasting facilities. Also well known are Les Ruchottes, Les Sorbets, Les Clos Sorbets, Les Millandes, Le Close des Ormes, Meix Rentiers, Monts Luisants, Les Bouchots, Clos Bussières, Aux Charmes and Les Chamières.

Chambolle-Musigny. The *grands crus* are Les Musigny and Les Bonnes Mares. Other known vineyards are Les Amoureuses, Les Charmes, Les Combottes and Aux Combottes. The local co-operative is run by M. Henri Ratheau, and is called 'GIE Union des Viticulteurs de Chambolle-Musigny *et* Morey-St-Denis', which produces AOC Bourgogne Grand Ordinaire, Bourgogne Passetoutgrain and Chambolle-Musigny Premier Cru. There are eighty-five local *vignerons* but only two offer tasting facilities. The monks of Citeaux created the first vineyards here. The 'Fête de St Vincent', *patron des vignerons*, is on 22 January.

Vougeot has the *grand cru* Clos de Vougeot. The local *cave co-opérative* produces AOC Vougeot. There are forty-eight *vignerons,* and five offer tasting facilities.

Vosne-Romanée has both *grands crus* and *premiers crus,* and there is a small local *cave co-opérative.*

Flagey-Échézeaux has La Romanée, Romanée-Conti, Les Richebourgs, La Tache, Les Verolles and Romanée St-Vivant. The AOC wines are Vosne-Romanée, Grand-Échézeaux and Échézeaux.

Nuits-St-Georges has Le St-Georges, Les Boudots, Les Cailles, Les Cras, Les Murgers, Les Porrets, Les Pruliers, Les Thorey and Les Vaucrains. The AOC wines of this large commune are Nuits, Nuits-St-Georges and Bourgogne vin-fin-de-Haute-Côte-du-Nuits. The annual auction of their Hospices wines (i.e. those actually owned by the Hospices de Beaune) takes place on the second Sunday before Easter.

Prémeaux-Prissey has a *cave co-opérative* producing AOC Nuits and Nuits-St-Georges. The village to the south, Corgoloin, marks the southern limit of the Côte de Nuits. There are eleven *vignerons,* all with tasting facilities.

• The Côtes de Beaune

Pernand-Vergelesses, Aloxe-Corton, Savigny-lès-Beaune, Pommard, Beaune, Volnay and Santenay are the major wine-growing areas of the Côtes de Beaune. The grape is the same as in the Côte de Nuits, but the soil is now lighter and more gravelly. At Volnay are to be found delicate and graceful red wines, and at neighbouring Meursault are the richest and most powerful white wines of Burgundy. The best vineyards are Les Maréchandes, La Toppe au Vert, La Coutière, Les Grandes Colières, Les Petites Colières and Basser-Mouriettes.

Savigny-lès-Beaune has three *têtes de cuvées*: Les Vergelesses, Les Marconnets, Les Jarrons and AOC Savigny-lès-Beaune. Other well-known vineyards are at neighbouring Chorey-lès-Beaune. There are three *grands crus* in the area — Corton, Corton-Charlemagne and Charlemagne — plus fourteen *premiers crus*, including Les Marconnets, Dominode, Serpentières, Vergelesses and Les Guettes; 99 per cent of the wines grown are red.

110

Pernand-Vergelesses produces AOC Aloxe-Corton and Pernand-Vergelesses, but their Île de Vergelesses is a *tête de cuvée*.

Aloxe-Corton. The *têtes de cuvées* vineyards are Le Corton, Le Clos du Roi, Les Renardes, Les Chaumes and Charlemagne. The AOC wines are Aloxe-Corton, Corton and Corton-Charlemagne. Other good vineyards are Les Valozières, Les Chaillots, Les Meix, Les Fournières, Les Maréchandes, Les Paulands, Les Vercots and Les Guérets. There is also a *caveau de dégustation*. There are thirty-three *vignerons,* four of whom offer tasting facilities.

Beaune is the *capitale des grands vins de Bourgogne*. The main vineyards are Les Fèves, Les Grèves, Les Cras, Les Champinets, Les Marconnets, Les Bressands, Clos de la Mousse and Clos des Mouches. The AOC wines are Beaune and Côte-de-Beaune. There are eighty local *vignerons,* twenty-two offering tasting facilities.

Pommard. The *crus* of Pommard have been known throughout Europe for centuries, and made famous by Ronsard and Victor Hugo. The main vineyards are Les Epenots, Les Rugiens Bas and Hauts, and Le Clos Blanc. The *cave co-opérative* produces AOC Pommard. There are fifty-four *vignerons;* twenty-one offer tastings.

Volnay, half a mile south, was originally a Celtic village. It has no less than twenty-six *premiers crus,* including Les Caillerets, Les Champains, En Chevret, Les Clos des Ducs, Les Fremets and Les Angles. There are thirty-three *vignerons*, all of whom offer tasting facilities.

Monthélie has an AOC Monthélie and a *cave co-opérative*, 'Les Caves de Monthélie', tel. 80.21.22.63 (please advise Mme S. Rudolph). There are twenty-five *vignerons* with three offering *caves de dégustation*.

Auxey-Duresses has an AOC Auxey-Duresses, red and white wines. There are twenty-six *vignerons*, one offering tasting facilities. The 'Fête des Vignerons' is on 24 August.

Meursault. The *têtes de cuvées* are Les Santenots du Milieu (red) and Les Perrières (white). The various Perrière and

111

Charmes vineyards are outstanding for their white wine. The vineyards La Goutte d'Or and Les Genevrières are well known. Meursault is rightly known as the *capitale des grands vins blancs de Bourgogne*. AOC wines are Meursault, Volnay-Santenots and Blagny, produced by a *cave co-opérative*. There are eighty-nine *vignerons*, thirteen of whom have *caves de dégustation*.

St-Aubin has an AOC St-Aubin. There are fourteen local *vignerons*, eight of whom offer tastings of red and white wines.

St-Romain has an AOC St-Romain. There are fourteen *vignerons*, seven of whom offer tastings of white and red wines.

Ste-Marie la Blanche has its own *cave co-opérative*.

Nolay and **La Rochepot** have a wine co-operative. The AOC is Bourgogne Haute Côte de Beaune. Nolay has eight *vignerons*.

Puligny-Montrachet. The best wine is Le Montrachet (part), one of the top white wines of Burgundy. There are twenty-two *vignerons*. All welcome visitors by appointment. AOC wines include Montrachet, Chevalier-Montrachet, Bâtard-Montrachet, Bienvenues-Bâtard-Montrachet, Blagny and Puligny-Montrachet.

Chassagne-Montrachet. The best wines are Le Montrachet (part) and Les Criots. The AOC wines are Bâtard-Montrachet, Criots Bâtard-Montrachet and Chassagne-Montrachet. Other vineyards are Le Cailleret, Les Combettes, Les Pucelles and Les Referts. Another Napoleonic museum is at the château. Both Montrachet villages are also known for their goat cheese.

Santenay is the southernmost village of the Côtes de Beaune. It is a *station thermale* with radioactive *thermales sources,* and an AOC Santenay. Their Les Gravières is a *tête de cuvée* wine. There are thirty-seven *vignerons*, all of whom offer tastings of red and white wines; though 90 per cent of production is red.

Wine co-operatives

Easily the largest and most important co-operative is **'Les Caves des Hautes-Côtes'**, with 130 *vigneron* members, founded in 1968, cultivating 450 hectares of vines. Their *chais* are on the route de Pommard, 3 km. due south of Beaune, tel. 80.24.63.12. M. Jean-Louis Giraud is the Délégue Commercial. M. Le Brun, who has a property at Villers-la-Faye, is vice-president of the Federation of Côte d'Or co-operatives. 'Les Caves des Hautes-Côtes' produce and sell a million bottles a year, 90 per cent red and 10 per cent white. Great Britain, with a dozen customers, takes 10 per cent per annum. The members' vintage is in early October and the co-operative brings their grapes in — carefully weighed and selected for *climat* or *appellation* — in their own trucks.

In addition there are small co-operatives to be found at Gevrey-Chambertin. M. Lucien Dupont at 1 rue de Paris has ten members and 9 hectares. Another is run by M. Marcel Jeanniard, rue de la Bidaude, Morey-St-Denis, tel. 80.34.32.12 with twelve members and 10 hectares but no *cave*. They sell only their grapes to *négociants,* and are called the 'Co-op Union des Propriétaires'.

M. Hubert Lignier runs the **'Co-op des Vins Fins'** of Morey-St-Denis, founded in 1911 at the rue de Très-Girard, 21220 Gevrey-Chambertin, tel. 80.34.31.79. Their eight members, with 12 hectares, produce fine wines in bulk and casks of 228 litres for sale to *négociants.* Their two-hundred-year-old caves with *pressoir* are near and under a good quality hotel-restaurant in Gevrey-Chambertin. Other small co-operatives are to be found at Chambolle-Musigny, run by M. Henri Ratheau, whose house is near the Post Office. There is a small co-op at Nuits-St-Georges and Marey-lès-Fussey, called 'Maison des Hautes-Côtes', and another 8 km. south-east of Beaune is the 'Cave Co-opérative Viticole de Ste-Marie-la-Blanche, tel. 80.26.60.60.

At Vosne-Romanée the **'Caveau St-Martin** is a '*groupement de viticulteurs*' with their own *cave* for '*visites et dégustation*'. There is also a small co-operative at Vougeot. South-west of Beaune there is a wine co-operative at La Rochepot (21340 Nolay) called 'Centre Co-opérative de Diffusion et Vente' at the famous Château de la Rochepot. Another is at Meloisey (219250), 5 km. west of Beaune. Yet another is at Monthiélie (21190) Meursault, south-west of Beaune, called 'Les Caves de Monthélie', run by Mme S. Rudolph, tel. 80.21.22.63. Nearer to Chalons (10 km. north-west) are 'Les Vignerons du Caveau de Mercurey', tel. 85.47.16.53. Both Nolay (21340) and Pommard (21630) have joint agricultural and wine co-operatives.

The smaller co-operatives have two methods of operation: (a) *metayage*, in which an elderly or non-resident owner concedes to the co-op the right to make his wine in the ratio of two-thirds of the weighed grapes to the 'grower' and one-third to the proprietor; and (b) *fermage*, when a *prix moyenne*, or average price, is agreed each April, several months before the *vendange*, between owner and co-op. Good and bad years in terms of quantity and quality are therefore evened out.

Two interesting 'Son et Lumière' tours of the vineyards can be made. One to the Côte de Nuits leaves from Dijon, Hôtel de Ville, nightly, except Sundays and holidays, July to 15 October, leaving at 9.30 p.m. in August, 9.00 p.m. in September and 8.30 p.m. in October. The other tour, of the Côtes de Beaune, leaves from Beaune Tourist Office on Tuesdays, Thursdays and Saturdays in July at 9.30 p.m. and in September at 9.00 p.m. The price is 100 francs for the two tours, and 60 francs for individual tours, including tasting. The highlights are the 'Son et Lumière' at the Clos de Vougeot château (Nuits trip) and at the Hôtel des Ducs de Bourgogne (Beaune trip).

Useful addresses

Fédération Interprofessionel Vins de Bourgogne, rue Henri Dunant, Beaune, tel. 80.22.62.95.

Assoc. des Viticulteurs de la Côte d'Or, 13 boulevard Maréchal Joffre, Beaune, tel. 80.22.67.95.

Co-op Agriculture et Viticole, Beaune, tel. 80.22.34.09.

Cave des Hautes Côtes et Co-op. M. Bernard Rocault, à Orches-et-Beaune, route de Pommard, tel. 80.24.63.72.

Fédération Co-opérative de la Côte d'Or. M. le Brun, vice-president, Villers-la-Faye.

The Comité Interprofessionel de la Côte d'Or et de l'Yonne pour les vins d'Appellation d'Origine Contrôlée de Bourgogne

(CIB), rue Henri Dunant, Beaune, tel. 80.22.21.35, runs specialist courses for wine lovers — usually one of five days in May and one of four days in November, in English. There are two stages, 'Initiation' and 'Perfectionnement'.

Modest hotels and restaurants

Dijon (pop. 160,000) is the préfecture city of the Côte d'Or and the capital of Burgundy. There are so many attractions here that a stay of at least two or three days is recommended. The choice of a hotel should theoretically be quite easy. The first problem encountered, however, is that of parking. The centre of Dijon is comprehensively metered, and side streets with free parking are only in the suburbs. The summary at the end of this chapter lists a number of one-star hotels, but most of them are in no-parking or metered areas. The other problem is that few hotels in Dijon have their own restaurant.

A recommended choice is the **Hôtel Monge,** 20 rue Monge, tel. 80.30.55.41. It has 24 rooms, its own small offstreet parking area, and is quiet. Mmes Agnes Tridon and Camille Vignaud run it most efficiently. Double rooms are priced between 73 and 103 francs. The hotel is open all the year round. The Hôtel Thurot, 4 passage Thurot, tel. 80.43.57.46, with 19 rooms from 90 to 150 francs and breakfast 15 francs, is also quiet and has free parking.

Restaurants with reasonable *prix fixe* menus at about 50 francs are the **Restaurant du Pressoir,** chemin de la Croix, tel. 80.41.45.86; **Restaurant Grande Taverne** Hôtel Terminus, 20 avenue Mar-Foch, tel. 80.43.58.33; **Restaurant Le Florentin,** 24 rue Bennelier, tel. 80.30.86.91; **Restaurant l'Entendart,** 4 rue des Perrières, tel. 80.41.51.32; and Le Moulin à Vent, 8 place François-Rude, tel. 80.30.81.43.

One characteristic of French towns with closed and open markets is the cluster of good low-cost restaurants close by. Dijon is no exception. **'Le Dôme',** 16 rue Quentin, tel. 80.30.58.92, has menus at 40, 45 and 55 francs. Wines are from 14–19.10 francs a bottle, and good value.

The **'Au Bec Fin'** restaurant, 47 rue Jeannin, tel. 80.66.17.85, has three excellent *prix fixe* menus. 'La

115

Fourchette', 77 rue Berbisey, has an excellent menu at 48 francs, as does 'Aux Chandeliers', 65 rue Jeannin, tel. 80.60.15.82. The rue Jeannin, 100 metres north of the 'Palais des Ducs', is easy to find. The 'Melodin' self-service restaurant, 6 avenue du Maréchal Foch, offers good value.

Beaune (pop. 20,000) is a very attractive and prosperous town, which has several attractive and prosperous hotels. Two good hotel-restaurants within the budget are the **Bellevue** and the **France et Terminus.** The Bellevue, 5 route de Seurre, on the east side of the town, tel.80.22.26.85, with 17 rooms from 90 francs, breakfast at 18 francs, and menus from 45 francs. Parking is easy and it is relatively quiet. The Hôtel de France et Terminus, 35 avenue du 8 Septembre, tel.80.22.12.99, has 22 rooms from 90 francs, breakfast at 18 francs and menus from 65 francs.

Two hotels without restaurants worth considering are **Hôtel Foch,** 24 boulevard Foch, tel. 80.22.04.29, with 10 rooms from 75 francs and breakfast at 19 francs; and **Hôtel St Nicolas,** 69 faubourg St Nicolas, tel. 80.22.18.30, with 13 rooms from 55 francs and breakfast at 17 francs.

Four restaurants within the budget are Auberge de la Toison d'Or, 4 boulevard Jules Ferry, tel. 80.22.29.62, menus from 45 francs; Brelinette, 6 rue Madeleine, tel.80.22.63.94, from 41 francs; Ciboulette, 69 rue Lorraine, tel. 80.24.70.72, from 40 francs; and Maxime, place Madeleine, tel.80.22.17.82, from 45 francs.

There are a number of other modest hotels and hotel-restaurants outside Beaune at Challonges, Meursault, Meloisey, St-Romain, Bligny-sur-Ouche, Nolay and Ivry-en-Montagne. There are good value restaurants at Montagne-de-Beaune, Chorey-lès-Beaune, Pommard, Ladois-Serrigny and Pernand Vergelesses.

Châtillon-sur-Seine (pop. 8,000) has two 'budget' hotels — the Hôtel le Cheval Rouge with 17 rooms, and Hôtel de la Montagne with 12 rooms.

Auxonne (pop. 6,500) has two 'budget' hotels. The Hôtel du Grand Cerf, 48 rue A, Masson, tel. 80.37.33.02, has 15 rooms and a menu from 45 francs; the Hôtel de la Poste, 89 rue E.

Gruet, tel. 80.37.31.32, has 9 rooms and a menu from 45 francs.

Nuits-St-Georges (pop. 5,000). An ideal situation from which to explore the wine country. The Hôtel des Cultivateurs, 12 rue du Général de Gaulle, tel. 80.61.10.81, has 9 rooms with a menu from 40 francs. The Hôtel Ibis, 1 avenue du Chambolland, tel. 80.61.17.17, has 52 rooms and a menu from 55 francs. The small Hôtel de L'Étoile, at neighbouring Montsauche, has 5 rooms from 60 francs.

Montbard (pop. 8,000) has the Hôtel de la Gare with 14 rooms, 10 avenue M-Foch, tel. 80.92.02.12.

Quetigny (pop. 7,500) has the Hôtel Climat de France, 14 avenue de Bourgogne, tel. 80.46.04.46, with 43 rooms priced at 90–100 francs and menus from 50 francs.

Saulieu (pop. 3,000) is a small town on a traditionally famous crossroads for travellers. There is an *embarras de richesse* in the way of small hotel-restaurants. 'La Tour d'Auxois', place Abreuvoir, tel. 80.64.13.30, has 30 rooms and a menu from 55 francs. 'Au Petit Marguéry', 4 rue d'Argentine, tel. 80.64.13.58, has 20 rooms and a menu from 45 francs. Hôtel de Bourgogne, 9 rue Courtépée, tel. 80.64.08.41, has 14 rooms and a menu from 60 francs. Hôtel la Renaissance, 7 rue Grillot, tel. 80.64.08.72, has 13 rooms and a menu from 60 francs.

Semur-en-Auxois (pop. 5,500) is one of the most attractive small towns in the whole of Burgundy. It has few hotels, and a telephone reservation in advance is recommended. On a recent visit two were closed for vacations, one was full and the last too expensive for the budget. There are three recommendations. **Hôtel des Gourmets,** 4 rue Varenne, tel. 80.97.09.41, has 15 rooms from 85–130 francs and menus from 65 francs. The **Hôtel de la Côte d'Or,** 3 place Gaveau, tel. 80.97.03.13, has 15 rooms from 70 francs, and breakfast at 18 francs. The **Résidence Dauphine,** tel. 80.97.13.36, is about 1.5 km. west of Semur off the D980. It has chalet rooms in the woods priced at 70–146 francs, and breakfast at 18 francs. Wines from 22 francs per bottle. Although the woods

117

make for a gloomy atmosphere, the excellent meals, good service, river, waterfall and owls make this a place well worth visiting.

Summary

Map ref.	Town	Hotel	No. of rooms	Tel. (prefix 86)
E–3	Aisey-sur-Seine 21400	du Roy	10	93.21.63 closed Tue. and Dec.
I–7	Arc-sur-Tille 21560	de la Tille	11	30.04.83
		des Marronières	12	37.01.22
D–9	Arnay-le-Duc 21230	Terminus, RN6	16	90.00.33
		du Dauphin, rue René Laforge	10	90.14.25
		de Paris, RN6	12	90.02.70 closed Feb.
		Relais St Jacques	10	90.07.33
J–9	Auxonne 21136	du Grand Cerf 48 rue A. Masson	15	37.33.02
		de la Poste, 89 rue E. Gruet	9	37.31.32
F–10	Beaune 21200	de France et Terminus, 35 avenue de 8 Septembre	22	22.12.99
		de Bretonnière, 43 faubourg Bretonnière	15	22.15.77 no restaurant
		Bellevue, 5 route de Seurre Foch, 24 boulevard Foch	17	22.26.85
			10	22.04.29 no restaurant
		St Nicolas, 69 faubourg St-Nicholas	13	22.18.30 no restaurant

I–6	Bèze 21310	de la Quat' Heurie	9	95.10.13
		le Bourguignon,	7	95.11.08 closed Tue. & Dec.
		rue la Porte Bessey		
		le Raisin d'Or	9	95.13.66
		2 place Verdun		
E–10	Bligny-sur-Ouche 21360	du Val d'Ouche	25	10.12.06 closed Nov.
		des Trois Faisons	7	20.10.14 closed Sun. and Dec-Feb
		rue du Pont		
E–2	Châtillon-sur-Seine 21121	du Jura, 19 rue Dr Robert	10	91.26.96
		le Cheval Rouge	17	
		de la Montaigne	12	
H–8	Chevigny-St-Sauveur 21800	au Bon Accueil, 16 avenue République	15	46.13.40
F–9	Collonges-lès-Bévy 21220	du Château	14	22.01.88 no restaurant
G–10	Comblanchien 21200	le Balcon	6	62.94.23
H–7	Dijon 21000	Monge, 20 rue Monge	24	30.55.41 no restaurant
		de France, 16 rue des Perrières	38	43.22.54
		Victor Hugo 23 rue des Fleurs	23	43.63.45
		Terminus, 20 avenue Foch	30	43.53.78
		de Pressoir, chemin de la Cras	21	41.45.86
		à l'Étendart, 4 rue des Perrières	12	41.51.32
		Thurot, 4 passage Thurot	19	43.57.46
B–6	Époisses 21460	de la Pomme d'Or rue des Forges	7	96.43.01 closed Fri. and Aug.
G–8	Fixin 21220	Chez Jeanette, 7 rue Noiset	11	52.45.49 closed Thurs. and 20/11–20/12

H–6	Gèmaux 21120	du Logis Neuf	9	95.34.14
I–8	Genlis 21110	de la Gare, 22 avenue de la Gare	19	31.30.11
G–8	Gevrey-Chambertin 21220	aux Vendanges de Bourgogne, 47 route de Beaune	18	34.30.24 closed Mon. and Feb.
G–7	Hauteville-lès-Dijon 21121	la Musarde	11	56.22.82 closed 25/1–15/2
E–10	Ivrey-en-Montagne 21340	Restau-Motel RN6	10	20.21.18
E–10	Lacanche 21230	au Bon Acceuil		90.05.81
D–2	Marcenay-le-Lac 21330	le Santenoy, Laignes	7	93.40.08 closed 20/1–28/2
H–6	Marcilly-sur-Tille 21120	de la Gare, place de la Gare	14	95.06.44
G–8	Marsannay-la-Cote 21160	Ibis, Dijon sud	48	52.86.45
J–7	Maxilly-sur-Saône 21270	le Tremblant, Pontailler		36.10.48
F–10	Meloisey 21190	à la Renaissance	3	26.00.76 closed Fri. and Jan.
F–11	Meursault 21190	des Arts	16	21.20.28 closed Mon. and Dec.
		du Centre	7	21.20.75
		Relais de la Diligence, 23 rue de la Gare	9	21.21.32
I–7	Mirebeau-sur-Bèze 21310	des Marronières	7	36.71.05
		la Gandeule, place d'Église	7	36.70.79
G–5	Moloy 21120	de l'Ecrevisse	15	95.11.79
		Hostellerie de l'Ignon	10	75.12.33
C–4	Montbard 21500	des Tilleuls	9	
		de la Gare	14	92.02.12
G–9	Morey-St-Denis 21220	Castel de Très Girard, rue du Castel	12	34.33.09
E–11	Nolay 21340	du Chevreul	9	21.71.89 closed 5/12–5/1
		de la Cloche d'Or	8	21.70.77 closed Thu.
		Ste-Marie	13	21.73.19 closed Jan.

H–7	Norges-la-Ville 21490	Tabaldini	34	35.72.17
G–9	Nuits-St-Georges 21700	des Cultivateurs, 12 rue du Général de Gaulle	15	61.10.81
		Ibis, 1 avenue du Chambolland de l'Étoile, Montsauche	52 5	61.17.17
F–8	Pont-de-Pany 21410	le Pont de Pany	14	23.60.59
J–8	Pontailler-sur-Saône 21270	du Marronières		36.12.70
E–8	Pouilly-en-Auxois 21320	du Bassin du Commerce	7 23	90.83.98 90.88.23
H–8	Quetigny 21800	Climat de France, 14 avenue de Bourgogne	43	46.04.46
B–6	Rouvray 21530	du Centre, la Roche-Brenil	8	64.75.22
H–7	St-Apollinaire 21000	Gril Campanile, 1 rue la Fleuries, Dijon	24	72.45.38
E–9	Ste-Sabine 21320	de Lassey	5	33.01.43
I–10	St-Jean-de-Losne 21170	Saônotel, 27 rue du Château	13	29.04.77 closed Nov.
		de la Marine	18	29.05.11 closed Mon. and Jan.
F–11	St-Romain 21190	les Roches	7	21.21.63 closed Fri. and Jan.
B–8	Saulieu 21210	la Tour d'Auxois, place Aubreuvoir	30	64.13.30
		au Petit Marguéry, 4 rue d'Argentine	20	64.13.58
		de Bourgogne, 9 rue Courtépée la	14	64.08.41
		Renaissance, 7 rue Grillot	13	64.08.72
		le Lion d'Or 7 rue Courtépée	12	64.16.33
		la Borne Impériale, 16 rue d'Argentine 16 rue d'Argentine	7	64.19.76

C–6	Semur-en- Auxois 21140	des Gourmets, 4 rue Varenne	15	97.09.41
		de la Côte d'Or, 3 place Gaveau	15	97.03.13
		Résidence de Dauphine, Bois de Montille	20	97.13.36
H–11	Seurre 21250	les Négociants, rue de la Républic	17	21.14.06 closed Sun.
E–8	Sombernon 21540	le Sombernon	10	33.42.23 closed Wed. and 15/1–15/2
		le Bellevue, rue Liberation	7	33.40.52
H–6	Til-Châtel 21120	de la Poste, rue d'Aval	12	95.03.53
G–7	Val Suzon 21121	la Chaumières	10	31.61.20
D–5	Venarey-Laumes- Alesia 21150	de la Gare, 6 avenue la Gare	25	96.00.46 closedq 1/10–15/10
J–9	Villers-lès-Pots 21130	du Cheval Rouge	10	36.34.11
F–3	Voulaines 21290	des Templiers, Recey	10	93.02.55

Camp sites

See general notes and prices on page 73. Camp site sizes range from Auxey-Duresses (25 *placements*) to Dijon (250 *placements*), and prices for two people per day from 9.50 francs at the former to 14 francs at the latter.

Map	*Town*		
D–9	Arnay-le-Duc 21230	Cam. mun. 'de Fouché',	tel. 80.90.02.23
F–11	Auxey-Duresses 21190 Meursault	Cam. 'du Moulin',	tel. 80.21.24.11
J–9	Auxonne 21300	Cam. 'de l'Arquebuse',	tel. 80.37.34.36
F–10	Beaune 21200	Cam. 'les Cent Vignes', 10 rue Dubois,	tel. 80.22.03.91
E–10	Bligny-sur-Ouche 21360	Cam. 'des Isles',	tel. 80.20.11.21
G–8	Chamboeuf 21220 Gevrey-Chambertin	Cam. 'du Relais des Hautes Côtes', M. Lanier,	tel. 80.51.81.83

F–6	Chanceaux	Cam. mun.,	tel. 80.35.02.87
	21440 St Seine l'Abbeye.		
H–10	Le Châtelet 21250 Seurre	Cam. 'Le Closeau',	tel. 80.21.12.38
		M. Hugot,	
E–2	Châtillon-sur-Seine 21400	Cam. mun.,	tel. 80.91.03.05
		Esplanade St-Vorles,	
G–7	Darois 21121 Fontaine	Cam. 'l'Orée-du-Bois',	tel. 80.35.60.22
H–7	Dijon 21000	Xam. 'du Lac',	tel. 80.43.54.72
		2 boulevard Kir,	
B–6	Époisses 21460	Cam. 'Les Libellules',	tel. 80.96.40.65
C–6	Flée	V.V.F. Flée,	tel. 80.97.12.99
	21140 Semur-en-Auxois.		
E–5	Frôlois 21150 Les Laumes	Cam. du G.C.U.	
G–4	Grancey-le-Château 21580	Cam. mun. Mairie,	tel. 80.95.60.30
J–7	Heuilley-sur-Saône	'Aire Naturelle de Cam.'	tel. 80.47.42.18
		M. Malou,	
	21270 Pontaillier		tel. 80.47.42.18
D–2	Marcenay-le-Lac	Cam. 'du Lac de	tel. 80.93.48.75
	21330 Laignes	Marcenay',	
H–5	Marey-sur-Tille	Cam. mun.,	tel. 80.95.61.70
	21120 Is-sur-Tille		
F–11	Meursault 21190	Cam. 'de la Grappe d'Or',	tel. 80.21.22.48
C–4	Montbard 21500	Cam. mun.,	tel. 80.92.21.60
J–5	Montigny-sur-Vingeanne	Cam. 'du Trou-d'Argot',	tel. 80.95.80.97
	21610		
C–6	La Motte-Ternant	Cam. mun. Mme Lesage,	tel. 80.64.22.18
	21210 Saulieu		
E–11	Nolay 21340	Cam. mun., route	tel. 82.21.73.40
		de Couches,	
H–10	Pagny-la-Ville 21250 Seurre	Cam. 'du Pont-de-	tel. 80.66.52.77
		Charrey',	
		Cam. 'les Peupliers',	tel. 80.66.52.77
J–8	Pontailler-sur-Saône	Cam. Plage 'La Chanoie'	tel. 80.36.10.58
	21290		
		Cam. 'Les Toiles',	tel. 80.47.48.06
C–6	Pont-et-Massène	Cam. 'du Lac de Pont',	tel. 80.97.01.26
	21140 Semur-en-Auxois		
E–8	Pouilly-en-Auxois 21320	Cam. mun. 'du Vert-	tel. 80.90.85.44
		Auxois',	
C–7	Précy-sous-Thil 21390	Cam. du Parc de	tel. 80.64.57.18
		l'Hôtel de Ville,	

G–9	Prémeaux-Prissey 21700 Nuits-St-Georges	Cam. 'du Plan d'eau de Saule Guillaume'	tel. 80.62.30.78
		Cam.'du Moulin-de-Prisse',	tel. 80.62.31.15
B–7	La Roche-en-Brenil 21530	Cam. mun.,	tel. 80.64.71.79
F–8	Ste-Marie-sur-Ouche 21410 Pont-de-Pany	Cam. mun.,	tel. 80.23.62.30
I–10	St-Jean-de-Losne 21170	Cam. 'les Herlequins',	tel. 80.39.22.26
		Cam. mun. 'de Chaugey',	tel. 80.29.08.84
F–6	St-Seine-l'Abbaye 21440	Cam. mun. Mme Mousseron,	tel. 80.35.00.09
E–11	Santenay 21590	Cam. mun.,	tel. 80.20.60.32
B–8	Saulieu 21210	Cam. 'le Perron',	tel. 80.64.16.19
F–10	Savigny-lès-Beaune 21420	Cam. mun.,	tel. 80.21.51.21
H–11	Seurre 21250	Cam. 'de la Piscine',	tel. 80.20.45.38
		Cam. 'de la Raie-Mignot'	
H–6	Til-Châtel 21120 Is-sur-Tille	Cam. 'Les Sapins'. RN74	tel. 80.95.16.68
B–6	Toutry 21460	Cam. mun. 'Le Serein',	tel. 80.96.43.93
E–8	Vandenesse-en-Auxois 21320 Poully-en-Auxois	Cam. 'du Lac de Panthier',	tel. 80.33.01.79
D–5	Venarey-les-Laumes 21150	Cam. mun.,	tel. 80.96.07.76
F–9	Veuvey-sur-Ouche 21360 Bligny-sur-Ouche	Cam. de la Gare,	tel. 80.33.04.50
G–10	Vignoles 21200	Cam. des Bouleaux,	tel. 80.22.26.88
D–7	Vitteaux 21350	Cam. St-Nicolas,	tel. 80.49.60.87
G–9	Vougeot 21640	Cam. du Moulin-du-Gentilhomme,	tel. 80.62.89.65

CHAPTER EIGHT:
THE RURAL DELIGHTS OF NIÈVRE

The Nièvre has the smallest population of the four Burgundian departments. Its quarter of a million inhabitants are spread over nearly 7,000 square kilometres. Before the Roman conquest, three tribes, the Berruyers, the Senons and the Eduens, dominated the area. Bibracte, on the top of Mont Beuvray, was their capital. They became allies of the Romans but took part in a disastrous Celtic revolt in 52 BC. Christianity was introduced to Nièvre in the second century. In the fifth century the region was incorporated into the Kingdom of Burgundy and then into the French Kingdom. During the Hundred Years War Nièvre was unhappily in the middle of the warring tribes – the Anglo-Burgundians and the French. It continued to suffer during the religious wars, the French Revolution and the First and Second World Wars. Many villages were destroyed by the German army in 1944.

Nevers is the préfecture capital of the department – a city that should not be missed. Spare time for pretty La Charité-sur-Loire and the Pouilly wine area north of Nevers. The department is one of the most wooded in France, with one-third of its area still forested. It also has many large lakes, sources of the rivers Almain du Nivernais and Aron, flowing into the mighty Loire, and in the north several tributaries of the river Yonne. Since it also incorporates most of the Morvan National Park, it is the ideal department for a mainly open-air holiday.

As Nevers is the capital, Préfecture and easily the largest city in the department, it makes a logical and pleasant place from which to make several regional tours. A tour-within-a-tour is suggested from **La Charité**, and **Clamecy** is another focal point for a tour.

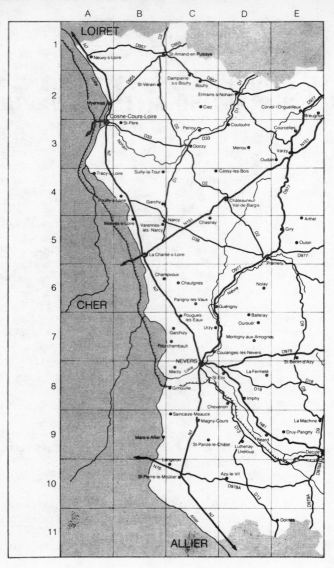

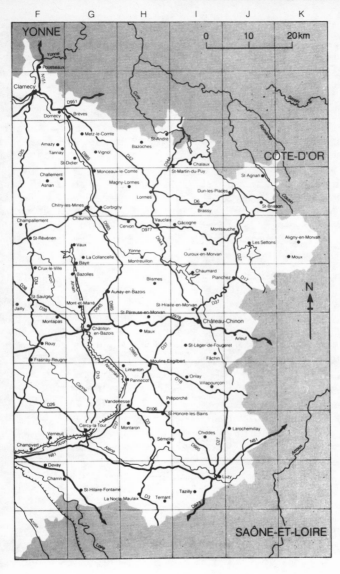

Nevers

The Tourist Offices are in the main square, place Carnot, tel. 86.61.27.75. They recommend a twenty-one-stage tour of the city of Nevers, which includes the convent of St Gildard, (where St Bernadette of Lourdes lies), the cathedral of St Cyr, various other major churches, excellent museums, an external look at the Palais Ducal, and the pottery/faience area between the cathedral and the station. Remember to track down and taste the seductively named confectionery: 'les Caraques', 'les Chardons', 'les Lolottes', 'les Négus', 'les Nougatines', 'les Roseaux' and 'les Skobeliffs'! Nevers being on the river Loire, the local fish dishes are excellent: *le sandre de Loire, la carpe à la Nivernaise, la friture 'Marins de Loire', la matelote 'Mariniers de Loire', le saumon de Loire au Pouilly Fumé,* and *les écrevisses de la Cure à la crème.* The local cheeses too should be tried – Pouilly, Tracy, d'Anost, Dornecy, Dornes, Lormes, Glux and Decize.

● Southern tour

The southern tour is the triangle between the river Alliers and the Loire. Start on the D13 to Sermoise, see the attractive château of Chevenon, follow the lateral canal via Luthenay-Uxeloup and Fleury-sur-Loire to Decize, which is on an island, and the meeting-point of several rivers, and see the church of St Are with its Merovingian crypt. From Decize go due south on the D978 to St-Germain-Chassenay, and the D182 to Dornes, and stop to look at the château and Romanesque church. Then drive due west on the D22 to the Château le Bessay, north to Azy-le-Vif and west to St-Pierre-le-Moûtier, where there are three interesting churches to look at. Go north on the D203 to St-Parize-le-Châtel, west on the D133 to Moiry and Mars-sur-Allier, due north on the D134 via the Château de Meauce near Saincaize, Gimouille, and via the D978 and N7 back to Nevers. The total circuit is 122 km.

● Northern tour

The northern tour starts west on the D266 and D131 to Marzy, where the church and folklore museums are worth a visit, then goes north to Fourchambault, Garchizy (château and Romanesque church) and Pougues-les-Eaux, where you can try the spa waters. Now drive east for 3 km and north on the D267 to Le Chazeau, Chaulgnes and Champvour (another early Romanesque church) to La Charité-sur-Loire.

La Charité-sur-Loire is an excellent place in which to stay a night in preparation for a Val de Loire-Puisaye-Donziais tour. This tour takes in the wine areas of Pouilly-sur-Loire, Cosne-sur-Loire, north to Myennes, on the D955 north-east to St-Amand-en-Puisaye (see the potteries) and either direct to Entrains-sur-Nohain or via Bitry, St-Vérand, Alligny-Cosne and Bouhy (Romanesque church) and back to La Charité via Vielmanay and Garchy on the D125. This circuit is 130 km. La Charité also has its own guided tour of the town.

The return to Nevers is due east from La Charité to Raveau, then following the D179 to St-Aubin-les-Forges, south to Guérigny (see the Château de Villemenant), east on the D26 via Balleray, Ourouër and Montigny-aux-Amognes. Pick up the D26 again to St-Jean-aux-Amognes, through St-Benin-d'Azy, and back west to Nevers via La Fermeté and Sauvigny-les-Bois. The total circuit is 110 km, excluding the local tour from La Charité described above.

- **Archaeological tour**

A grand archaeological tour of 300 kilometres is also possible from Nevers. Initially, go due south to St-Parize-le-Châtel, east to Decize, and further east on the N478 to Luzy, then north to Mont-Beuvray and St-Leger, north on the D500 to Arleuf and Les Bardiaux, west to Château-Chinon, north on the D944 and west to Corbigny, on to Champallement, north to Brinon-sur-Beuvron, north-east to Sur-Yonne and Brèves on the D34 to Clamecy, west on the D957 to Entrains-sur-Nohain, and on the D168 to Cosne-Cours-sur-Loire. Then south via La Charité-sur-Loire and Pougues-les-Eaux back to Nevers. All these towns and villages have archaeological sites, museums and/or exhibitions. The local archaeological society is called the GRA – ask at the Tourist Offices for local addresses.

Clamecy

The town of Clamecy has its own guided tour, and it is also suggested as a centre for a regional tour. This follows the river Yonne south to Amazy on the D34 to Tannay (see the Romanesque church), south on the D985 to Monceaux-le-Comte, Corbigny and the Château de Villemolin and south to the Château de Marcilly. Then cross the river and drive west on the D197 over the Canal du Nivernais to the lake of Baye, north and then west to Vitry-Laché (see the St Révérien Romanesque church), the splendid little hamlet of Champalle-ment, through Neuilly to Brinon-sur-Beuvron, north-west on the D5 to Varzy (where the château and church of St Pierre are definitely worth a stop), then back to Clamecy, either direct on the N151 or via Menou, La Chapelle-St André and Corvol l'Orgueilleux, following the west bank of the river Sauzay on the D19 and D977. The total circuit is 131 km.

Decize and Guérigny also have their own guided tours of the town.

Places of interest

Alligny-en-Morvan (K–5). Napoleon stayed here on his triumphant return from Elba.

Arleuf (J–7) has vestiges of the Gallo-Roman era, called 'des Bardiaux'.

Arthel (E–5). The Château d'Apremont was a stronghold of the Anglo-Burgundian army in the Hundred Years War, but was besieged, destroyed, and later rebuilt.

Asnan (F–4). A little hamlet named after the monks of Hubans, who came here to collect drinking-water mounted on *des ânes,* or asses!

Baye, Étang de (G–5). This large inland lake has regattas every Sunday in the summer.

Bouhy (C–2) is the site where poor St Pèlerin (pilgrim), Bishop of Auxerre, was decapitated in AD 259. The fountain and church of St Pèlerin are still visited on pilgrimages.

Brassy (I–4). The Abbey of Cluny founded a Benedictine priory here in the eleventh century.

Breugnon (E–2). At the edge of the woods, 6 km out of Clamecy on the N151, is a menhir, or dolmen, called the 'Pierre Fiche', one of the rare megaliths of the Nièvre.

Cercy-la-Tour (G–9). This twelfth-century stronghold was the original *rendezvous de chasse* of the old dukes of Nièvre, as was the nearby Château de Briffault. It is still well known for its breeding of racehorses at the famous *Haras* (stud farm) *de Cluny*.

Cessy-les-Bois (C–4). A Benedictine priory of St Baudèle was founded here by St Didier, Bishop of Auxerre, which subsequently became a celebrated pilgrimage centre.

Chalaux (I–3). In the Second World War the farm 'des Goths' and the neighbouring woods were the headquarters for the local resistance of the Maquis 'Camille', and an English parachutist camp.

Champallement (F–5). Approaching St Révérien one sees the remains of a large Gallo-Roman village set on a Roman road.

La Charité-sur-Loire (B–5). This town was so named in the Middle Ages because of its charity to pilgrims passing on their way to St James (Jacques) of Compostella. Pope Pashal II came from Aix-la-Chapelle in 1107 to consecrate the priory 'La Charité des Bons Pères'. During the Hundred Years War the English troops occupied the town, and the French, led by Joan of Arc, besieged it in 1429, but failed to take it. This is a delightful town overlooking the Loire, with narrow streets, gabled houses, a convent, ramparts, towers and cloisters. Worth a visit.

Chasnay (C–5). This small hamlet has an annual pilgrimage to the chapel of St Anne on the second Sunday in August.

Chevenon (D–8). The annual Burgundian championship of cyclocross (cross-country motor bike racing) is held here.

Chiddes (I–9). The annual fête includes the tasting and eating

131

of *andouilles*. On 8 September there is an annual pilgrimage to Mont Charlet.

Clamecy (F–2) is one of the prettiest towns in the Nièvre, dating from AD 600. In the sixteenth century a Jean Rouvet invented a system of floating trees from the forests upstream on the several rivers which flow down into Clamecy, for timber for house-building, pulp and chemicals.

Corbigny (G–4) has many old buildings, cellars and galleries, and is known as a *'village fleuri'*.

Cosne-Cours-sur-Loire (A–3). Remains of the second-century Gallo-Roman city of Condate can still be seen here.

Coulange-lès-Nevers (C–7). Legend has it that St Aré, Bishop of Nevers, returning from Aquitaine, sent a priest called Ours on ahead to announce his return. On crossing the river Nièvre, Ours was swept under and almost drowned, but was saved by the fervent prayers of St Aré. Ours (who became a saint himself) recovered. There are still water mills at the Pont St Ours nearby. An annual pilgrimage is made to St-Expédit on the Sunday after Easter.

Courcelles (E–3). One of Napoleon's generals, Allix, is buried here. The annual Fête of St Jean with fireworks on the 'route de Flez' is accompanied by gifts of wine and *beignets* (doughnuts).

Crux-la-Ville (F-6). In August 1944 severe fighting took place here between the retreating German troops and the French Maquis.

Decize (E–9). St Aré is buried in the church which bears his name. The town was mentioned by Caesar in his war commentaries. There are old fortifications, circular towers, a clock tower, an attractive 'Promenade des Halles' and many châteaux overlooking the canals of the Loire, Acolin and Nivernais.

Devay (F–10). This *'village fleuri'* celebrates on the first Sunday of October with a parade of flower-covered floats.

The Queen of the commune is elected in the second week of March.

Donzy (C–3) dates from AD 600 and there are many old timbered buildings with dovecots, narrow, picturesque streets, old mills, towers and châteaux. There is a firm that treats feathers for the Folies Bergères dancers in Paris.

Druy-Parigny (E–9). The Château de Druy was burnt in 1944 during fighting between the German troops and the Resistance.

Dun-les-Places (J–4). On 26 June 1944 the Germans set fire to the village and shot twenty-seven Frenchmen. A granite monument to the victims marks the place of the mass murder. A retired and wealthy pirate called Xavier Feuillet lived here, and in 1851 had built at vast expense by the Parisian architect Louis Lenormand a church of the eleventh-century Roman-esque style in granite. This was to purchase *le rachat de son âme*, i.e. to make his peace in heaven! The donor may not have reached Paradise but his body rests in the coffin in his church.

Entrains-sur-Nohain (D–2) was once a small, prosperous Gallo-Roman town. From it comes the largest Gallo-Roman sculpture in the Museum of National Antiquities, a seated 'Apollo with a Lyre', 2.65 metres high. The excavations have revealed a vast theatre and artisans' district with dwelling houses, cellars, courtyards, wells, cesspool and streets.

Fourchambault (C–7). The forges at work from 1818 gave this town the nickname in the mid-nineteenth century of 'Manchester de la France'.

Frasnay-Reugny (F–7). The Virgin of Pity of Frasnay was an object of pilgrimage in the Middle Ages. As late as 1870 many pilgrims prayed to her to preserve Nièvre from the advancing German troops.

Langeron (C–10) has many houses from the Middle Ages and a circular keep called the 'Tour de Langeron'.

Luzy (I–10) has in the Hôtel de Ville eight beautiful Aubusson tapestries from the seventeenth century. In the old keep of the barons of Luzy is an archaeological exhibition.

La Machine (E–9). In 1670 a machine drawn by horses was installed here to extract coal. Jean-Baptiste Machecourt, one of its inventors, also invented a parachute which saved many lives. The Fête Ste-Barbe is for the miners in December, and the Fête Ste-Cécile is celebrated by local musicians.
musicians.

Marzy (C–8). The car industry has a factory here. The Pilgrimage of St Christopher, patron saint of travellers, on 25 July ends with a blessing on all locally made vehicles!

Maux (H–7). The waters from the spring near the Chapelle St-Donat-d'Abon are said to have the same properties as those of Évian.

Monceaux-le-Comte (G–4) is a fortified village with ramparts and towers.

Montaron (H–9). On 10 July 1944 German troops killed twenty-three members of the Maquis of Montaron here.

Montreuillon (H–5). In 1845 the Aquaduc de Montreuillon was built, with thirteen arches; 33 metres in height and 170 metres in length. The village is famous for its freshwater trout.

Montsauche (J–5). The town was almost entirely destroyed by the Germans on 25 June 1944.

Moulins-Engilbert (H–8) took its name from the many water mills in the vicinity, built around an old Roman camp. There are several interesting châteaux, convents and an old hospital. The town is sited in heavily wooded country along the valleys of the rivers Guignon, Garat and Dragne.

Neuvy-sur-Loire (A–1). The town was severely bombarded in 1944 but has been reconstructed.

Nevers (C–8). The Préfecture town, which is twinned with St Albans in England, suffered severely in the revolt of the

Gauls against Julius Caesar in 52 BC, again during the Hundred Years War, the Wars of Religion in the sixteenth century and the 1944 bombardments. Nevertheless a considerable number of interesting old houses survive, many from the fifteenth century. Nevers is famous for Le Couvent St-Gildard, founded in 1680. Bernadette Soubirous of Lourdes came there on 7 July 1866 to live as a Sister of Nevers. She was born in Lourdes on 7 January 1844 and in 1858 saw eighteen apparitions of the Virgin Mary. She died in Nevers on 16 April 1879, aged 35. Her corpse was exhumed many times and found to be in the original state of conservation as at her death. Tens of thousands of pilgrims come each year to see her lying in the Convent chapel. Nevers has the ancient quarters of St Étienne around the cathedral, the Porte du Croix and other bastions, the old clock tower, priory, convents and many old 'hotels', or mansions.

Nolay (D–6). The pilgrimage of St Solange takes place on Pentecost Monday. During the Revolution her relics were miraculously preserved from the mobs.

Oudan (E–3). The bishops of Auxerre built a stronghold here, which the French inhabitants of Varzy destroyed in 1358 for fear of the marauding English army. St Germanus (Germain) is the local saint, following the legend that he became lost in the forest of Oudan and, surviving, became patron of the commune. There is a statue of him, and the *fête patronale* on the second Sunday in August is named after him.

Planchez (j–6). The German troops fired the village in 1944 before they left.

Pougues-les-Eaux (C–7). Legend has it that Hercules came here to take the waters to improve his health and strength. Certainly Henri IV and Louis XIV took the waters here for their curative effects; the calcium bicarbonate in the water is reputedly good for hepatitis sufferers. There is a casino here.

Pousseaux (F–1) has a prehistoric grotto, 'La Founetière'.

St-Agnan (J–4) has an artificial lake of 142 hectares (over 300 acres).

135

St-André (H–3), set in the Morvan National Park, has attractive windmills and many old Morvan-style houses.

St-Benin d'Azy (E–7). Benignus, a Christian evangelist of Bourgogne, was martyred at Dijon by the Roman troops of Marc Aurelius, and gave his name to this town.

St-Honoré-les-Bains (H–9) has a *parc thermal* with springs containing sulphur and arsenic; it is a recognized spa.

St-Martin-du-Puy (I–3) is another Morvan village surrounded by woods, lakes and rivers.

St-Parize-le-Châtel (C–9) is known for its sparkling mineral waters 'des Fonts-Bouillants'.

St-Pierre-le-Moûtier (C–10). Joan of Arc retook the village from the English troops in 1429 and a statue records the fact. The town was once fortified and flanked by moats and circular towers. There are pretty Renaissance houses and a *plafond*, cellars and windmills.

Ternant (J–10). In the modest church are two remarkable Flemish triptychs of the fifteenth century.

Tracy-sur-Loire (A–4). In the sixteenth century a Scottish family called Stutt, originally living in the Berry area, moved to the Château of Tracy.

Varzy (E–3). A small town which dates from the fifth century with towers, vaulted cellars, an old college, covered wells and statues.

Vaux (G–5). The lake covers 200 hectares (nearly 500 acres) and has good fishing.

Vignol (G–3). John d'Estutt (of the same Scottish family as in Tracy) in 1629 owned the Seigneurie and lands of Lallemande at Vignol.

Villapourçon (I–8) is another Morvan village with water mills set amidst wooded hills of Mont Genièvre and Boûquet de la Gravelle, near the waterfall on the river Dragne.

Castles and châteaux

The old battle-weary defensive strongholds that still have an interesting site are Motte-Josserand, Meauce, Chevenon, Rosemont, Passy-les-Tours, Bazoches, Champidoux, Vandenesse and Giry. The transient Italian phase produced the splendid ornamental ducal palace at Nevers, La Motte-Farchat, Dornes, Les Granges and St-Armand-en-Puisaye. The late seventeenth- and eighteenth-century châteaux worth a visit are Chassy, Vesigneux, Quincize, La Roche and the bishops' palace at Urzy. I have included only exceptional buildings, classified as MH (*Monument Historique*) or IMH (*Inscrit à l'Inventaire des Monuments Historiques*). Would-be visitors are advised to check opening times either with the nearest tourist information office or with the Association Nièvre Tourisme, Préfecture de la Nièvre, 58019 Nevers, tel. 86.57.80.90, or at the Office de Tourisme, 31 rue du Rempart, tel. 86.59.07.03.

Aunay-en-Bazois (G–6) was built in the sixteenth century and reconstructed over the two suceeding centuries. It has three corner towers, a courtyard, classic gates, a vaulted kitchen, and an orangery.

Bazoches (H–3) was built in the fifteenth century and repaired in the seventeenth. It was owned by Marshal Vauban in 1703 and has main walls in a polygonal shape with circular towers, a gate tower, keep, courtyard, vaulted rooms, etc.

Blismes (H–6). The Château de Quincize, built in the fifteenth century and repaired in the eighteenth, was an ancient stronghold. It has circular towers, terraces, gardens and inner rooms in good condition, including a bathroom!

Châtillon-en-Bazois (G–7). The Château de Châtillon was a stronghold fortress in 1280, and has been restored. It has a high keep, circular corner towers and a Gothic chapel.

Chevenon (D–8) was built in the fourteenth century, and repaired and restored in the sixteenth and nineteenth in the style of Vincennes. It is well worth a visit.

137

Chitry-les-Mines (G–4) was repaired in the seventeenth century. The Galerie des Sybilles, with paintings and tapestries, is of note.

Corbigny (G–4) has the châteaux of Chitry and Villemolin.

Dornes (E–11), which was reconstructed in the sixteenth century, has circular towers, a dovecot, an Italian-style façade, a stone staircase and tapestries on view.

Gimouille (C–8) has the Château du Marais, built in the fourteenth century with many circular towers, chapel, etc.

Giry (E–5) has a fourteenth-century château with towers, a fortified porch, a courtyard with a gallery, pavillions, etc.

Guérigny (C–6). The Château du Villemenant is a fifteenth-century manor house with a good façade, towers, chimneys, and old forges on view.

Larochemillay (J–9). The Château de la Roche was reconstructed in 1720 by Marshal Villars. It is on a rocky promontory with terraces, pavilions, staircases, etc.

Luthenay-Uxeloup (D–9) was built in the thirteenth century. Seven circular towers can still be seen, but the famous old castle of Rosemont is sorely battered.

Menou (D–3) was built in the seventeenth century. It has a huge courtyard, pavilions, and a park known as 'Les Tuileries Nivernaises'.

Nevers (C–8) has the magnificent Ducal Palace, built in the fifteenth century, overlooking the Loire. It is in excellent condition, but can only be seen from the outside.

Perroy (C–3). The Château de la Motte-Josserand was built in the fourteenth century. It was occupied by the Captains of the Grand Companies, and later by the *routiers*. The quadrilateral main walls surround an inner courtyard with four round corner rooms, a castle chapel, and a fourteenth century well.

Prémery (D–5) was the old castle of the bishops of Nevers in the fourteenth to sixteenth centuries. It has many towers, and interesting inner and outer walls.

Saincaize-Meauce (C–9). The Château de Meauce was built in the thirteenth century and repaired in successive centuries. It has circular walls, an inner courtyard, hexagonal tower and fifteenth century battlements.

St-Amand-en-Puisaye (B–1). The Château Renaissance was built in the sixteenth century of brick and stone.

St-Léger-de-Fougeret (I–7) was built in the sixteenth century and later reconstructed. It has towers, pavilions, elegant furnishings, formal gardens, a park, a dovecot, etc.

St-Martin-du-Puy (I–3). The Château de Vesigneux was reconstructed in the sixteenth and seventeenth centuries. It has a crenellated keep, circular towers, a castle chapel, chimneys and many tapestries.

Suilly-la-Tour (B–4). The Château des Granges was built in the fifteenth century and has a castle chapel, pavilions, courtyard, murals, etc.

Tracy-sur-Loire (A–4) was built in the fifteenth century and later repaired. The *pavillon d'entrée* is noteworthy, as is the high, round keep.

Urzy (C–7) is another château which was owned by the bishops of Nevers. The neighbouring Château des Bordes was reconstructed in the fifteenth century. Both are worth a visit.

Vandenesse (H–8) was built in the fifteenth century. It has a polygonal outer wall, a crenellated keep, several towers, Renaissance chimneys, and tapestries.

Varennes-lès-Narcy (B–5). The fourteenth century Château de Passy-les-Tours has a keep, corner towers, etc.

Cathedrals, abbeys and splendid churches

The main Romanesque churches in the department are at Béard, Jailly, Jaugenay, St-Parize-le-Châtel, St-Agnan-de-Cosne, Mars-sur-Allier, St-Révérien, St-Pierre-le-Moûtier, and

139

notably at La Charité-sur-Loire. The Gothic architectural style can be seen in the churches of St-Amand-en-Puisaye, Prémery, Surgy, St-Père, Corbigny, Challement, Varzy, St-Saulge, part of the Cathedral of Nevers, and the collegiate of Clamecy.

Alligny-Cosne (B–2) is described as 'sixteenth century flamboyant Gothic'.

Amazy (F–3) has the sixteenth century church of St Franchy.

Balleray (D–7) has the twelfth century Romanesque church of St Blaise, which contains a painting of St Hubert's chase. Each year the hunting community celebrates its patron saint here.

Béard (D–9) has the twelfth century Romanesque church of St Laurent. The clock tower is built in three stages with a steeple. This little church has been recently restored.

Cervon (H–5). This eleventh century Romanesque collegiate church has also been restored. The west door is noteworthy.

Challement (F–4). This hamlet, with a population of ninety, has the sixteenth century Gothic church of St Hilaire.

Champvoux (B–6) has the eleventh century Romanesque church of St Pierre. The high choir is flanked by side-aisles; the transept and carved pillar heads are of note.

La Charité-sur-Loire (B–5) has the eleventh century church and Benedictine Priory annexe of Cluny. Although much damaged through the centuries, this church remains a most interesting example of Cluniac architecture. The tower 'Sainte Croix' is ornamented with multifoil blind arcades and a curious frieze. On the tympanum of one of the walled-up doorways, Christ is seen in Majesty blessing the Priory monks at the request of the Virgin; scenes from the life of the Virgin also decorate the lintel. The fifteenth century door leads to the Place Sainte-Croix, where the ten-bay nave once stood. The present church stands on the site of the first four bays. The false triforium arcades of the six bays, now destroyed, can still be seen embedded in the walls of the neighbouring houses. The ambulatory leads to a ring of five radiating chapels around the elegant chancel, the columns of which are capped by very beautifully historiated capitals. Over the pointed arches, stone carvings of eight beasts can be seen, and above this a false triforium with multifoil arcades. From the Square des Benedictines there is a fine view of the *chevet* and the octagonal tower above the transept crossing.

Chevenon (D–8) has the twelfth century Romanesque church of Jaugenay, now in course of restoration.

Clamecy (F–2) has the thirteenth century collegiate church of St Martin, restored in the nineteenth century by Viollet-le-Duc with a noteworthy '*façade flamboyante*'. The twelfth century cathedral of Bethléem is worth a look, even though it is now a hotel-restaurant.

Cosne-Cours-sur-Loire (A–3) has the Romanesque church of St Agnan built by Hugh, Abbot of Cluny. The main door is richly sculptured. The Gothic church of St Jacques was built in the fifteenth century. Finally the old convent of the Augustins, mainly seventeenth century, is of note.

Crux-la-Ville (F–6). The church has a noteworthy painting by Philippe de Champaigne, 'L'Ange gardien', which depicts the crowning of the Virgin.

Dampierre-sous-Bouhy (C–2) has a flamboyant sixteenth century Gothic church.

Decize (E–9). The church of St Aré, built in a cruciform shape, has a choir, a Merovingian crypt and a stone altarpiece. The thirteenth century chapel of St Thibault and the seventeenth century convent of Minimes are also worth a visit.

Donzy-le-Pré (C–3). The Priory of Donzy-le-Pré was attached to Cluny in 1109. Three-quarters of the church is in ruins, but its fame remains owing to the tympanum with a crowned Virgin at its centre, carrying the child Jesus, sheltered under a canopy upheld by two columns decorated with chevron patterns and flutings. On the right is a censer-bearing angel, on the left the emaciated figure of the Prophet Isaiah holds a palm and a parchment. A delicate pattern of flowers, palm

141

leaves and balls decorates the covings of the doorway. Beautiful rosette frieze.

Garchizy (C–7) has a twelfth century Romanesque church of St Martin, dominated by a fine octagonal Cluniac clock tower.

Garchy (B–4) has a twelfth century Romanesque church.

Jailly (F–6). The twelfth century Romanesque church of St Sylvestre has a choir and transept of that period. The west doorway is noteworthy.

Mars-sur-Allier (B–9). The Romanesque church of St Julien dates from the eleventh century and has a noteworthy tympanum above the main door.

Marzy (C–8) has a twelfth century Romanesque church dominated by a handsome square clock tower called the 'bec d'Allier'.

Metz-le-Comte (G–3) has the twelfth century Romanesque church of Notre Dame.

Montigny-aux-Amognes (D–7) has a twelfth century Romanesque church with an arched façade.

Moulins-Engilbert (H–8) has a recently restored twelfth century Romanesque priory of Commagny, 2 km outside the town.

Narcy (B–5). The twelfth century church of St Marcel has a choir worth looking at.

Nevers (C–8), as one might expect, has half a dozen MH classifications. The cathedral of St Cyr and Ste Juliette has the remains of an early Christian baptistry of the sixth-eighth centuries. The church of St Étienne, of pure Romanesque style of the eleventh century, has a nave 18 m high on three levels – the outside *chevet* is well-nigh perfect. The church of St Pierre was a seventeenth century Jesuit college chapel; the wall paintings are unusual. All these, with the twelfth century Romanesque church of Notre Dame de St Genest, the chapel of Ste Marie, founded in 1620, and the old chapel of the oratory, make Nevers a centre of superb ecclesiastical architecture. The Convent of St Gildard, which houses the body of St Bernadette, is situated in the north-west of the town, near the large municipal park.

Ourouër (D–7) has a fine twelfth century Romanesque church, with a notable stone cross of the fifteenth century and octagonal clock tower.

Prémery (D–5). The church of St Marcel, of Gothic style of the thirteenth century, contains a remarkable statue of the Virgin.

Rouy (F–7) has a twelfth century Romanesque church with elegant clock tower and decorated *chevet*.

St-Amand-en-Puisaye (B–1) has a thirteenth century church with fittings and paintings worth a visit.

St-Éloi (D–8) commemorates St Eligius, patron of metal workers. The twelfth century Romanesque church of Chaluzy has a fortified clock tower.

St-Parize-le-Châtel (C–9) has a twelfth century Romanesque church of St Patrick (St Parize). Below the choir is a huge crypt with massive columns surmounted by carved images – a woman acrobat, animal musicians, a mermaid, an archer killing a stag, a miser holding his purse tightly – inspired by the bestiaries of the Middle Ages.

St-Père (B–3) has a sixteenth century church with a nave on three levels, also the ancient Commanderie of Villemoison and a twelfth century Romanesque chapel.

St-Pierre-le-Moûtier (C–10). The ancient church of the ninth century Benedictine Abbey has retained from the Romanesque era two fine capitals, worthy of being attributed to a Burgundian workshop, and two doors. The one on the north side has a tympanum showing Christ with the four Evangelists framed by an archivolt of four angels bearing censers and candlesticks.

St-Révérien (F–5). The earlier church was built in the twelfth century on the spot where an oratory had been dedicated to

143

St Révérien, a third century martyr, who had come to spread the Gospel to the Eduens. The *chevet* is remarkable for the arrangement of its chapels and the elegant tiered roofing. The choir, the ambulatory and the radiating chapels are considered to be one of the gems of Nivernais architecture. The capitals are amongst the most beautiful of Romanesque art; their subjects are most varied: geometrical patterns, foliage, well-known figures of the Old Testament and fantastic animals.

St-Vérain (B–2) has an ancient priory with a choir, an old clock tower and beautiful stained-glass windows.

Semelay (H–9) has a twelfth century Romanesque church of St Pierre, with a very long choir and an apse with rich decorations of foliage, rosettes, bestiary animals, etc.

Suilly-la-Tour (B–4) has a church with a Renaissance clock tower and scuptured door.

Tannay (F–3) St Léger, an ancient collegiate church, has a *bas-relief* representing the legend of St Hubert.

Ternant (H–10) has a modest church with two remarkable fifteenth century Flemish triptychs.

Varzy (E–3). The thirteenth century church of St Pierre has two clock towers, and a nave 50 m long. A sixteenth century triptych and the treasury are of note.

Verneuil (F–9) has a twelfth century Romanesque church with wall paintings and a crenellated clock tower.

Museums

The Nièvre is proud of its archaeological sites, and its museums reflect this. The activities of the following eight regional societies are co-ordinated by M. Bouthier of the Comité département RA Nivernais, 20-22 rue Richier, 75009 Paris, tel. (16)14.264.70.17:

G–2 Brèves. Association Culturelle du Mont-Beuvrois, Mairie de Brèves, 58530 Dornecy.

F–5   Champallement. Les Amis de Compierre, 21 rue des Perrières, 58000 Nevers, tel. 86.57.31.98, or 29.63.57 at Neuilly.

E–2   Corvol l'Orgueilleux, Les Amis du Vieux Corvol. M. Jarreau, Mairie de Corvol, 58460 Corvol.

A–3   Cosne-Cours-sur-Loire. GRA Condate. M. Bouthier, as above.

E–9   Decize. GRA du Sud Nivernais. Dr Pages, 11 place Hanoteau, 58300 Decize.

D–2   Entrains-sur-Nohain. GRA d'Entrains. M. Meissoι.ηier, 8 boulevard du Massacre, 44800 St-Herblain, tel. 40.30.84.95.

I–10   Luzy. GRA Nivernais, Hotel de Ville, 58170 Luzy. M. Arnoux, Tel. 86.30.05.89.

E–3   Varzy. GRA Proto-historique, Haut-Nivernais. Mairie, 58210 Varzy.

Brèves (G–2). Consult the Mairie. There is an exhibition of excavations from a Merovingian necropolis, where over two hundred tombs have recently been discovered. Burial objects (ceramics, glassware, jewellery, weapons) give invaluable indications of the life of an early Frankish community. Open mid-summer.

Cervon (H–5). The Musée de la Mer à la Vallée de Certaines is a museum of marine zoology.

Champallement (F–5) has a museum of archaeology.

La Charité-sur-Loire (B–5). At the Hôtel Adam, rue des Chapelains, tel. 86.70.16.12, there is a collection of medieval archaeology. Open every day except Tue.

Château-Chinon (I–7). The Musée rue de Château, tel. 86.85.06.58, has objects from Neolithic to Gallo-Roman times gathered during recent excavations at several sites in the Haut-Morvan, in particular the Île du Lac des Settons, Fou de Verdun, Huis l'Abbé and Les Bardiaux. Also folklore and costumes. Open Wed., Sat. and Sun. To visit, apply to the town hall.

Clamecy (F–2) has the Musée Romain Rolland at the Hôtel de Bellegarde, tel. 86.27.02.51. In addition to the burial furnishings (torques and fibulae) originating from a protohistoric tumulus, the museum exhibits items from Gallo-Roman sites of Entrains and Compierre: bronzes, lapidary sculptures (Eduen couple, radiating sun head, god with mallet), ceramics and two coins from the mid-third century. Open every day except Tue., all year.

Corvol-lOrgeuilleux (E–2). At the church of St-Vincent-de-Corvol are four sarcophagi, three of which are decorated, dating from the sixth and seventh centuries. They come from the old cemetery of St Maurice at Corvol.

Cosne-Cours-sur-Loire (A–3). At the Palais de Justice is the 'Maison des Chapelains', tel. 86.28.11.85. It contains various small domestic objects of bronze and bone, stone sculptures, coins, ceramics (including wine amphorae), equipment of everyday life, remains of iron and bronze-working (crucibles, charcoal), a large fragment of mosaic from Pouilly-sur-Loire and building utensils. Also pottery and metal implements from the Merovingian, Carolingian and medieval eras. Open during summer. Information at town hall.

La Machine (E–9). At 2 avenue de la République is an exhibition of mines and mining activities. Open Jun.–Sep. except Tue.

Marzy (C–8). At 22 place de l'Église is the museum of folklore and local history. Open Sun. only, throughout the year.

Nevers (C–8). The Musée Municipal, 12-16 rue St-Genest, has an exhibition of faience, tel. 86.57.37.86. Closed Jan. The Musée Lapidaire at the Porte du Croix has an exhibition of Greek marbles, Roman sculpture and gems. Open all year.

St-Brisson (J–4). The Musée de la Résistance, Maison du Parc du Morvan, is open every day except Tue. for most of the year, but in winter at weekends only.

Varzy (E–3) has a museum of faience and paintings, rue St-Jean. Closed Tue.

CHAPTER NINE:
A FEAST FOR THE PALATE

There is much good locally produced food. Poultry and game are bred at Bouhy (C–2), whichis known for pigeons, hares and quail, Couloutre (D–3), which specializes in pheasants, Aunay-en-Bazois (G–6), known for rabbits and poultry, and Cosne-sur-Loire (poultry). Lormes (H–4) is renowned for ham, *rosett du Morvan* – a kind of sausage – and cheeses. It holds fairs for sheep, veal and poultry during the year. Entrains-sur-Nohain (D–2) also has regular fairs for horses, cattle and poultry. Clamency produces its own *andouillettes*. Towns and villages by the river Loire have fish, including salmon, *sandre*, pike and eel.

Many small villages specialize in the growing of mushrooms and the making of cheese, especially goat cheese, and St-Hilaire-Fontaine (G–10) should be visited for a sample of 52jambon de Morvan and cream cheese. Other Morvan gastronomic specialities can be found at Onlay (I–8), a *village fleuri*. Dornecy (F–2) and Chaulgnes (C–6) are known for bee-keeping and honey. Azy-le-Vif (D–10) grows walnuts, and Cessy-les-Bois (C–4) makes walnut oil. Myennes (A–2) makes biscuits known as *croquets de Myennes*, Never makes *nougatine* and *négus*, and St-Nenin-d'Azy produces *Saupiquet des Amognes*.

Perroy (C–3) makes cider, and there are distilleries for Marc de Bourgogne at Préporché (H–8), Montapas (F–7), Ciez (C–2) and Cosne-sur-Loire.

Local wines

The Nièvre is the Cinderella of the wine-producers of Burgundy. Nevertheless there are over thirty villages in the region which cultivate table wine grapes or, in two cases, which have distilleries for Marc de Bourgogne. The most important area, with the only co-operative, is at Pouilly-sur-Loire, halfway between La Charité and Cosne-Cours-sur-Loire. The wines of 'Pauliacum' were known in the ninth century and were initially planted by Benedictine monks; even now there is a 4-hectare vineyard at Pouilly called 'La Loge aux Moines'. Surplus production was shipped on the river Loire to Paris.

Before the ravages of the disease phylloxera in the nineteenth century, the total area under vines at Pouilly totalled 1,500 hectares. After replanting about 1900 there are now 500 hectares producing either Chasselas grapes, which give a clear, light, white wine with 10-11 degrees of alcohol and 3-4 grammes of acidity per litre, or Sauvignon, with tight little bunches of small, egg-shaped grapes. The latter produce a grey-white coloured wine, the colour of smoke, thus called 'Blanc-Fumé', with 12 degrees of alcohol and 5 grammes of acidity per litre. This is a higher quality wine but both *crus* have been given *appellation contrôlée* status.

The villages which grow and supply grapes to the co-operative are Loges, Bouchot, Berthiers, St-Andelain and Tracy. The Château du Nozet has the largest single vineyard of 50 hectares, which produces 5,000 hectolitres of Blanc-Fumé, more than 25 per cent of the total in the region, much of it exported. The Château de Tracy, which has a fifteenth-century fortress keep, is also worth visiting.

Pouilly: Les Cornets, La Loge aux Moines, Varigny, Les Fouinelles, Les Bas Coins, Les Vignes des Pierres, Les Griottes and Les Vignes de Berge.
St-Andelain: Le Désert, La Charnoie, Le Champ du Clou, Les Chailloux, La Renardière and Les Chaudoux.
Tracy: Le Travers des Plantes, Les Champs de Cris, Le Champ Billard, Les Champs de la Croix and Château de Tracy.

The *cave co-operative* of Pouilly-sur-Loire (58150) is at Les Moulins à Vent, tel 83.39.10.99. It was created in 1947 and buys, in grapes, nearly all the local production of the small *vignerons* – currently 500 hectolitres of Chasselas and 2,000 hectolitres of Blanc Fumé. In addition, the co-operative markets a good quality Rouge de Cosne from the villages further north, of Neuvy-sur-Loire, Myennes, St-Père-Pougny (its own VDQS wine) and Châteauneuf Val-de-Bargis. The Cosne red and *rosé* wines are known as Vins des Coteaux du Giennois VDQS. The *caves*, which are open for tasting and sales every day except Sunday, are easily reached by the RN7, 40 km from Nevers. They overlook the river near the centre of the town, and are quite near the main bridge over the river. M. Paul Mollet is the President des Vignerons and M. Bernard Bouchie is the Chef des Caves. Two villages to the east – Nannay and La Celle-sur-Nièvre – also produce white wines.

The keen *amateur de vin* should follow leisurely the recommended 'Route des Vins', starting in Pouilly and going east to Bouchot d'en Bas, north to Bouchot d'en Haut, Le Nozet, Bois Renaud to St-Andelain, Le Grand Soumard, north to Boisfleury, west to Tracy and south back to Pouilly via Les Girarmes and Les Loges. Most of the local farmers offer tasting facilities. St-Andelain and Alligny-Cosne have a 'Fête des Vignerons' for St Vincent on 22 January.

The secondary area for wine production in the Nièvre is in the region around and mainly south of Clamecy. Tannay produces an acceptable white wine. There is a *confrérie vineuse* called 'Les Chanoines de Tannay'. Other wine-producing villages are Vignol, Teigny, Talon, St-Germain-des-Bois, St-Aubin-des-Chaumes, Pouques-Lormes, Nuars, Moissy-Moulinot, La Maison-Dieu, Courcells and Asnois. Finally, on the southern borders with the Saône-et-Loire, one finds *vin de pays* at St-Hilaire, Lucenay-les-Aix, Livry, Devay and Charrin.

Modest hotels and restaurants

Nevers (pop. 50,000), the capital of the Nièvre, has eleven hotel-restaurants, fifteen hotels without restaurants and six officially endorsed 'tourist restaurants'. In addition, there are over thirty small café-restaurants, *crêperies* and *pizzerias*. Most of the hotels are located in the south-west of the town, near the railway station and the river Loire. A recommended hotel is the Terminus, 57 avenue Charles de Gaulle, tel. 86.57.09.22, with 25 rooms. It is two hundred metres from the station and is thus easy to find. Technically it is a two-star hotel, but the current prices fall within our budget. Ask for an inside room. Parking: turn right out of the hotel and there is a quiet side street first right. There are two alternatives listed in the summary at the end of this chapter. If you choose one of the fifteen one-star hotels without a restaurant, try the d'Artagnan, 25 quai de Mantoue; the Coquillat, 84 rue de Nièvre, or l'Étable, 56 *bis* rue 13e de Ligne, which all offer good value *prix fixe* menues for around 50 francs.

Cosne-Cours-sur-Loire (pop. 12,000) is in the north-west corner of the department, 50 km from Nevers, on the river Loire. Of the six hotel-restaurants, five are shown in the summary. The Hôtel de la Gare is good value, but the restaurant is closed on Saturday and Sunday. The Grand Hôtel Moderne, 52 rue du Commerce, tel. 86.28.17.86, has 24 rooms and is also good value.

La Charité-sur-Loire (pop. 6,000) halfway between Nevers and Cosne-Cours, is one of the most attractive towns in the Nièvre, overlooking the Loire. The two recommended hotels, l'Union and Terminus, are close together on the avenue Gambetta. The Terminus, tel. 86.70.09.61, has 10 rooms but is closed on Mondays. Parking is easy. In both hotels rooms are well within the budget. Breakfast is 16 francs. L'Union's *prix fixe* menu is 50 francs; closed Tuesday.

Decize (pop. 7,500) is 35 km south-east of Nevers on the river Loire. Both hotel-restaurants there give reasonable value. The Hôtel de l'Agriculture and the Hôtel le Centre are both well within the budget, with *prix fixe* menus about 50 francs.

Fourchambault (pop. 6,000) is an industrial town, 10 km north-west of Nevers. The Hôtel du Berry is listed in the summary.

Clamecy (pop. 6,000) is a charming old town, well worth a visit. It is situated on the northern boundary with the Yonne department, on the river Yonne, 75 km north-east of Nevers on the main road from Auxerre. There are three hotel-restaurants. Especially good value is the Hôtel de la Boule d'Or, 5 place Bethléem, tel. 86.27.11.55, with 26 rooms (closed first fortnight in February and September). Both the Boule d'Or and the Hostellerie de la Poste, 9 place Émile-Zola, tel. 86.27.01.55, have *prix fixe* menus about 50 francs and easy parking.

Château-Chinon (pop. 3,000) is 60 km due east of Nevers, near the boundary with the department of Saône-et-Loire, on the road from Autun, and is a key town for exploring the Morvan National Park. The Hôtel au Vieux Morvan, 8 place Gudin, tel. 86. 85.05.01, has 23 rooms. It has two stars and rooms start at 70 francs. If you can obtain the cheapest double then you will be just within the budget. The Hostellerie l'Oustalet, route de Lormes, tel. 86.85.15.57, with 16 rooms, is well within the budget.

Imphy (pop. 5,000), a small industrial town on the Loire, is well known for its freshwater fish. It is 15 km south-east of Nevers. Both the Hôtel du Commerce, 14 rooms, and the Central, 13 rooms, are suitable.

Prémery (pop. 2,800) is 30 km north-east of Nevers and has many local events and gastronomic specialities. The fair for foals and fillies is on the first Tuesday of every month; the fair for the earliest calves is on 5 November, and the poultry fair of St Nicolas is on 6 December. Visit the Tuesday and Saturday morning markets. The Hôtel de la Poste, 27 Grande-Rue, tel. 86.68.12.30, has 16 rooms (closed Friday and February) and gives good value. Full pension per person is not more than 150 francs.

St-Pierre-le-Moûtier (pop. 2,250) is 30 km south of Nevers and is part of the *étape gastronomique*. It is near the border with the departments of Cher and Allier. The inhabitants are proud of the fact that Joan of Arc recaptured the town from the English Army in 1429. They have a statue of her and a fête

151

commemorating the victory on the second Sunday in October. The Hôtel au Bon Labourer, tel. 86.37.41.30, has 10 rooms and is one of the twelve 'Auberges du Nivernais-Morvan'.

Pouilly-sur-Loire (pop. 2,000) is halfway between Cosne-Cours-sur-Loire and La Charité-sur-Loire. The centre of the Nièvre wine area, it is well worth a visit. The Hôtel de l'Écu de France, tel. 86.39.10.97, has 10 rooms and is within the budget. The Hôtel le Relais Fleuri is a two-star hotel on the avenue de la Tuilerie, tel. 86.39.12.99 with 9 rooms (closed Thursday night). It is just within the budget, and has a *prix fixe* menu about 50 francs.

St-Honoré-les-Bains (pop. 1,000), 30 km due south of Château-Chinon, is a spa town, known to the Romans and still a source of *eaux sulfurées arsenicales* (definitely curative!). Gastronomic specialities of the Morvan, such as game and fish, are to be found here. There are some one-star hotel-restaurants within the budget of which two are given in the summary.

Other small towns with appropriate good value hotel-restaurants include **Châtillon-en-Bazois** (pop. 1,150), 20 km west of Château-Chinon; **Chaulgnes** (pop. 850), 20 km north of Nevers; **Corvol-l'Orgueilleux** (pop. 1,000), 10 km west of Clamecy, known for its pheasant breeding, goat and other cheeses; **Donzy** (pop. 2,000), 20 km due east of Cosne-Cours, known for its snails and mushrooms; **Dun-les-Places** (pop. 550), 30 km north of Château-Chinon, known for its folklore festival on 3 August; **Luzy** (pop. 2,750), 40 km due south of Château-Chinon on the borders of the Saône-et-Loire, a *ville fleurie* at the south of the Morvan National Park; **Marzy** (pop. 2,800), 6 km west of Nevers, known for its Charollais cattle and poultry; **Montsauche** (pop. 850), 30 km north-east of Château-Chinon, known for its fish and other gastronomic specialities. In the Morvan National Park, **Moulins-Engilbert** (pop. 1,850), 15 km south-east of Château-Chinon, known for its fish and '*tir aux jambons*'. **Neuvy-sur-Loire** (pop. 1,200), in the furthest north-west corner of the Nièvre, known for its 'fête de Roses' on 18 May, its poultry and wine; **Ouroux-en-**

Morvan (pop. 1,000), 15 km north of Château-Chinon, known for its fish, its many fairs and the folklore group of the 'black Montagnes'. **Pougues-les-Eaux** (pop. 2,000), 15 km north-west of Nevers, is another small spa town, with '*eaux bicarbonatées calciques*' for hepatitis and stomach sufferers, and folklore fêtes. **Tannay** (pop. 750), 15 km due south of Clamecy, has gastronomic specialities and local wine, and **Varzy** (pop. 1,500), 20 km south-west of Clamecy, is an interesting old town with various fairs and fêtes.

There are good-value low-cost restaurants to be found in Chaulgnes (Grill Courte Paille), Clamecy (Le Cercle), La Marche (Les Routiers), Montigny-aux-Amognes (Auberge des Amognes), Moux (Beau Site), Pouilly-sur-Loire (Relais Grillade, La Vieille Auberge) and Urzy (Auberge du Pont-St-Ours).

Restaurants

There are good-value low-cost restaurants to be found in Chaulgnes (Grill Courte Paille), Clamecy (Le Cercle, La Marches (Les Routiers), Montigny-aux-Amognes (Auberge des Amognes), Moux (Beau Site), Pouilly-sur-Loire (Relais Grillade, La Vieille Auberge) and Urzy (Auberge du Pont-St-Ours).

Summary

Map ref.	Town	Hotel	No. of rooms	Tel. (Prefix 86)
B-5	La Charité-sur-Loire 58400	l'Union, 8 avenue Gambetta	11	70.08.58 closed Tue. pm.
		Terminus, 22 avenue Gambetta	10	70.09.61 closed23/12–31/1
		du Cygne	7	70.10.29 closed Mon.
I-7	Château-Chinon 58120	l'Oustalet, route de Lormes	16	85.15.57 closed 21/9-31/10

153

		au Vieux Morvan, 8 place Gudin	23	85.05.01
G-7	Châtillon-en-Bazois 58110	de la Poste, rue Charles-Duret	12	84.14.68 closed Sun. pm. and 20/12-20/1
C-6	Chaulgnes 58400	la Chance au Roy	8	68.80.08
F-2	Clamecy 58500	de la Boule d'Or, 5 place Bethléem	26	27.11.55 closed Sep. and 1/2-15/2
		de la Poste, 9 place Émile-Zola	17	27.01.55 closed Mon. and 20/12-20/1
		au Bon Accueil, 3 route d'Auxerre	10	27.06.32 closed Tue. and Dec./Jan.
E-2	Corvol-l'Orgueilleux 58460	du Dr-Minxit	12	29.12.81
A-3	Cosne-Cours-sur-Loire 58200	à la Ferme, les Gatines	11	28.15.85
		de la Gare, 3 place de la Gare	24	28.22.78 closed Oct. restaurant closed Sat. and Sun.
		La Charrue, place Foch	19	28.15.76 closed 20/12/-10/1
		le St-Christophe, place de la Gare	15	28.02.01 closed Fri. and Feb.
		Grand Hôtel Moderne, 52 rue du Commerce	24	28.17.86 closed 15/1-15/2
E-9	Decize 58300	de l'Agriculture, 20 route de Moulins	18	25.05.38 closed 1/10-2/10
		le Centre, 6 place de la République	7	25.13.87 closed Mar.
C-3	Donzy 58220	du Grande Monarque	17	39.35.44

J-4	Dun-lès Place 58230	le Mont Vélin, Montsauche	10	84.61.82 closed Wed. and 1/12-15/4
D-8	La Fermeté 58160	Nivernaise	7	58.40.37
C-7	Fourchambault 58600	du Berry	10	58.84.26
D-8	Imphy 58160	du Commerce, 44 avenue Jean-Jaurès	14	68.70.13 restaurant closed Jul.
		Central, 7 rue Édouard-Vaillard	13	68.71.57
D-8	Luzy 58170	du Centre, 26 rue de la République	11	30.01.55 closed Mon. 20/10-30/10 and 20/11–15/1
		du Morvan, 73 rue du Dr Dollet	11	30.00.66
		de la Gare, place de la Gare	8	80.04.03
C-8	Marzy-sur-Loire 58000	du Val-de-Loire	24	57.12.24
J-5	Montsauche 58230	Idéal, route des Settons	17	84.51.26 closed Easter to 1/11
H-8	Moulins-Engilbert 58290	du Bon Labourer, place Boucamont	20	84.20.55
A-1	Neuvy-sur-Loire 58450	de la Gaieté, 39 rue Jean-Jaurès	11	39.20.55 closed Sat. and Nov.
C-8	Nevers 58000	Terminus, 57 avenue Charles de Gaulle	25	57.09.22
		de la Gare, 44 avenue Charles de Gaulle	14	57.06.59
		Villa du Parc, 16 rue Lourdes	28	61.09.48
		de l'Avenue, 38	16	61.01.97

155

		avenue Colbert des Deux Gares, 9 rue Charleville	13	57.20.70
I-5	Ouroux-en-Morvan 58230	de la Poste	10	78.21.86
C-8	Pougues-les-Eaux 58320	Central, 62 route de Paris	13	68.85.00 closed Fri. and and 15/11-15/12
		Normandy	8	68.83.33
B-4	Pouilly-sur-Loire 58150	de l'Écu de France	10	39.10.97
		le Relais Fleuri, avenue de la Tuilerie	9	39.12.99 closed Wed. pm.
D-5	Prémery 58700	de la Poste, 27 Grande-Rue	16	68.12.30 closed Fri. and Feb.
H-9	St-Honoré-les-Bains 58360	Rose-Marie, avenue Dr Segard	20	30.70.88 closed 1/10-28/4
		Anne-Marie, 1 allée des Garennes	19	30.76.89 closed 23/9-22/3
C-10	St-Pierre-le-Moûtier 58240	au Bon Labourer	10	37.41.30
F-3	Tannay 58190	de la Gare, place de la Gare	15	29.87.51
E-3	Varzy 58210	de la Gare, place de la Gare	7	29.44.16

Camp sites

See general notes and prices on page 73. *Placements* range from 10 francs at Châteauneuf-val-de-Bargis to 150 francs at Nevers, La Charité and Montsauche.

Map ref.	Town		
G-6	Bazolles 58110 Châtillon-en-Bazois.	Cam. mun. 'Baye',	tel. 86.38.97.83
G-2	Brèves 58530 Dornecy.	Cam. 'Les Fontaines'. Mairie, or	tel. 86.27.05.26 tel. 86.27.14.21
G-9	Cercy-la-Tour 58340	Cam.mun. 'du Port'. Mairie,	tel. 86.50.50.69

F-9	Champvert 58300 Decize	'Le Rio Gaillard', 'La Mme Lafond,	tel. 86.25.09.08
B-5	La Charité-sur-Loire 58400	Cam. 'de la Saulaie',	tel. 86.70.00.83
F-10	Charrin-la-Varenne 58300	M. Jean-Paul Aurousseau,	tel. 86.50.30.14
I-7	Château-Chinon 58120	Cam. 'de Perthuy- d'Oiseau'. Mairie,	tel. 86.85.15.06
D-4	Châteauneuf-Val-de Bargis 58350	'Le Bourg'. Mairie,	tel. 86.69.22.79
G-7	Châtillon-en-Bazois 58110	Cam. mun.,	tel. 86.84.14.76
G-4	Chaumot-Chitry- Corbigny 58800	Rte de Germenay, 'L'Ardan'. M. Senn, L'Arden'. M. Senn,	tel. 86.20.11.39
D-8	Chevenon 58160 Imphy.	Cam. mun.,	tel. 86.68.71.71
F-2	Clamecy 58500	Cam. 'du Pont-Picot',	tel. 86.27.05.97
G-5	La Collancelle-Mondain 58800	M. Bernard Goguelat, La Collancelle,	tel. 86.20.41.89
A-3	Cosne-Cours-sur-Loire 58200	Cam. 'de l'Île- de-Cosne',	tel. 86.28.17.92
E-9	Decize 58300	Cam. mun. 'Les Halles',	tel. 86.25.14.05
C-3	Donzy 58220	Cam. mun., rue A. Audinet,	tel. 86.39.30.28
J-4	Dun-les-Places 58230 Montsauche.	Cam. 'du Montal', 'Aire naturelle de cam. Haut du Château',	tel. 86.84.61.38
D-2	Entrains-sur-Nohain 58410	Cam. 'de St-Cyr'. Mairie,	tel. 86.29.26.38
C-7	Fourchambault 58600	Cam. 'de Fourchambault,	tel. 86.58.86.68
H-4	Lormes 58140	Cam. 'de l'Étang-du- Goulot',	tel. 86.20.80.60
I-10	Luzy 58170	Cam. mun. 'de la Bédure', rte d'Autun,	tel. 86.30.02.34
C-9	Magny-Cours 58470	Cam. mun. 'La Plaine'. Mairie,	tel. 86.58.13.36
B-5	Mesves-sur-Loire 58400 La Charité-sur-Loire.	Cam. 'Les Charmilles',	tel. 86.70.14.87
F-7	Montapas 58110 Châtillon-en-Bazois	Cam. Caravan 'de la Chênaie',	tel. 86.58.34.32

157

J-5	Montsauche 58230	Cam. 'Plage-du-Midi',	tel. 86.84.51.97
H-8	Moulins-Engilbert 58290	Cam. mun. Mairie,	tel. 86.84.21.48
		Cam. Caravan 'de l'Escame'. Mairie,	tel. 86.84.21.48
K-5	Moux-Chevigny 58230 Montsauche	Cam. 'de l'Hermitage-de-Chevigny',	tel. 86.84.50.97
C-8	Nevers 58000	Cam. mun.	tel. 86.57.56.95
H-10	La Nocle-Maulaix 58250 Fours.	Cam. 'les Parcs',	tel. 86.30.84.44
I-5	Ouroux-en-Morvan 58230 Montsauche.	Cam. mun.,	tel. 86.78.21.02
H-8	Pannecot-Limanton 58290 Moulins-Engilbert.	Cam. mun.,	tel. 86.84.21.20
J-6 t	Planchez-en-Morvan 58230 Montsauche.	Cam. 'du Renard'. Mairie,	tel. 86.78.42.03
C-7	Pougues-les-Eaux 58320	Cam. 'les Chanternes',	tel. 86.68.86.18
B-4	Pouilly-sur-Loire 58150	Cam. mun. 'Malaga', bord de Loire,	tel. 86.39.63.72
D-5	Prémery 58700	Cam. mun. 'Les Prés de la ville',	tel. 86.68.12.40
B-1	St-Amand-en-Puisaye 58310	Cam. 'de la Vrille', route de St-Sauveur,	tel. 86.39.63.72
H-9	St-Honoré-les-Bains 58360	Cam. 'des Bains', 15 avenue J. Mermoz,	tel. 86.30.73.44
		Cam. Bonneau, avenue Eugène-Collin,	tel. 86.30.76.00
H-7	St-Péreuse-en-Morvan 58110 Châtillon-en-Bazois	Cam. Caravan 'Bezolle'. M. Lequime,	tel. 86.84.42.55
C-10	St-Pierre-le-Moûtier 58240	Cam. mun., route Courbelon,	tel. 86.68.42.55
F-6	St-Saulge 58330	Cam. mun. 'Aire naturelle'. Mairie,	tel. 86.58.30.33
J-5	Les Settons 58230 Montsauche.	Cam. 'des Braniasses', base nautique,	tel. 86.84.51.98
F-3	Tannay-St-Didier 58190	Cam. 'Les Grandes Îlottes'. Mme Jalquin,	tel. 86.29.86.02
I-10	Tazilly 58170 Luzy.	Cam. 'de Chigy',	tel. 86.30.10.80
H-8	Vendenesse-St-Étienne 58290 Moulins-Engilbert.	Mme J. Jeandaux,	tel. 86.30.71.96
E-3	Varzy 58210	Cam. 'du Moulin-Naudin',	tel. 86.29.43.12

CHAPTER TEN: THE HEART OF THE WINE COUNTRY

The Saône-et-Loire was peopled by the tribe of the Eduens. Their capital town was Bibracte (modern Mont Beuvray). In 52 BC they revolted unsuccessfully against Caesar's legions, and afterwards enjoyed the prosperous years of the *Pax Romana*. In the fifth century, after the Romans had left, the region was invaded by the tribe called les Burgondes, who have been living there ever since. In the ninth century Richard le Justicier, Count of Autun, became the first duke of Burgundy. The tenth century saw the establishment of the Abbey of Cluny. From 1364 the Duchy was ruled by the Valois, and this powerful dynasty transformed Burgundy from a province of France into a grand state, by political alliances and marriages, until the ambition of Charles the Rash and his rivalry with King Louis XI caused the eventual downfall of the Valois rulers. The department takes its name from the two great rivers which form part of its borders – the Saône to the east and the Loire to the west.

Highlights

In addition to the famous wine region around Mâcon, the capital and préfecture city, the department is famous for its religious centres – poor, ravaged Cluny, Paray-le-Monial, visited by millions of pilgrims each year, and modern Chapaize. The archaeological sites of Solutré, Chassey and Autun should also be visited. In the department there are five centres for regional tours – Mâcon in the south, Louhans in the north-east, Chalon-sur-Saône in the north, Autun in the north-west and Digoin in the west. This is the major region for wine co-operatives!

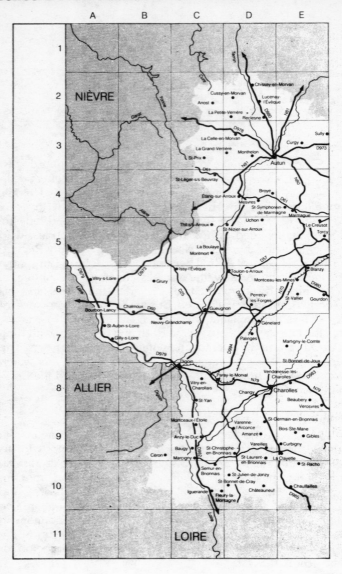

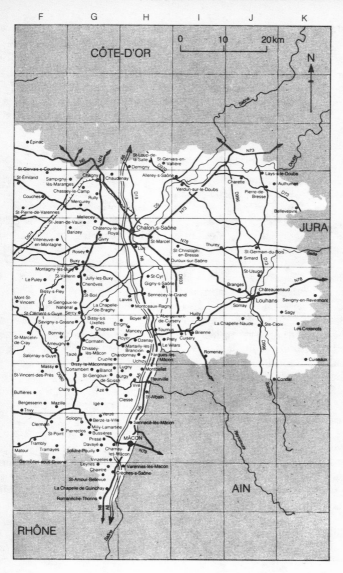

Mâcon

The Syndicat d'Initiative is in a smart, glass-plated building, 187 rue Carnot, tel. 85.38.06.00, opposite the church of St Pierre. It recommends a one-and-a-half-hour tour of the town on foot, which includes the eleventh-century bridges over the Saône, the Hôtel de Ville, the church of St Pierre, La Charité tower, La Maison de Bois, the old cathedral of St Vincent, the Ursuline convent, the Maison Mâconnaise des Vins, overlooking the river.

● North-west circuit (Tournus)

There are two circuits north-west of Mâcon, both of 90 km distance. Go due north on the D103 to Sancé, (thirteenth-century château and twelfth-century Romanesque church), then on to Charbonnières, with its fine view over the valley of the Saône, Clessé (eleventh-century Romanesque church with octagonal tower), and Peronne, a *village perché*, with château and Romanesque church. Next comes Viré-Verizet, a typical Mâconnais wine village, and Burgy, which has a Romanesque church perched on a hill overlooking the wine village. Drive north, east, and north again, with a short detour via Montbellet (four small châteaux, Romanesque church and the old Templar temple of St Catherine), to Mercey on the D210 and north to Uchizy, which is a classic old Mâcon village with galleried houses, Château de Grenod, Romanesque church, and AOC Pinot-Chardonnay-Mâcon.

Drive through Fargues-lès-Mâcon (eleventh century Romanesque church) towards your main objective – beautiful Tournus. The Syndicat d'Initiative is in the place Carnot, tel. 85.51.13.10. You may feel inclined to stay overnight here, since there is much to be seen, including the abbey of St Philibert, the chapel of St Michel, the cloister of St Ardain and many other churches, old houses and museums. The return to Mâcon is west and south-west via the Col-de-Beaufer and Ozenay (Romanesque church and château) on the D14 to Martailly-lès-Brancion, which is a medieval fortified hilltop village with a feudal castle, fifteenth-century marketplace and Renaissance houses – a most attractive ensemble. There is a 'biological' market there on the first and third Sunday of each

162

month. The grotto of Four-de-la-Baume is in the nearby valley 'des Tranchées'.

Now travel south on the D161 to Cruzille (seventeenth-century château and wine museum), then south-east to Lugny, with its château, old Mâconnais houses, notable sixteenth-century stone altarpiece of the Apostles in the church, and one of the major wine co-operatives in Burgundy. Now go west to Bissy-la-Mâconnaise, which has a Romanesque church with a rectangular tower overlooking the vineyards of Mâcon-Lugny, and south to St-Gengoux-de-Scissé (eleventh-century Romanesque church, fine old houses and another wine co-operative). Continue south to Azé, with its caves and grottos, and then south-east on the D82 to St-Maurice-de-Satonnay, with its château, old wash-houses and Gothic church, and Laizé, which is a typical Morvan village and has two châteaux. Then drive south to Hurigny, another pictur-esque village with four small châteaux, and back to Mâcon.

● North-west circuit (Cluny)

The next north-west tour from Mâcon starts by a route due west on the N79 to Charnay-lès-Mâcon, where the Château of St Léger overlooks the town. See also the other châteaux and the watermills, and visit the wine co-operative. Then continue on the N79 with a small detour south to Prissé (three châteaux and another wine co-operative). La Roche-Vineuse can be seen on the north side of the N79. You could now branch off on a small detour to Milly-Lamartine (Romanesque church), Sologny (a picturesque small village with a twelfth-century church and wine co-operative) and Berzé-la-Ville, with its Grotto des Fortins, Château des Moines, old wash-houses, Roman chapel and small wine co-operative.

Alternatively, continue north on the N79 to Berzé-le-Châtel to see the twelfth-century feudal castle with seven towers, drawbridge and two embattled keeps. The road winds a lot now, but is well signposted to your main objective, which, via the D980, is Cluny. Apart from seeing the famous abbey of St Pierre and St Paul, visit the Gothic church of Notre Dame, the two museums – Farinier and Ochier – and examine the ramparts, Romanesque houses, and perhaps the famous horse stud-farms.

Head north from Cluny on the D981 to Massilly, to Taizé to see the contrast between the twelfth-century Romanesque church and the modern 'Église de la Reconciliation', the centre of the 'Reformed Community' founded in 1943 by Pastor Roger Schutz. Continue, via Ameugny (eleventh-century Romanesque church), to Cormatin, to see the six *salles d'orées* and Louis XIII furnishings in the seventeenth-century Renaissance château.

Now drive due east on the D187 to Lys, and either make a dog-leg north to Chapaize, with its eleventh-century Romanesque church of St Martin, or continue east to Chissey-lès-Mâcon, a village with old houses, a Romanesque church and chapel, until you link up with the D187 again, heading south to Blanot, with its eleventh-century Romanesque church and Cluniac priory near the 600-metre Mont St-Romain. Stop and venture into the extensive grottoes of La Cailleverdière. Next, travel south on the D446 to Donzy-le-Pertuis (eleventh-century Romanesque church and panorama), towards Mont Joux, south-east on the D15 to Azé, but this time south on the D85 to Igé and Verzé, both wine villages with co-operatives. Then go south-east to Chevagny-les-Chevrières on the D194, and back on the N79 to Mâcon.

• South-west wine tour

The final tour from Mâcon is south-west to the wine-growing villages of the Pouilly white wine area and northern Beaujolais. Start by driving west on the N79, and then fork left and southward on the D54 under the Autoroute A6 until the D89 takes you south to Vinzelles, Chaintré, Chanes and St-Amour. Go north to St-Vérand, Leynes and Chasselas (which introduced the famous grape of that name) on the D31 to Solutré, where the towering rock will remind you of the unpleasant wild-horse hunts in the paleolithic era. Most of the little wine villages have a small Romanesque church, a château and a wine co-operative. Next, go east to Davayé, west on the D54 to Vergisson, to see the dolmen 'Menhir de Chancerons', and through the Mâcon vineyards growing Pouilly-Fuissé, to

Pierreclos via the D177. The fourteenth-century château with its keep and chapel overlooks the valley of the Petite Grosne river. You now have a choice of returning to Mâcon via Milly and the N79 or venturing by the D45 to the hills of the 'Col de Grand Vent' and 'La Mère Boitier'.

Louhans

Louhans is due east of Tournus, and is the picturesque capital of northern Bresse. The main street is lined with arcades, and the Towers of St Peter and St Paul are worth seeing. The famous Bresse poultry, pigs, calves and other livestock are bought and sold at the large open-air market on Monday mornings. The hospital apothecary is noted for its collection of sixteenth-century pottery. From Louhans tours can be made south-east on the D972 to Cuiseaux, like Louhans an attractive small town with grottoes, narrow streets, ramparts, Renaissance houses, the Château of the Princes of Orange and the Chapelle St Jacques. From Cuiseaux, head west on the D11 to Dommartin and Varennes-St-Sauveur, on the D2 to St-Trivier-de-Courtes. Then go north on the D975 to Romenay, a fortified town, next to Brienne, and west to Cuisery, which is worth a stop to see the châteaux and the flamboyant Gothic church of Notre Dame. The market, where the Bresse food specialities are to be found, is on Tuesdays. Next, drive north on the D933 to Simandre and St-Germain-du-Plain, and east on the N78 back to Louhans.

● Northern circuit

The northern circuit from Louhans is by the N78 and D23 to Montcony, Sens-sur-Seille, St-Germain-du-Bois (market day Saturday) to Mervans (see the Maison des Arcades), and back south to Louhans on the D996.

Chalon-sur-Saône

Chalon-sur-Saône is worth a visit and overnight stay. The Syndicat d'Initiative is in the Square Chabas on the corner of the boulevard de la République and the avenue Nicéphore

Niépce, tel. 85.48.37.97. Its grand tour of the town on foot takes in thirty-two points of call. See the St Vincent Cathedral and cloisters, the Doyenne Tower, Denon and Niépce Museums, the quaysides along the river Saône, and the rose garden in the St Nicolas Park (five minutes by car from the town centre).

From Chalon-sur-Saône visit Chagny, to the north-west, on the intersection for the Dheune river and Canal du Centre; and the famous Châteaux of Rully, Couches and Germolles near Millecey. From Chalon-sur-Saône to the north-east, visit the fortified Verdun-sur-le-Doubs (try the *pochouse* – a dish of freshwater fish stew cooked in local white wine) and the villages of Sermesse, Charette, Terrans and Pierre.

Digoin

Digoin is on the western border, and is a cheerful, bustling town. The Office de Tourisme is at 8 rue Guilleminot, tel. 85.53.00.81. See the ceramic workshops and the aqueduct bridge over the Canal du Centre. The local market is on Fridays and Sundays. Paray-le-Monial is due east on the N79, the centre for pilgrimages to the Basilica of Sacré-Coeur. There are many villages, mainly to the south of Paray-le-Monial, which are well known for their Brionnais Romanesque churches, and there is the incomparable château of La Clayette. A few miles further east, still on the N79, is Charolles, dominated by the Château des Comtes de Charollais. As this is the centre for the famous Charollais cattle, there are frequent fairs. Drive south on the D34 via Poisson, Varenne and St-Christophe, and west on the D989 to Semur and Marcigny, a pretty town with towers and museum. Head north to Anzy-le-Duc (eleventh-century church), and return to Digoin via Monceaux and St-Yan.

• Circular tour

North of Digoin there is an interesting circular tour. Start west on the D979 to St-Agnan and continue to Gilly-sur-Loire, St-Aubin-sur-Loire and Bourbon-Lancy, where there are many attractions – archaeological remains, ramparts, watchtower, old town houses, minor châteaux, the church of

St Nazaire, a good museum and spa water therapy! The rest of the circuit needs careful map-reading. Drive east to Mont, north to Maltat and Cressy-sur-Somme, east to Issy-l'Evêque (see the twelfth-century Romanesque church), south to Uxeau, north to Ste-Radegone and Toulon-sur-Arroux, and south back to Digoin via St-Romain, Perrecey-lès-Forges, Gueugnon and Rigny-sur-Arroux. Most of these villages have a minor château and a Romanesque church.

Autun

Autun is in the north-west of the department. The Office de Tourisme is at 3 avenue Charles de Gaulle, tel. 85.52.20.34. It recommends a twenty-point tour of the town, but some points, such as the Temple of Janus, the Roman theatre, Roman gates, the Porte St-André and the Porte d'Arroux, are on the outskirts of the town, and you will need a car to reach them. The cathedral of St Lazare, which dominates the town, the Musée Lapidaire and the Musée Rolin (of medieval art) are clustered together in the centre.

To the west of Autun lie the hills, valleys and rivers of the Morvan, to the south-east the industrial cities of Le Creusot and Montceaux-les-Mines. The glamorous châteaux of Sully (north-east), Nolay and Couches (east) are within easy striking distance.

Places of interest

Anzy-le-Duc (C–9) was ravaged by the Black Prince in 1366.

Authumes (J–4) is a typical village of the Bresse area in the north-east of the department, with brick-built houses with huge roofs; fortified walls, moat and sacred fountain.

Autun (D–3) was originally known as 'Augustodunum' and was built in the year 10 BC by the Emperor Augustus as a capital town instead of Bibracte. It became the third city in Gaul after Nîmes and Trèves. Evangelized in the second century, it became a bishopric in the third century and knew great prosperity under a succession of illustrious bishops. As

167

with every major city in France, it suffered from the invasions of the Vandals, Francs, Saracens, Normands and, of course, the English, who burned the city in 1379. Talleyrand was Bishop of Autun when the Revolution started. Autun is one of the major sights in Burgundy. Its archaeological sites, the Roman theatre, the Temple of Janus, the Pyramid of Couhard and the Portes St-André and d'Arroux are worth a visit. So, too, are the town quarter called Marchaux, the Passage de la Terrasse, the Promenade des Marbres, the squares of St Louis and the Terreaux, the tower of St Leger, the Ursuline Collège des Jesuites, Fontaine St-Lazare, the clock tower, and many other attractive buildings and sites.

Azé (G–8). The prehistoric grottoes of Rizerolles extend over 1,500 metres; one has 300,000-year-old skeletons of a bear and a lion, another a subterranean river; near the river La Mouge, open Easter–Sep. Entrance 15 francs.

Beaubery (E–8). The French Resistance was particularly strong and effective in this area during the Second World War. A monument to their bravery can be seen on Mont Chatelard.

Bellevesvre (K–4) is a village of the Jura style, with huge, brick-built houses. It is on the border of Bourgogne and Franche-Comté, and was once an important fortified town.

Blanot (G–8) is an ancient hamlet with galleried houses, an old fountain, wash-house, ovenhouse, priory, polygonal tower and *murgers* – dry stone walls. There are also caves and caverns and a sixth-century necropolis with twenty-two sepulchres at the foot of Mont St-Roman (580 m) overlooking the village. Open Apr. to Sep. Entrance 12 francs.

Bourbon-Lancy (A–6). Orginally known as 'Aquae Nisinei', this was an important thermal water spa in Gallo-Roman times. As late as the sixteenth and seventeenth centuries the waters were taken by Henri III, Louise de Lorraine and Richelieu. It is a picturesque old town with half-timbered houses, galleries, clock tower and belfry, priory, hospice and Hôtel de Ville. There are hot spring baths and a casino.

Buffières (F–8). Once the centre of a religion entitled 'Des Blancs', who were *'anti-concordataires'*, a harsh and severe sect that still exists.

Buxy (G–5) is a pretty wine village overlooking the 'Route du Vin'.

Chagny (G–4). During the Hundred Years War, *les écorcheurs*, or *grandes compagnies*, made this town their headquarters. Étienne-Jules Marey (1830–1904), a notable physiologist and inventor, studied bird flight from the hill, called 'La Folie', where he lived.

Chalon-sur-Saône (H–5). The Romans created a garrison and depot town here in 58 BC. It was evangelized by St Marcel in the second century, and made a bishopric in the fifth century. It was the capital of the Merovingian kings of Burgundy, and has always known prosperity. In the Middle Ages important fairs were held here regularly. The construction of the Canal du Centre in 1784–92 accelerated its trading interests. The people of Chalon were ardent *bonapartistes*, and in 1814 resisted the Austrian invasion. In recompense the town was awarded the *Légion d'honneur*. Well worth a visit on the wine route from Beaune to Mâcon. Now a thriving commercial centre, Chalon is also known for its gastronomic specialities. It borders the river Saône and has many interesting buildings. The spring carnivals are called the 'Goniots du Mardi Gras.'

La Chapelle-Naude (J–7) was evangelized by a German monk of the sixth century called St Arnaud or d'Eudes.

Charnay-lès-Mâcon (G–9). A town perched on a hill which overlooks rivers and the Mâcon vineyards and which was the home of Claude Brosse, who first took the wines of Mâcon to Paris by river for sale to the court. The poet Seneca (1643–1737) lived in the Château de Condemine.

Charolles (D–8) has known prosperity since the Middle Ages, not only for its forge metal working, its wine, wood and potteries, but of course for its world-famous Charollais cattle. Cattle fairs take place on the second and fourth Wednesday of each month in this picturesque town. Calf fairs are on the fourth Friday in October and first Thursday in January.

Chassey-le-Camp (G–4). This site, 'Le Chasséen', revealed Neolithic culture including ceramics with geometric motifs. There is also a small Gallo-Roman sanctuary.

Chatenoy-le-Royal (H–5) was known for its curious marriage and courting traditions from the Middle Ages up to the nineteenth century.

La Clayette (E–9) was and is still famous for its breeding of race horses. Henri IV purchased his well-known white horse here in the sixteenth century.

Cluny (G–8). In AD 910 Guillaume le Pieux, Duke of Aquitaine and Count of Mâcon, gave the lands of Cluny to Abbot Bernon, who was installed there with twelve Benedictine monks. Thanks to the dynamism of its abbots – St Odon, St Mayeul, St Odilon, St Hugues de Semur and Pierre le Vénérable, the Abbey became of considerable importance, not recognizing any other authority, secular or religious. More than 1,500 monasteries were founded and funded by donations of money and lands. Rivalry with Citeaux diminished Cluny's importance. In the seventeenth and eighteenth centuries Richelieu, a Prince de Conti and Mazarin were all made Abbots of Cluny, but delegated all power to their Priors. The Revolution closed down the Abbey, the Directoire sold it, and the next Monarchy destroyed it. In the course of twenty-five years, 1798 to 1823, the Republic, the Empire and the Monarchy destroyed the greatest Christian church of all time – after nine hundred years of grandeur! It is essential to visit Cluny to see the many historical sites and its famous horse-breeding stud.

Couches (F–4). Six menhirs (dolmens) of the Époigny Megaliths have been found here. They are now regrouped at the crossroads of the D225 and CV4. They date from the late Neolithic period. The tallest is 7.35 metres high.

Le Creusot (E–5) has been an industrial centre for centuries. Despite its background of mines, cannon (eighteenth century) crystal (eighteenth century) and metallurgical industries, it is now a city of parks, trees and gardens. It was heavily bombed in the Second World War by the Allies, and the large town has been almost completely rebuilt since then – so much so that the local fairs are mainly devoted to chickens and turkeys!

Cuiseaux (K–7) is a most picturesque village on the frontier of Burgundy and Franche-Comté. It has many narrow and tortuous lanes and a square with arcades, ramparts, towers, gatehouse and old houses. Visit the Grotte de la Balme, and view the panorama over the Jura and Bresse.

Digoin (C–8) has been a trading centre from the Middle Ages, being on road and river 'crossroads'. An aqueduct bridge takes the Canal du Centre over the Loire. Digoin's ceramics industry is still the most important in France.

Épinac (F–3) was burned by the English troops in 1359.

Gibles (E–9) was a centre of the French Resistance in the Second World War.

Givry (G–5) was sacked by the Tard-Venus (the latecomers) of the *grandes compagnies* in 1360. Henri IV's favourite wine was called (AOC) Givry Rouge. The first Sunday in September is the 'Fête de la Vigne'. Givry is worth visiting for its architectural beauties, the Hôtel de Ville, its fountains, market-place, monks' cellar and churches.

Gourdon (E–6) is perched on a hill with lovely views. There is a treasure of Merovingian jewellery in a cabinet of medals (ask at the Town Hall).

Geugnon (C–6) is an industrial town which has the ceramic centre of the Gallo-Roman era, called 'Vieux-Fresné', dating from the first to the fourth centuries.

Huilly (I–7) has a monument to the brothers Mathy executed by the Germans in 1944 at Moley.

Louhans (J–6) is worth a detour to see its arcades, timbered houses, Hôtel-Dieu, bridges, hospital-apothecary, Tour St Pierre, and Hôtel de Ville. It is the capital of northern Bresse,

171

and a well-known poultry fair is held there every Monday morning.

Lugny (H–8) The *château fort* was besieged in the Hundred Years War by the *grandes compagnies*, but survived only to be burned at the Revolution.

Lux (H–5). According to legend, it was here that the Emperor Constantine, on his way to do battle with Maxence, saw a vision of the Holy Cross.

Mâcon (H–9) was evangelised in the third century and promoted to a bishopric in the sixth century after the relics of St Vincent had been brought to the town. The cathedral of St Vincent is named after the saint – now patron of the *vignerons*; so too is the 'Confrérie des Vignerons de St-Vincent de Mâcon'. The *quartiers anciens* include the Hôtel-Dieu, Hôtel de Ville, an apothecary's shop, the Pont St-Laurent and many *hôtels*, including the Maison de Bois. The national wine fair is on 20 May – a very important event. Mâcon is known as the birthplace and home of Alphonse Lamartine (1790–1869), poet and novelist.

Marcigny (C–9) has an unusual fortified windmill tower, 'Des Moines', and many old houses with dovecots.

Martailly-lès-Brancion (H–7) was once a fortified royal town of the dukes of Burgundy, built on a hill overlooking the river Grosne. The notable ruins of the *château fort*, a Romanesque church, attractive old houses with galleries and dovecots and the grotto 'Four de la Baume' make this village worth a detour.

Mercurey (G–4). A temple was erected here to the God Mercury at the time when the vineyards belonged to the Emperor Probus.

Mesvres (D–4). Pierre de Beaufort was prior of this town in 1357, and became the last French pope, Gregory XI, in Avignon during the years of the dual papacy.

Montagny-lès-Buxy (G–6) now has vestiges of a military camp – not Roman, but German from the Second World War!

Montceau-les-Mines (E–6) has been known for centuries as an industrial town. In Gallo-Roman times there were forges here for the manufacture of roofing tiles.

Montceaux-Ragny (H–6) is the smallest commune in Burgundy, with a population of sixteen. It is a *village perché* and has several old houses and the chapel of St Isodore with a rustic campanile. Its *caprins* (goats) make excellent cheese, and AOC Mâcon Rouge is grown here. The *fête patronale* is on the Sunday nearest Armistice Day.

Monthelon (D–3). Ste Jeanne de Chantal, grandmother of Madame de Sévigné, founder of the convent of the Visitation, lived here in 1602–9 and received a visit from St François de Sales.

Montmort (C–5) took its sad name, 'Montes Mortuorum', from the site of the battle here, where Julius Caesar beat the Swiss tribesmen.

Paray-le-Monial (C–8). In AD 973 Lambert, Count of Chalon, founded a priory here. His son Hugh, bishop of Auxerre, gave it to the abbey of Cluny in AD 999. From 1673 to 1689 St Marguerite-Marie Alacoque, a nun of the Convent of Visitation, had many repeated visions of Christ. Paray-le-Monial became an important pilgrimage centre to the Sacré-Coeur de Jésus. A third of a million pilgrims wend their way here every year. (*Monial* means 'monastic'). There are several interesting buildings in Paray, which overlooks the river Bourbince and the Canal du Centre. Certainly worth a visit.

St-Christophe-en-Brionnais (D–9). Since the fifteenth century this has been the largest market in Burgundy for Charollais cattle. One of their fêtes is called 'du pot-au-feu'. The fairs, market days and *fêtes aux bestiaux* are well known.

St-Emiland (F–4). In AD 725 the saint of that name, a bishop of Nantes, came to defend Autun against the Saracens and beat them, but was killed during the ensuing pursuit.

St-Gengoux-de-Scissé (G–8). Charlemagne gave the village and church to the chapter of St Vincent of Mâcon.

173

St-Gervais-en-Vallière (H–3). After Gervais du Mans was martyred and subsequently canonized, a church was founded here by St Loup, bishop of Chalon.

St-Legér-sous-Beuvray (C–4). Mont Beuvray was the Gaulish town of Bibracte, capital of the tribe of Eduens. Their pagan fêtes on the summit of the mountain were denounced by St Martin, who had come to evangelize the region. The treasures from the archaeological site can be seen in the museums of Autun and St-Germain-en-Laye.

St-Marcel (H–5). A priory from Cluny was built here, where St Marcel was martyred for his faith in AD 179. Abelard spent his last days here before he died in 1142. Traces of both their lives can be seen in the town in the church of St Marcel.

St-Vallerin (G–6) was named after the Christian martyr decapitated in AD 178 at Tournus, nearby.

Sampigny-lès-Maranges (G–4). The monks of Beaune cultivated vineyards here in the early Middle Ages. The society of 'Vignerons de St-Vincent' was formed here.

Savigny-en-Revermont (K–6) is known for its curious marriage customs!

Solutré-Pouilly (G–9 is a prehistoric village perched on top of a famous rocky promontory, called 'La Roche de Solutré'; at the foot were discovered the grisly skeletons of about 100,000 horses plus many human bones!

Taizé (G–7). This small hamlet is the centre – created in 1940 – of the monastic 'Reformed Community'. It has become an ecumenical sanctuary whose members, the 'Frères de Taizé', include artists, potters, painters, writers and engravers. The Church of the Reconciliation, built in 1962 by volunteers of all nationalities, is near a Romanesque church.

Tournus (H–7). The Roman castle and environments of 'Trenorchium' were evangelized in AD 177 by St Valérien. After invasions by the Normans and by the Hungarians, the town knew an era of prosperity. For its courageous resistance to the Austrians in 1814, Tournus received the cross of the *Légion d'honneur*. Greuze, the famous French painter, lived and worked here. Besides the superb Abbey and Roman Abbatiale St philibert, there are many narrow streets with old buildings. It is a most attractive town along the banks of the river Saône. It is essential for any visitor to spend at least half a day here.

Uchizy (H–7). The legend is that the 'Chizerots', the original inhabitants, were a Saracen or Illyrian colony who settled here in the eighth century.

Castles and Châteaux

The early feudal era is represented in this department by the defensive stronghold fortresses of Couches, Sercy, La Clayette, Berzé-le-Châtel, Rully and Martailly-lès-Brancion. For the Renaissance period one should see the Hôtel de Ville in Paray-le-Monial, the old houses of Mâcon, and the château of Sully. The seventeenth century saw the building of Chaumont at St-Bonnet-de-Joux, and Pierre-de-Bresse and Cormatin. The eighteenth-century buildings are the Hôtel de Ville of Givry, the château of Digoine at Palinges and that of St-Aubin-sur-Loire. The Château de la Verrerie in Le Creusot represents the era of industrial architecture. There are sixty châteaux worth seeing in the department. Most of them are lived in, and not open to the public. With the major châteaux it is easy to establish if and when they open, and this has been noted; with the lesser-known châteaux it is best to enquire at the local Syndicat d'Initiative. Nevertheless all those listed are worth a visit, irrespective of whether a guided tour is permitted. I have included only exceptional buildings, classified as MH (*Monument Historique*) or IMH (*Inscrit à l'Inventaire des Monuments Historiques*). Would-be visitors are advised to check opening times either with the nearest tourist information office or with the Association Saône-et-Loire Tourisme, Hôtel du Département, 187 rue Carnot, 71025 Mâcon, tel. 85.38.06.00.

Amanzé (D–9) has a twelfth century château.

Beaubery (E–8) has the sixteenth century Château de Corcheval – a massive building with circular corner towers.

Berzé-le-Châtel (G–8) of the thirteenth century has five round towers in the outer walls. Terraces open from Apr. to end Oct.

Bissy-sur-Fley (F–6) was a feudal fortress with massive circular towers and chimneys.

Broye (D–4). The Château de Montjeu was reconstructed in the seventeenth century and is set in attractive gardens and a huge park.

Changy (D–8), **Charnay-lès-Mâcon** (G–9), **Cortambert** (G–8) and **Cruzille** (G–7) all possess minor châteaux of interest.

La Clayette (E–9) was a stronghold in the fourteenth century, later repaired by Viollet-le-Duc. It has many attractive towers, flanked by a moat. Well worth looking at, but not open to the public.

Cormatin (G–7) is a Renaissance château. The interior apartments, furnishings, sculpture and paintings are excellent. Open Jul. to Sep. Entrance 18 francs.

Couches (F–4). The château is named after Marguerite de Bourgogne. The keep is twelfth century, the round towers thirteenth. Open midsummer. Entrance 15 francs.

Le Creusot (E–5) has the unusual Château de la Verrerie, which was originally a glass-making factory owned by Marie-Antoinette. Two old kilns have been turned into a theatre and a chapel. The U-shaped château houses the Eco Museum.

Curbigny (E–9) has the Château de Drée, constructed in the fifteenth century by the Duke of Lesdiguières. It is set in formal gardens.

Épinac (F–3). The ruins of the old priory of Val-St-Benoît, founded in the tenth century and partly destroyed by the English in 1259, are well worth a visit, as is also the Château de Monestoy.

Étrigny (H–7) has the Château de Balleure.

Fleurville (H–8) has two châteaux, du Vieux-Fleurville and Marigny.

Germolles-sous-Grosne (F–9) has the seventeenth century Château de Gorze.

Martailly-lès-Brancion (H–7) is a small hamlet between Mâcon and Chalon on the D14. The feudal village and the remains of the tenth-century feudal fortress, which include two keeps and a fortified gate-house, and the manor house of Beaufort, overlook the valley of the Grosne. Open Easter to mid-Nov. Signposted tour. Entrance 10 francs.

Mellecey (G–5) has the fourteenth century Château de Germolles, which has interesting apartments, a Gothic chapel, frescoes, and excellent sculptures by Marville and Sluter. Open midsummer, but closed Tue. Entrance 13 francs.

Monthelon (D–3). The fifteenth century château, 6 km west of Autun, has a typical Burgundian tiled roof, circular towers, chapel, gallery, etc.

Neuvy-Grandchamp (B–7) has the Château de Lavault et de Beauchamp, with nearby water mills.

Ozenay (H–7). The thirteenth century château has one circular and two square towers, mullioned windows and is unique in that the roof has flat stones, known locally as '*lava*' stones.

Palinges (D–7). The Château de Digoine was reconstructed in the eighteenth century. It has two rounded towers with domes, lanterns and slate roof. The windows have iron balconies.

Paray-le-Monial (C–8). The Hôtel de Ville Jayet dates from the sixteenth century. The Renaissance façade is decorated with medallions, shells and statuettes. There are several towers of note – St Nicolas, another in the place Guitault, and a third in the old abbatial palace.

Pierreclos (G–9). The fourteenth century château was rebuilt in the seventeenth. It is perched on a promontory surrounded by vineyards and meadows. Twelfth century chapel, watchtower, *cour d'honneur* and crenellated keep.

Pierre-de-Bresse (J–4). The seventeenth century château buildings are surrounded by a moat. The massive outhouses, the U-shaped central house and the four domed corner towers are of note. Open daily. No charge, but external viewing only. The nearby Château de Terrans, with its feudal-age moat, can also be seen.

Rosey (G–5) has the eighteenth century Château de Meloisey.

Rully (G–4) has a twelfth-century fortress-château, converted in the fifteenth century. It has quadrilateral surrounding walls, crenellated keep, huge round corner towers, and interesting residential rooms running from the keep to the three main towers. The roof is of flat '*lava*' stones. Open mid-Apr. to mid-Oct. Entrance 13 francs.

St-Aubin-sur-Loire (A–7) has an eighteenth century château with massive outhouses, set in formal gardens and park overlooking the river Loire. Open mid-Jul. to mid-Sep., but closed Tue. Entrance 8 francs.

St-Bonnet-de-Joux (E–8). The Château de Chaumont was built in 1510 by Pierre de la Guiche, and rebuilt in the nineteenth century. It has a Renaissance façade, the tower of Amboise, a sixteenth century wing in the style of Louis XII, stables for ninety-nine horses, and two monumental staircases.

St-Émiland (F–4) has the twelfth century stronghold of Château d'Épiry, repaired in the sixteenth and eighteenth centuries. Four round twelfth century towers guard the main fifteenth century building which has mullioned windows, a classical façade, and watermills in the grounds. Open by request to Mme Vazelhes, tel. 85.49.65.25.

St-Pierre-de-Varennes (F–4). The fourteenth-century Château de Brandon, a former stronghold of the Dukes of Burgundy, was rebuilt in the succeeding centuries. It has a polygonal surround, with crenellated towers and a fortified gatehouse. The battlements, fortified walls and turrets preserve the original feudal fortress's identity. Open by request to M. de Masin, tel. 85.55.45.16.

St-Point (F–9) has the fifteenth century fortress of Château de Lamartine, rebuilt in the style of the 'Gothic troubadour'. It has a clock tower and two medieval towers. The salons are of note, with souvenirs of the poet Lamartine and his family. Open Mar. to mid-Nov., except Wed. Entrance 10 francs.

St-Racho (E–10) has the sixteenth century Château de Chevannes, which has a timbered gallery and two towers with mullioned windows. Local Brionnais craft exhibitions are held there in the summer. Open Jul. to Aug. Entrance 13 francs.

Semur-en-Brionnais (C–10) has the fortified twelfth century Château de St Hugh, which has a Roman keep. Open Apr. to Nov. Entrance 8 francs.

Sennecey-le-Grand (H–6) has the remains of an ancient *château-fort* and the Château de Ruffey with its tenth century towers, moat, etc.

Sercy (G–6) is another good example of medieval architecture. Built in the twelfth century, it has a high, circular tower topped with a timber gallery, one of the oldest in France. It overlooks a small lake. Open by request Apr. to Nov. M. de Contenson, tel. 85.47.67.68.

Sully (E–3). The château was constructed in the sixteenth century by Gaspard de Saulx-Tavannes, Governor of Provence. It is called the 'Fontainebleau de la Bourgogne'. The moat is fed by the river Drée, which surrounds the four sides of the castle. Angled towers are set into each corner. There is a chapel. Open for outside views and courtyard only, Easter to Sep. Entrance 8 francs.

Tramayes (F–9). The sixteenth century château has a high, crenellated tower, a gatehouse, two corner towers and a dovecot.

Uchizy (H–7) has the sixteenth century Château de Grenod, with its chimneypiece.

Verosvres (E–8) has the fourteenth century Château du

179

Terrau with moats and circular towers, *cour d'honneur*, formal gardens and park.

Cathedrals, abbeys and splendid churches

This department has no less than three hundred Romanesque churches built in the eleventh and twelfth centuries – almost every single village or hamlet has one! The four 'greats' are at Cluny, Autun, Tournus and Paray-le-Monial, followed by those at Brancion, St-Martin-de-Laives, Chapaize, Semur-en-Brionnais and Anzy-le-Duc. Some of them are built of warm ochre limestone – absolute architectural gems.

Ameugny (G–7) has an eleventh century Cluniac church of ochre limestone. It has a unique nave, a huge fortified clock tower and, most unusually, an inscription on the main door, made by the original builder, of his name.

Anzy-le-Duc (C–9) has a three-tiered octagonal bell tower of Lombard influence of the eleventh century as the main feature of this elegant church – one of the loveliest of the Brionnais area. The neighbouring priory is also a *site classé*. Well worth a visit.

Autun (D–3). The cathedral of St Lazare was built between 1120 and 1130 – one of the major Cluniac works of art. It is famous for the Gislebertus Romanesque sculptures, the tympanum on the main door, glass windows, statues, tapestries and chapter house. This Gallo-Roman city has other treasures: the church of Notre Dame; the ancient Jesuit college and chapel; the Roman hospital; the chapel of St Nicolas de Marchaux, now a museum; the old church of St Pierre l'Estrier just outside the town, and the Carolingian crypt of the Abbey of St Andoche. Autun has more beautiful Gallo-Roman sites than any other city in Burgundy. Essential for a visit, therefore.

Barizey (G–5) has an eighteenth century church by Gauthey with a sixteenth century polychrome statue in wood of St Marguerite.

Baugy (C–9) has an eleventh century Romanesque church.

Bergesserin (F–8) has a twelfth century church with a Romanesque choir and a clock tower.

Berzé-la-Ville (G–9). St Hugh built a small Romanesque chapel in the Château des Moines in the twelfth century. It was the residence of the Abbots of Cluny. The wall painting of Christ in Majesty, 4 m high, is justly well known.

Bissy-la-Mâconnaise (G–8). A huge clock tower with a turret dominates this late Romanesque church.

Blanot (G–8) has a twelfth century Romanesque church with a tall eleventh-century clock tower of Lombard style.

Bois-Ste-Marie (E–9). The twelfth century church of Notre Dame has an eleventh century Romanesque altar, a sculptured tympanum (the Flight into Egypt) and a fortified clock tower. This church has been meticulously preserved and restored.

Bonnay (F–7) has an eleventh century fortified Romanesque priory church, with the transept and clock tower together forming a castle keep.

Bourbon-Lancy (A–6) has the eleventh century priory church of St Nazaire, which has a five-bay nave surmounted by a massive square tower; it is now the museum.

Burgy (H–8). There is a twelfth century Romanesque church in this small *vigneron* village.

Bussières (G–9) has a Romanesque church with an interesting bishop's tomb.

Chagny (G–4) has a twelfth century Romanesque church with a triple nave and a fortified clock tower.

Chalon-sur-Saône (H–5). The church of St Vincent was once a twelfth century cathedral with Romanesque, Gothic and Renaissance architecture. The vaulted fourteenth century cloister is of note.

Chapaize (G–7) is dominated by a high rectangular three-storey clock tower of the twelfth century, and can be seen from far off in the Mâconnais vineyards. Chapaize is a small village of 134 inhabitants, but it boasts a second classified church of Lancharre, built of the remains of a once powerful twelfth century abbey.

Châteauneuf (D–10) has an eleventh century Romanesque church with a sculptured frieze of the twelve apostles, flamboyant pillar-head carvings and a fortified belfry.

Chissey-lès-Mâcon (G–7) has a twelfth century Romanesque church with a nave and fortified clock tower of that date, and unusual capitals with historical subjects.

Clessé (H–8) has an eleventh century Romanesque church with an octagonal clock tower, with Lombard bands around it.

Cluny (G–8). The ancient abbey of St Pierre and St Paul was built in AD 910. It mothered fifteen hundred other ecclesiastical establishments and more than ten thousand monks. Thanks to the revolutionaries, three-quarters of the greatest abbey in the world was destroyed between 1798 and 1823. The south transept and 62-metre-high octagonal tower, 'L'Eau Bénite', still stand proudly, as does the large thirteenth-century monks' mill and granary.

Cluny has two other surviving churches of note: the thirteenth century Gothic Notre Dame, and the twelfth-century church of St Marcel, with its octagonal cupola and octagonal Romanesque clock tower.

Cuisery (I–7) has the fifteenth century flamboyant Gothic church of Notre Dame, with polygonal choir, sixteenth-century triptych, clock tower and nave – all of note.

Curgy (E–3) has the eleventh century Romanesque church of St Ferréol, made of granite, with a narrow, four-bay nave surmounted by a strong, square tower.

Épinac (F–3). The remains of the old priory of the Val-St-Benoît is a *site classé*.

Fargues-lès-Mâcon (H–7) has a small eleventh century church, an example of early Mediterranean Romanesque art, surmounted by a two-storey square tower.

Givry (G–5) has an eighteenth century classical church built by Gauthey on an octagonal plan with a fortified clock tower.

Gourdon (E–6) has an eleventh century Romanesque church made of granite; its square tower faces Mont-St-Vincent.

Iguerande (C–10) has an eleventh century Romanesque church overlooking the Loire, with a triple nave, an octagonal cupola, a massive clock tower and sculptures of note.

Issy-l'Évêque (C–6) has a twelfth century Romanesque church. A compromise between Cluniac and Brionnais art, it has a six-bay nave, frescoes and a castellated clock tower.

Laives (H–6) has an eleventh century Romanesque church of St Martin standing proudly on a hill overlooking the A6 motorway – probably not envisaged by Sanctus Martinus in Monte in the ninth century.

Mâcon (H–9) has the thirteenth century cathedral of St Vincent with Roman narthex, frescoes, sculptured tympanum and two very high towers – visible from afar.

Martailley-lès-Brancion (H–7) has a late Romanesque church of the twelfth century – a masterpiece of Romanesque art. It stands on a promontory overlooking the valley of the Grosne, and is noted for its fourteenth century frescoes, fortified clock tower, in a fortified medieval village, and the tomb of Jocerand, last Lord of Brancion.

Massy (F–8) has a small eleventh century church representing early Lombard Romanesque art. It has a single timbered nave, a fine two-storey bell tower and a Romanesque font.

Mazille (F–8) has an early thirteenth century church with an elegant square tower and a platformed nave.

Mercurey (G–4) has the thirteenth century Gothic Église de Touches.

Montceaux-l'Étoile (C–9) has a twelfth century Romanesque church with a remarkable portal, tympanum and lintel over the main door showing the Ascension of Christ, with the apostles.

Mont-St-Vincent (F–6) has an eleventh century priory of St Vincent, perched on one of the highest points in the department. It has an interesting tympanum and sculptured capitals.

Ozenay (H–7) has a twelfth century Romanesque church with a notable porch.

Paray-le-Monial (C–8) has the famous twelfth century basilica of Sacré-Coeur, the church of Notre Dame – a real gem of the Romanesque Cluny style. The octagonal belfry towers over the transept crossing. It was built by Hugh de Semur about 1100, said to be a smaller reproduction of the great Abbey of Cluny. The *chevet* is in three tiers. Two hundred metres away is the Parc des Chapelains, one of the focal points of the major pilgrimages for St Marguerite Marie Alacoque, whose visions in 1673 brought the Catholic world to see her shrines.

Perrecy-les-Forges (D–6). This church was built in AD 1130 and has a most remarkable twelfth century narthex. Its three two-bay naves are built on two floors. Its sculptured tympanum over the front doors, historic capitals and fine two-storeyed Brionnais bell tower make this a most interesting church.

Le Puley (F–6) has a twelfth century Romanesque priory church with an octagonal bell tower and Lombard-style main façade.

St-Albain (H–8) has a thirteenth century Romanesque church.

St-Bonnet-de-Cray (D–10) has a Romanesque church with a twelfth-century choir.

St-Clement-sur-Guye (F–6) has a twelfth century Romanesque church with an unusual bell tower.

St-Germain-en-Brionnais (D–9). This eleventh century Romanesque church is built of sandstone, and was restored in 1582.

St-Gervais-sur-Couches (F–4) has a Gothic church of the thirteenth century with a fifteenth century altarpiece.

St-Julien-de-Jonzy (D–10). Originally a Romanesque church, this has a twelfth century Brionnais bell tower and tympanum/lintel carved out of sandstone; the sculpture is notable.

St-Laurent-en-Brionnais (D–9). This Romanesque church of the twelfth century has an early Romanesque choir, carved clock tower and an octagonal dome.

St Marcel (H–5). The Cistercian monks rebuilt this priory church of St Marcel at the end of the twelfth century. A Latin inscription commemorates the death of Abelard.

St-Marcelin-de-Cray (F–7) has an eleventh century Romanesque church next to the Château de Lamartine. The church has the poet's tomb and that of his family.

St-Vincent-des-Près (F–8) has an eleventh century Romanesque church, one of the oldest in Burgundy, with a Lombard-style façade and a three-storeyed square belfry.

Semur-en-Brionnais (C–10) has the twelfth century Romanesque church of St Hilaire, of Cluniac style, built on three storeys with an exquisite *chevet* crowned by a two-tiered octagonal tower.

Sennecey-le-Grand (H–6). The twelfth century Romanesque church of St Julien has a fifteenth century two-storeyed square bell tower and nave.

Taizé (G–7). The twelfth century Romanesque church has a single nave, an octagonal cupola, and a carved clock tower. It is near the modern Église de la Réconciliation, where religious offices are held for three different Christian churches.

Toulon-sur-Arroux (D–6) has the eleventh century Romanesque church of St Jean Baptiste, which has a fourteenth-century watchtower.

Tournus (H–7). Lombard masons built this tenth century abbey of St Philibert, one of the finest works of Bungundy Romanesque. It has a notable crypt, above which stands a narthex with round pillars. The monks' refectory, the Grandes Caves and the cellar are twelfth century. The upper storey has

185

the Chapelle St-Michel. Every traveller to Burgundy should visit this superb church, the pre-Romanesque chapel of St Laurent, and the Romanesque churches of St Valérien and de la Madeleine. Tournus is a veritable gem.

Uchizy (H–7) has an eleventh century Romanesque church with three naves and a square belfry above the transept; the statuary is sixteenth century and the frescoes seventeenth.

Vareilles (D–9) is of twelfth century origin, with some restorations. The bell tower and spire are strong and delicate.

Varenne l'Arconce (D–9) has an eleventh century Romanesque church with striking sandstone carvings, square belfry and sculptured tympanum.

Le Villars (H–7) has the eleventh century priory church of St Madeleine. There are two parallel naves, one of which also serves the parish church, the other the ancient chapel of the Benedictine monks. The cloister and statues are of note.

Museums

Autun (D–3). The Musée Rolin, rue des Bancs, tel. 85.52.09.76, displays archaeological collections originating from the excavations at Bibracte, especially native and imported ceramics, metalwork, evidence of craftwork and agriculture, and coins. Numerous items found at Autun evoke different aspects of the Gallo-Roman civilization (burial rites, religion, economic activities, intellectual, artistic and everyday life). There are also medieval and Gothic collections. The St-Nicolas lapidary museum, 10 rue St-Nicolas, tel. 85.52.35.17, is partially installed in a Romanesque chapel, whose apse is decorated by a mural painting: Gallo-Roman and medieval lapidary collections, steles, architectural elements. There are also the Musée Régional Verger-Tarin, the Musée d'Histoire Naturelle, 14 rue St-Antoine, tel. 85.52.09.15, and the Musée de la Salle Capitulaire. The Bibliothèque Municipale, Hôtel de Ville, tel.85.52.20.34, has more than 70,000 volumes, illuminated manuscripts, etc.

Azé (G–8). The Society of the Caves of Azé exhibits in the Musée Archéologique collections from prehistoric times to the Middle Ages.

Barizey (G–5) has a small museum of wine-growers' implements over the centuries.

Blanzy (E–6) has a museum devoted to mines and old mining equipment.

Bois-Ste-Marie (E–9) has a museum of the folklore and customs of La Grenette.

Bourbon-Lancy (A–6). The Musée St-Nazaire, rue du Musée, tel. 85.89.23.23, is divided between archaeology, the fine arts and local history.

Chagny (G–4) has a similar museum to that at Bourbon-Lancy.

Chalon-sur-Saône (H–5) has very rich archaeological collections at the Musée Denon, rue Denon, tel. 85.48.01.70, including the eighteen-thousand-year-old Volgu flint – the finest example in the world – as well as the Bronze Age collection of swords, daggers and jewellery – all found on the bed of the Saône river. Documents from the excavations of early habitats are also exhibited: from Épervans, Ouroux (late Bronze), Bragny, St-Marcel (Halstatt) and Verdun-sur-le-Doubs (La Tène). Also, rich Gallo-Roman collections and objects from the Merovingian period. Open all year. The Musée Nicéphore Niépce, 28 quai des Messageries, tel. 85.48.41.98, concentrates on early photographic equipment and cameras, including the first darkroom invented by the 'father of photography'.

Charolles (D–8) has a museum devoted to the work of a well-known sculptor, René Davoine, promenade St-Nicolas, tel. 85.24.06.40; and the Musée Jean Laronze, displaying his paintings, archaeological finds, old prints, furniture and ceramics.

Chauffailles (E–10) has a Musée de l'Automobile.

La Clayette (E–9) has a Musée de l'Automobile.

187

Cluny (G–8). The Musée Ochier, place de l'Abbaye, tel. 85.59.05.87, has historical items from Cluny's glorious past, and engravings by Prud'hon, the eighteenth-century local artist. The Musée du Farinier has gemstones and archaeological finds.

Couches (F–4) has collections of local folklore and history, to be seen in the Château.

Le Creusot (E–5) has the Écomusée de la Communauté, tel. 85.55.01.1; a collection of early industrial machines can be seen at the Château de la Verrerie, and an exhibition of art at the chapel there.

Cruzille (G–7) has a museum of artisans' implements at the Domaine des Vignes du Maynes, tel. 85.33.20.15, with tools for woodwork, ironwork, leathercraft, clothmaking and wine-barrel coopering.

Digoin (C–8) has a permanent exhibition of ceramic manufacturing through the ages. Consult the Syndicat, 8 rue Guilleminot, tel. 85.53.00.81.

La Grande Verrière (D–3) has the Musée Minéralogique du Morvan, Les Vernottes, tel. 85.82.51.01.

Igé (G–8) has a museum of wines and vines at the Chapel of Domange.

Issy-l'Évêque (C–6) has a small geological exhibition of artefacts from Mont-Dardon.

Mâcon (H–9) has the Musée Lamartine, rue Bauderon, tel. 85.38.06.00. The Musée des Ursulines, 5 rue des Ursulines, tel. 85.38.18.34, houses the municipal collection of fine arts and prehistoric artefacts. The Apothecary of the Hôtel Dieu has faience, old furniture, etc.

Marcigny (C–9) has the Musée de la Tour du Moulin, tel. 85.25.39.49, with pottery, sculptures, etc. There is also a small exhibition of 111 pieces of *faiences de Nevers* in the hospital pharmacy.

188

Martailley-lès-Brancion (H–7) has a small museum of the Middle Ages.

Matour (F–9) has a museum of natural history with over ten thousand plants and collections of stones and birds.

Mont-St-Vincent (F–6) has a museum in the Grenier à Sel of artefacts from Chassey camp.

Paray-le-Monial (C–8) has the Musée d'Art Sacré le Hiéron, rue de la Paix, tel. 85.81.10.92, which is devoted to eucharistic works and sacred art, with a twelfth-century tympanum from Anzy-le-Duc (open May to Sep.); and the Musée Municipal, which displays local antiquities, coins and paintings.

Pierre-de-Bresse (J–4). The ecological museum, tel. 85.76.27.16, is housed in the attractive Château de Pierre (open Jun. to Sep.).

Romanèche-Thorins (G–9) has the Musée Guillon, or Compagnonnage, of carpentry through the ages. Apply to the Mairie, tel. 85.35.50.26. Open Easter to end Oct.

Romenay (I–7). The Musée du Teroir – the museum of Bresse art created by the 'Amis du vieux Romenay' – displays archaeology from Bresse: the Mesolithic industry of Sermoyer (6500 BC), Neolithic flints, protohistoric implements and weapons, Gallo-Roman remains from Romenay, and objects carved from antlers discovered in the excavations of the early medieval defensive moat at Loisy. Open during summer.

St-Bonnet-de-Joux (E–8) has a museum of prehistoric, Celtic, Gallo-Roman and Merovingian artefacts.

St-Léger-sous-Beuvray (C–4). The Salle Bibracte at the Mairie has a collection of coins, amphorae and artisans' implements.

Sennecey-le-Grand (H–6). The Château de Ruffey has an exhibition of paintings and sculptures.

Solutré-Pouilly (G–9) has an exhibition of flints, arrowheads and an ossuary in the Musée Archéologique.

Tournus (H–7). The Musée Greuze, rue du Collège, has works and engravings by that painter, who was born here. Closed in winter. The Musée Perrin de Puycousin concentrates on local folklore, customs and costumes. The Apothecary of the Hôtel Dieu has seventeenth-century faience and other ceramics. The library has an excellent collection of manuscripts and books. There is also the Musée Bourgnignon, rue A. Thibaudet. For information on any of the Tournus museums, apply to the Office de Tourisme, Tel. 85.51.13.10.

Trambly (F–9) has a museum devoted to stones, gems, etc., open Jul. and Aug. only.

Uchon (D–5) has a summer exhibition of the work of local artists and craftsmen.

Verdun-sur-le-Doubs (I–4) has a museum specializing in bread, corn and wheat, and the history and culture of flour.

CHAPTER ELEVEN: THE CULINARY CHARMS OF THE COUNTRYSIDE

Local wines

The wines of this department fall into two main regions: La Côte Chalonnaise and Le Mâconnais. The northern part, La Côte Chalonnaise and Le Couchois, is in the region between Santenay through Chagny and Montagny to St-Boil and Santilly in the south. The other main region, Le Mâconnais, joins the Côte Chalonnaise at its southern point and, taking in an area extending roughly from Tournus to Cluny, runs south to join the Beaujolais region south of Mâcon and Fuissé.

● La Côte Chalonnaise

The *vigneron* villages in this region are Aluze, Barizey, Bissey-sous-Cruchaud, Bouzeron, Buxy and Chagny, and Chalon-sur-Saône is the headquarters of the area. At the Maison des Vins de la Côte Chalonnaise, on the promenade Ste-Marie, one can taste and buy AOC Aligoté, Aligoté de Bouzeron, Montagny, Rully, Mercurey (white and red), Givry (white and red), Passe Tout Grains and Bourgogne. Open weekdays, tel. 85.41.64.00, M. Guepey. There is a restaurant on the first floor serving regional speciality meals from 45 to 65 francs, tel. 85.41.66.66, M. Dauvergne. Park in front of the Maison des Vins.

● Wine villages

Other wine villages in the area are Change, Chassey-le-Camp, Chaudenay, Cheilly-lès-Maranges, Couches, Culles-lès-Roches, Dennevy, Dezize-lès-Maranges, Dracy-lès-

191

Couches, Fontaines, Géanges, Genouilly, Givry, Jambles, Jully-lès-Buxy, Mellecey, Mercurey, Montagny-lès-Buxy, Moroges, Paris-L'Hôpital, Rosey, Rully, St-Boil, St-Denis-de-Vaux, St-Désert, St-Jean-de-Vaux, St-Léger-sur-Dheune, St-Martin-Sous-Montaigu, St-Maurice-Lès-Couches, St-Semin-du-Plain, St-Vallérin and St-Ythaire, Sampigny-lès-Maranges, Saules and Savigny-sur-Grosne. The wines of Mercurey, Givry, Rully and Montagny are well known. Red wines account for three-quarters of the annual production.

• Co-operatives

The first co-operative is at Bissey-sous-Cruchaud (71390 Buxy), 'Cave Co-opérative des Vignerons'. The president is M. Perriaux, tel. 85.42.12.16. Their tasting *cave* is open on Sundays and holidays. They produce Bourgogne Blanc, Aligoté, Passe Tout Grains, Bourgogne Rouge and sparkling Mousseux Blanc de Blanc. The 'Cave des Vignerons de Buxy' is much larger. The president is M. Legros. It was formed in 1931 and now has 100 *vigneron* members owning 600 hectares of vineyards. They stock over 1½ million bottles. The 'Chai de St-Gengoux-le-National', also known as 'La Grande Agasse', tel. 85.47.61.75, and the 'Chai de Buxy', known as 'Les Vignes de la Croix', tel. 85.92.03.03, make substantial quantities of wine. Their *appellations* are Montagny, Aligoté, Bourgogne Rouge, Passe Tout Grains and Rully, as well as sparkling Mousseux Rosé and Crémant de Bourgogne. Other specialities include Fine Eau de Vie de Bourgogne, Crème de Cassis and Crème de Framboise. Tasting takes place at their *caveau*, 'La Tour Rouge', place Carcan, Buxy, tel. 85.42.15.76, open all year. Snacks, such as *cassecroute* and pizzas, can be obtained. This is the most important co-operative in the Côte Chalonnaise. The third co-operative is the 'Cave Co-opérative de Genouilly', tel. 85.49.23.72, which offers standard AOC wines. The president is M. Davanture.

Chagny (G–4) has a *cave co-opérative* and produces AOC Rully. The tasting is in an old '*grenier à sel*' (literally, a large salt-cellar!).

Mercurey (G–4) has a medium-sized co-operative with 180 members farming 120 hectares, founded in 1930. Run by M. Hubert. Chambounard, tel. 85.47.10.01, it is called 'Les Vignerons du Caveau de Mercurey', 71460 Givry. Their AOC Mercurey red and white, Marc and Fine de Bourgogne can be tasted at the *caveau*. Annual production is 7,000 hectolitres, 70 per cent red, 30 per cent *rosé*. They supply a leading wine club in the UK.

● **Le Mâconnais**

This is the second major production area in the department. About 240,000 hectolitres of wine are made each year – about five times that of the Côte Chalonnaise. Two-thirds of the total is AOC Blanc, of which the *caves co-opératives* make three-fifths, or nearly 100,000 hectolitres. Of the balance of AOC Rouge, the co-ops make two-thirds, or about 52,000 hectolitres. The co-op share is increasing each year because of their production, quality control and superior marketing. The five co-ops in the Côte Chalonnaise produce about 28,000 hectolitres, and in Le Mâconnais about 150,000 hectolitres (out of 250,000 total). Including sparkling Crémant of 7,000 hectolitres, all made by the co-ops, the grand total made by the co-ops was 155,000 hectolitres.

The wine villages are Azé, Blanot, Bray, Burgy, Bussières, Chaintré, Chanes, La Chapelle de Guinchay, Chardonnay and Chasseles (homes of the famous grapes of those names), Charnay-lès-Mâcon, Clessé, Crèche-sur-Saône, Cruzille, Davayé, Fargues-leÌ€s-Mâcon, Fuissé, Hurigny, Igé, Jalogny, Leynes, Lournand, Lugny, Mâcon, Mangey, Massy, Milly-Lamartines, Mont Bellet, Peronne, Pierreclos, Pontanevaux, Préty, Prissé, La Roche-Vineuse, Romanèche-Thorins, St-Amour-Bellevue, St-Maurice-de-Satonay, Sennecey-lès-Mâcon, Serrières, Sologny, Solutré-Pouilly, Uchizy, Varennes-lès-Mâcon, Vergisson, Verzé, Vinzelles and Viré. At the Maison Mâconnaise des Vins, avenue de Lattre de Tassigny, 71000 Mâcon, Tel. 85.38.36.70, one can not only taste and buy any or all of the AOC wines of the department, but also sample some or all of the regional specialities – spare ribs, *andouillette*, many and varied cooked meats, onion soup and goat cheese. Information from Mme Feyeux. The villages of La Chapelle-de-Guinchay, Leynes, Pruzilly and Romanèche-Thorins also make AOC Beaujolais-Villages, overlapping with the next department of the Rhône.

Azé (G–8) 15 km north-west of Mâcon, has a 'Cave Co-op Vinicole', tel. 85.33.30.92. M. Bouchard is president. At the *caveau* one can taste AOC Mâcon or Pinot-Chardonnay-Mâcon wines. This is a small co-operative, which has recently joined the Fédération des Caves Co-opératives. Besides Mâcon Villages Blanc, Mâcon Rouge and Bourgogne Rouge, they produce Grand Vin Mousseux – *brut* and *demi sec*. Closed Fri.

Chaintré (G–10) has a co-op a few km south-west of Mâcon, tel. 85.35.61.61. M. Laneyrie is president. They produce AOC Montagny, Bourgogne Rouge, Bourgogne Alitogé, St-Vérand, Pouilly-Fuissé and Blanc de Blanc Méthode Champenoise. Their modern *caveau* for tasting is in the Moulin à d'Or (windmill). The 160 members farm 200 hectares, of which 170 produce white wine, 30 red: 12,000 hectolitres each year.

Chardonnay (H–7) has given its name to the famous grape which makes Bourgogne Blanc, Mâcon Blanc, Pouilly-Fuissé, Montagny, St-Vérand and the sparkling Brut de Bourgogne. The *cave co-opérative*, tel. 85.51.06.49, is run by M. R. Gaudez. It is a few miles south of Tournus. Founded in 1928, it now has 300 *vigneron* members farming 200 hectares, of which 80 per cent of production is white wine. They also make Mâcon red, *rosé* and Crémant de Bourgogne.

Charnay-lès-Mâcon (G–9) has the 'Union des Co-opératives Vinicoles de Bourgogne', tel. 85.34.21.97. The president is M. Mazille. The co-op produces AOC Mâcon, Pinot-Chardonnay-Mâcon and Sparkling Mousseux. Sica Bourguignons Producteurs BP225 is the marketing headquarters for the seventeen Saône-et-Loire co-operatives.

Clessé (H–8). The *cave co-opérative* at La Vigne Blanche, tel. 85.36.93.88, produces AOC Mâcon Clessé, or Pinot-

Chardonnay-Mâcon. M. Jean Luzy is their president. They have ninety *vigneron* members farming 115 hectares, of which 85 per cent of the production is white wines. They also produce white and *rosé* sparkling wines, *brut* or *demi sec*. The co-op was founded in 1927. Their *chai* holds 14,000 hectolitres and they produce 6,000 hectolitres each year. Clessé is equidistant from Mâcon and Cluny, and near the A6 and RN6.

Cluny (G–8) has a small co-op at Les Barabans, called the 'Union des Producteurs de vins Mâcon', place St-Pierre, 71000 Mâcon. One can taste AOC Mâcon, red, white and *rosé* wines from Jul. to mid-Sep. Park in the place de l'Abbaye.

Igé (G–8) has a cave co-op called 'Les Vignerons', tel. 85.33.33.56. M. J. F. Dafre is president. The thirty member *vignerons* farm 250 hectares, of which 100 are Gamay, 100 Chardonnay, 39 Pinot Noir and 11 Aligoté. Of their annual production of 1,500 hectolitres, 55 per cent is red and 45 per cent white. The highly modern co-op produces Mâcon Village Blanc, St-Vérand, Mâcon Rosé (of the Gamay grape), Mâcon Superior Rouge, Bourgogne Passetoutgrains, Bourgogne Rouge, Mousseux Rosé and Blanc Brut and Crémant de Bourgogne. The *caveau de dégustation* the Musée du Vin, is the old Chapelle de Domange, situated in the vineyards. The monks of neighbouring Cluny built it in the eleventh century. Open Sat., Sun. and holidays.

Leynes (G–10). The co-operative produces Mâconnais-Beaujolais wines – AOC St-Vérand, Mâcon or Pinot-Chardonnay-Mâcon. M. Duperron, Tel. 85.35.11.39, is in charge of the 'Caveau Relais le Cru St-Veran', 71570 La Chapelle-de-Guinchay.

Lugny (H–8) has the largest co-operative in the department. It is a large modern complex called 'Caveau St-Pierre', tel. 85.33.20.27, in the heart of the vineyards. Founded in 1926, it is now called 'Caves de St-Gengoux de Scissé et de Lugny'. There are 475 members and 200 owner/growers farming 900 hectares of vineyards. Annual production is 55,000 hectolitres. They store 1 million still wines in bottle and 400,000 Crémant de Bourgogne. Three-quarters of the production is

195

white wine, the rest red. Les Charmes, Cuvée Eugène Blanc and Cuvée Henri Boulay are their well-known white wines. There are tasting facilities in the village at 'Le Vieux Logis', open weekends, and 'Caveau St-Pierre' in the main buildings. M. Ch. Jousseau is the president and M. Brunet is the commercial director.

Mancey (H–7) has a co-operative called 'Les Vignerons de Mancey', which produces a wide range. The president is M. Dupuis, tel. 85.51.00.83. The *caveau* is at the *cave co-opérative*, open all the year. In addition to Passe Tout Grains, Mâcon red and white, they make Crémant de Bourgogne, Marc and Fine de Bourgogne, Cassis and Framboise. Their popular basic wine is Mancillon-Bourgogne Grand Ordinaire, with a price of 10 francs per bottle TTC. They sell in bulk at prices from 3.80 francs per litre.

Prissé (G–9) has the co-operative called 'Groupement de Producteurs de Prissé', 71960 Pierreclos, *cave*, tel. 85.37.82.53, and *chais-bureau*, tel. 85.37.88.06. M. Duvert is the president of this co-op, founded in 1918, which has 250 members and farms 380 hectares of vineyards. Production is considerable – 27,000 hectolitres, half white, half red. They export 50 per cent of production to Benelux, the USA and elsewhere. Their AOC white wines are St-Vérand, Mâcon Villages, Bourgogne Aligoté and Pouilly-Fuissé. The red are Bourgogne, Passe Tout Grains, Mâcon Rouge and Mâcon Rosé. They also produce three sparkling wines – Crémant de Bourgogne, Bourgogne Mousseux and Mousseux Rosé. This is one of the oldest and most respected of the co-operatives.

Romanèche-Thorins (G–10) is on the southern borders of the department with the Rhône. They have a 'Maison des Viti-culteurs du Moulin à Vent', and a 'Caveau du Moulin à Vent', tel. 85.35.51.03, where AOC Moulin à Vent and Beaujolais can be tasted and purchased.

St-Amour-Bellevue (G–10) has a *caveau* – 71570 La Chapelle-de-Guinchay, tel. 85.37.15.98 – which is the co-operative 'du Cru St Amour'. *Appellation* St-Amour and Beaujolais can be tasted and purchased from Mar. to 20 Dec., Sun. and holidays only.

St-Gengoux-le-National (G–6). The co-op here, tel. 85.47.61.75, produces AOC Mâcon.

St-Gengoux-de-Scissé (G–8). The co-op here, tel. 85.33.20.35, produces AOC Mâcon, and Pinot-Chardonnay-Mâcon Henri Boulay.

Sennecey-le-Grand (H–6). The co-op is actually at Mancey.

Sennecey-lès-Mâcon (H–9) has a *cave co-opérative* run by M. Galland, tel. 85.33.39.73, which offers AOC Pouilly-Vinzelles, Pouilly-Loché and Mâcon. This is a relatively new co-op.

Sologny-Berzé la Ville (G–9) has a *cave co-opérative* with 150 members farming 350 hectares, of which M. Mauguin is the president. The tasting *caveau*, Lamartine, is in Sologny opposite the modern *chais* and is open all the year except holidays, tel. 85.36.60.64. Their AOC wines are Mâcon white, *rosé* and red, Bourgogne Aligoté and sparkling Mousseux Blanc de Blancs (priced at 28 francs).

Solutré-Pouilly (G–9) has a 'Caveau de Pouilly-Fuissé', run by M. André Forest of Vergisson and M. Joanny Guérin of Solutré-Pouilly, tel. 85.37.84.23.

Vinzelles (G–9) has the 'Cave des Grands Crus Blancs' owned by the 'Co-op. Vinicole de Vinzelle-Loché', tel. 85.35.63.06. M. Bourdon is the president of this co-op, which was founded in 1928 and now has 133 *vigneron* members farming 118 hectares, of which 100 produce white wine, and 18 red wine. Their annual production is 2,500 hectolitres of Pouilly-Vinzelles-Loché Blanc, 2,000 hectolitres of Mâcon Vinzelles-Loché Blanc, and the remaining small amount Beaujolais Villages and sparkling Mousseux.

Viré (H–8) has a *cave co-opérative*, founded in 1928, with 250 members farming 300 hectares, tel. 85.33.12.64. M. Philippe is the president. Annual production is 25,000 hectolitres, of which nearly half is exported to the USA,

Canada, UK, Benelux and Germany. Production is entirely of white wine – Mâcon Viré, Crémant de Bourgogne, Crème de Cassis and Liqueur de Framboise. The Modern *chais* hold 40,000 hectolitres. A thousand years ago the archives of Cluny mention the *'vin blanc de Viré'*. The *caveau de dégustation* is called 'Le Virolis', tel. 85.33.10.57.

Minor co-operatives are to be found at the following:

Davayé (G–9) is 10 km from Mâcon. The *groupement de producteurs*, 'Les Vignerons des Côtes Mâconnaises et Beaujolais', tel. 85.37.82.23, produces AOC St-Vérand, Mâcon or Pinot-Chardonnay-Mâcon wines.

Étrigny (H–7) is halfway between Chalon and Mâcon. The *cave co-opérative* produces AOC Mâcon.

Milly-Lamartine (G–9) has a *cave co-opérative* for Mâcon. Their tasting *caveau* is open all the year.

Varenne-lès-Mâcon (H–10) has a co-op, tel. 85.34.77.49, which makes AOC Mâcon.

Verzé (G–9) has a *cave co-opérative*, tel. 85.33.30.76, which produces AOC Mâcon-Verzé. The president is M. Janald.

Other co-ops are at **Berzé-la-Ville** (G–9), **Couches** (F–4) and **Cruzille** (G–7).

The vineyards of the Pouilly-Fuissé white wines are clustered to the west and south-west of Mâcon, and include the villages of Vergisson, Solutré, Chaintré, Vinzelles, Leynes and St-Amour. Mme Boivin is the secretary of the Fédération des Caves Co-opératives of the Saône-et-Loire, at the Maison de l'Agriculture, boulevard Henri Dunant, 71000 Mâcon, tel. 85.38.50.66. Of the seventeen members, that of Lugny is the largest, followed by Buxy, Prissé and Viré.

Modest hotels and restaurants

Chalon-sur-Saône (pop. 61,000) is a major commercial and industrial centre on the main route south from Beaune to Tournus and Mâcon. There are two good-value hotels. One is

Le Regal, 7 rue Dr Mauchamp, tel. 85.46.59.98, with 14 rooms and menus from 40 francs. It is reasonably quiet and there is no parking problem. Good pension terms for three-day stays. The Hôtel de la Gare, 17 avenue Jean-Jaurès, tel. 85.43.36.83, has 52 rooms and a three-course menu from 40 francs. It is rather noisy and parking is not easy. The Hôtel le Petit Chef, 4 rue de Dijon, tel. 85.46.66.56, and the Hôtel Rive Gauche, 1 avenue de Verdun, Tel. 85.48.76.25, are within the budget. There are several modest hotels without restaurants given in the summary. There are a dozen or more restaurants with menus for less than 50 francs, including La Courte Paille, Maître Pierre, Brasserie Lyonnaise, Chez Jules, L'Eau à la Bouche, Le Neptune, Cafeteria Medicis and Le Piranha.

Mâcon (pop. 41,000) has, like Beaune, a reputation for rather expensive hotels, but there are four hotel-restaurants within the budget. Les Tuileries, quai des Marans, tel. 85.38.19.91, has 13 rooms and a menu from 42 francs. La Renaissance, 115 rue Rambuteau, tel. 85.35.15.98, has 11 rooms and a menu from 45 francs. Le Charolais, 71 rue Rambuteau, tel. 85.38.36.23, has 12 rooms and a menu from 48 francs. Le Pape, 74 rue Dufour, tel. 85.38.38.78, has 11 rooms and two menus below 50 francs, excellent value. The *pichets* of wine were about 10 francs. Reasonably quiet, with easy parking. The Relais Fleuri, 28 rue des Minimes, tel. 85.38.36.02, has 24 rooms starting from 75 francs. A double room including breakfast for 2 was 100 francs, but there is no restaurant. So try the SICA Maison Mâconnaise des Vins, avenue de Lattre de Tassigny, tel. 85.39.09.84. It has a menu for under 50 francs, and you can taste any wine of the region!

Autun (pop. 23,000) has several low-cost hotel-restaurants. Hôtel le Commerce et Touring, 20 avenue de la République (opposite the station), tel. 85.52.17.90, has 23 rooms from 70–132 francs and breakfast at 18 francs. The nearby Hôtel de la Tête Noire, 3 rue de l'Arquebuse, tel. 85.52.25.39, has 20 rooms from 80 francs, breakfast for 18 francs and menus from 55 francs. The Hôtel de France, place de la Gare, tel. 85.52.14.00, has 23 rooms from 60–140 francs. Breakfast is 18 francs, and there is a *brasserie* with a wide range of hot plates and snacks.

Tournus (pop. 8,000) offers a good choice. The Hôtel de la Madeleine, 15 rue D. Mathivet, tel. 85.51.05.83, has only 4 rooms, at 75–105 francs, and excellent meals from 40 francs. It is in a quiet street near the river with easy parking. In the continuation of this street, called the avenue du 23 Janvier, are the Au Terrasses at no. 18, tel. 85.51.01.74, with 12 rooms at 50–132 francs and menus from 50 francs, and Le Pas Fleury, tel. 85.51.00.78, with 9 rooms at 70–80 francs and menus from 40 francs – both are quiet and there are no parking problems. Good restaurants abound: L'Abbatoir, Au Bon Accueil, Le Grill, Grill de la Gaieté. Tournus is a small, compact town, and one can walk easily from the sights to the hotels and restaurants, all near the flowing Saône.

Montceau-les-Mines (pop. 28,000) is a commercial and industrial centre and has several modest hotels. Du Lac, 58 rue de la Loge, tel. 85.57.18.22, has 20 rooms; Hôtel du Nord, 13 rue du 11 Novembre, tel. 85.57.05.33, has 12 rooms; and the Hôtel de France, 7 place Beaubernard, tel. 85.57.26.64, has 11 rooms. Only the last has a restaurant.

Digoin (pop. 11,000) has two 'budget' hotels. Hôtel Terminus, 76 avenue Général de Gaulle, tel. 85.53.17.26, has 17 rooms and a menu from 53 francs. The Modern Hotel, 6 rue de la Faiencerie, tel. 85.53.05.80, has 12 rooms and menus from 60 francs.

Paray-le-Monial (pop. 12,000), as befits a major pilgrimage centres, has a good choice. Hôtel Terminus, 57 avenue de la Gare, tel. 85.81.08.80, has 22 rooms with *prix fixe* menus from 48 francs, Hôtel du Val d'Or at La Beluze, 2 km outside the town, tel. 85.81.05.12, with 15 rooms, has a *prix fixe* menu at 48 francs. Hôtel du Champ-de-Foire, rue Desrichard, tel. 85.81.01.08, and Hôtel St-Roch, 39 avenue de la Gare, tel. 85.81.15.74, should be considered.

Le Creusot (pop. 33,500) is a well-known industrial city. The Hôtel des Voyageurs, 5 place Schneider, tel. 85.55.22.36, has

15 rooms and a *prix fixe* menu at 50 francs.

Chagny (pop. 5,700) has the Hôtel Central, 1 rue de la République, tel. 85.87.20.18, with 8 rooms and a *prix fixe* menu at 48 francs.

Cluny (pop. 4,500) has the Hôtel du Commerce, 8 place du Commerce, tel. 85.59.03.09, with 17 rooms but no restaurant. The Hôtel de l'Abbaye, 14 avenue de la Gare, tel. 85.59.11.14, has 18 rooms and a menu at 75 francs.

Louhans (pop. 7,250) has the Hôtel du Cheval Rouge, 5 rue d'Alsace, tel. 85.75.21.42, with 14 rooms and a menu from 50 francs.

Charolles (pop. 4,400), the famous centre of the Charollais cattle country, has the Hôtel du Lion d'Or, 6 rue de Champagny, tel. 85.24.08.28, with 20 rooms and a menu from 50 francs. The Nouvel Hôtel, 1 Place du Champ-de-Foire, tel. 85.24.02.20, has 7 rooms and a menu from 45 francs.

Gueugnon (pop. 10,800) is another industrial centre. The Hôtel Centre, 34 rue de la Liberté, tel. 85.85.21.01, has 18 rooms from 75–140 francs.

Summary

Map ref.	Town	Hotel	No. of rooms	Tel. (Prefix 85)
D-3	Autun 71400	de la Tête Noire, 1/3 rue de l'Arquebuse.	20	52.25.39 closed Mar.
		Commerce et Touring, 20 avenue de la République.	23	52.17.90 closed Oct.
		de France, place de la Gare.	23	52.14.00
E-8	Beaubery 71220	l'Auberge de Beaubery, St-Bonnet-de-Joux	5	24.80.21 closed Fri. and 15/12-15/1
F-8	Bergesserin 71250	le Relais	7	59.01.52

E-6	Blanzy 71450	du Centre, l rue Joseph Lambert.	12	57.38.21
		le Plessis, 33 route de Mâcon.	11	570774
A-6	Bourbon-Lancy 71140	du Pont de Loire, Le Fourneau.	7	89.20.18
G-4	Chagny 71150	Central, l rue de la République	8	87.20.18 closed Sat. and Nov./Dec.
H-5	Chalon-sur-Saône	Le Regal, 7 rue Dr Mauchamp.	14	46.59.98 closed Sun. and and Jan.
	71100	Rive Gauche, 1 avenue Verdun.	18	48.76.25 closed Sun.
		de la Gare, avenue Jean Jaurès.	17	43.36.83
		le Petit Chef, 4 rue de Dijon.	8	46.66.56
		du Kiosque, 10 rue des Jacobins.	28	48.12.24 no restaurant
		Gloriette, 27 rue Gloriette.	18	48.23.35 no restaurant
		le Relais Bourguignon, Le Gauchard, RN6.	10	43.10.69 closed Fri.
		Ma Campagne, quai Bellevue.	12	48.33.80 closed Mon. and and Oct.
J-4	Charetté 71270	Doubs-Rivage, rue de la Chapelle	8	76.23.45 closed Fri. and 20/12-20/1
D-8	Charolles 71220	du Lion d'Or, 6 rue de Champagny.	20	24.08.28 closed Sun. and Mon.
		Nouvel Hôtel, 1 place du Champ-de-Foire	7	24.02.20 closed Mon. and Mar.
J—6	Château Renard 71500	la Poularde, 5 rue du Jura	8	75.03.06 closed Fri. and 15/12-15/1

E-10	Chauffailles 71170	du Commerce, 48 rue du 8 mai 1945	18	26.01.43 no restaurant
D-2	Chissey-en-Morvan 71540	Auberge Fleurie	7	82.62.05
E-9	La Clayette 71800	de la Gare, 38 rue de la Gare	11	28.01.65 closed Mon.
G-8	Cluny 71250	de l'Abbaye, avenue de la Gare.	18	59.11.14 closed Jan. and Feb.
		du Commerce, 8 place du Commerce	17	59.03.09
F-4	Couches 71490	des Trois Maures place République	10	49.63.93 closed Mon. and 15/2-15/3
E-5	Le Creusot 71200	des Voyageurs, 5 place Schneider	15	55.22.36 closed Jul. and Aug.
K-7	Cuiseaux 71480	du Nord, 1 Grande Rue.	25	72.71.02 closed Thur. and and Nov.
		du Commerce, 36 Grande Rue	9	72.71.79 closed 10/6-20/6
C-8	Digoin 71160	Terminus, 76 avenue Général de Gaulle. Modern, 6 rue de la Faiencerie	17 12	53.17.26 closed 6/1-6/2 53.05.80 closed Tue. and Nov.
H-8	Fleurville 71260	le Fleurvil	10	33.10.65 closed Tue. and 15/11-15/12
D-7	Génelard 71420	du Commerce, rue Nationale	7	79.20.87 no restaurant
A-7	Gilly-sur-Loire 71160	la Gare, 13 place de la Gare	7	53.91.13
G-5	Givry 71640	de la Halle, place de la Halle	10	44.32.45 closed Sun., Mon. and Nov.

E-6	Gourdon 71690	le Grilloir, Le Plain-Joly	7	57.37.19 closed Fri.
B-6	Grury 71760	du Centre	10	89.81.32
C-6	Gueugnon 71130	du Centre, 34 rue de la Liberté	18	85.21.01 no restaurant
C-6	Issy-L'Évêque 71760	des Voyageurs, rue du 8 Mai	8	89.85.35 closed Mon. and 1/7-18/7
J-6	Louhans 71500	du Cheval Rouge, 5 rue d'Alsace	14	75.21.42 closed Mon. and 22/12-5/1
H-9	Mâcon 71000	les Tuileries, quai des Marans.	13	38.19.91
		le Renaissance, 115 rue Rambuteau.	11	34.15.98
		le Charolais, 71 rue Rambuteau.	12	38.36.23
		le Pape, 74 rue Dufour.	11	38.38.78
		le Savoie, 87 rue Rambuteau.	19	38.42.22
		du Centre, 45 rue Franche.	16	38.05.34 no restaurant
		la Boiserie, 56 rue Victor Hugo.	9	38.00.90 no restaurant
		le Relais Fleurie, 28 rue des Minimes.	24	38.36.02 no restaurant
C-9	Marcigny 71110	St-Antoine, place 11 Novembre	13	25.11.23
H-8	Montbellet-St-Oyen 71260	le Miranbel, Lieu dit Mirande	8	33.10.24 closed Fri.
E-6	Montceau-les-Mines 71300	de France, 7 place Beaubernard.	11	57.26.64 closed Mon. and and Aug.
		du Nord, 13 rue du 11 Novembre.	12	57.05.33 no restaurant
C-8	Paray-le-Monial 71600	Terminus, 57 avenue de la Gare.	22	81.08.80 closed Nov.
		du Val d'Or (La	17	81.05.07

		Beluze, Volerres).		closed Mon. and Oct.
		aux Vendanges de Bourgogne, 5 rue Denis Papin.	14	81.13.43 closed Sun. and Mon.
		du Nord, 45 avenue de la Gare.	15	81.05.12 closed Jan.
		Champ de Foire, rue Desrichard.	8	81.01.68
		St-Roch, 39 avenue de la Gare.	9	81.15.74
D-2	La Petite-Verrière 71400	au Bon Accueil	5	82.74.48 closed 15/12-6/1
J-4	Pierre-de-Bresse 71270	de la Poste, place des Hôtels	7	76.24.47 closed Mon., Tue. and Oct.
G-10	Romanèche-Thorins 71576	Relais Beaujolais-Bresse, RN6	12	35.51.96 closed Thur. Fri. and Nov.
I-7	Romenay 71470	Moderne, place du Champ-de-Foire	7	40.35.23 closed Mon.
E-8	St-Bonnet de Joux 71220	le Val de Joux	8	24.72.39 closed Mon. and 15/12-15/2
H-6	St-Cyr 71240	Relais de Grosne	15	44.20.05 closed Sun. and and 21/9-21/10
J-5	St-Germain du Bois 71330	Hostellerie Bressane, route Sens	9	72.04.69 closed Fri. and 3/6-21/10
G-6	St-Gengoux-le National 71460	de la Gare, avenue de la Gare	10	47.68.39
E-4	St-Symphorien-de-Marmagne 71710	la Rose des Vents, Montecenis	17	78.20.86
J–6	St-Usuge 71500	Boivin, au Bourg	8	72.10.95 closed 10/9-5/10

E-6	St-Vallier 71230	de la Saulle, 136A rue F. Roosevelt	33	57.10.71
C-8	St-Yan 71600	Motel de la Gare, 6 rue de la Gare	15	81.17.64
H-6	Sennecey-le Grand 71240	Lion d'Or, rue de la Gare	12	44.83.75 closed Mon. and 15/12-15/1
H-7	Tournus 71700	au Terrasses, 18 avenue 23 Janvier.	12	51.01.74 closed Mon.
		l'Abbaye, 12 rue Leon Godin.	23	51.11.63 closed 1/11-15/3
		de Bourgogne, rue Dr Privey.	12	51.12.23
		Gras, 2 rue Fénelon.	8	51.07.25 closed Sun.
		le Pas Fleury, avenue 23 Janvier.	9	51.00.78 closed Fri.
		de la Madeleine, 15 rue D. Mathivet.	4	51.05.83 closed Sun and and Mon.
H-7	Uchizy 71700	du Nord	9	51.00.92
F-5	Villeneuve-en-Montagne 71390	des Quatre Vents	8	96.99.25 no restaurant
A-6	Vitry-sur-Loire 71140	des Acacias, le Bourg	10	89.71.36

Camp sites

Thil-sur-Arroux is the smallest site, with six *placements*. The costs per day for two people are 16 francs and 19 francs respectively.

Map ref.	Town		
D-3	Autun 71400	Cam. mun. du Pont d'Arroux,	tel. 85.52.10.82
G-8	Azé 71260 Lugny.	Cam. 'des Grottes',	tel. 85.33.32.23
A-6	Bourbon-Lancy 71140	Cam. 'St-Prix',	tel. 85.89.14.85

H-7	Boyer 71700 Tournus	Relais du Jonchet, RN6. M. Morant,	tel. 85.51.01.02
I-7	Brienne 71290 Cuisery	'Les Sénons', M. Pagand, tel. 85.40.10.52	
D-3	La Celle-en-Morvan 71400 Autun.	Cam. 'Les Deux-Rivières' tel. 85.52.43.15	
G-4	Chagny 71150	Cam. Mun. du Pâquier- Fané,	tel. 85.87.21.42
H-5	Chalon-sur-Saône 71380 St-Marcel.	Cam. mun. de la Butte,	tel. 85.48.26.86
D-8	Charolles 71120	Cam. mun., rte de Viry,	tel. 85.24.04.90
E-10	Chauffailles 71170	Cam. 'Les Feuilles',	tel. 85.26.48.12
E-9	La Clayette 71800	Cam. 'Les Bruyères,	tel. 85.28.09.15
G-8	Cluny 71250	Cam. mun. St. Vital, rue des Griottons,	tel. 85.59.08.34
G-10	Crèches-sur-Saône 71680	Cam. mun. du Port d'Arciat,	tel. 85.37.11.83
K-7	Les Crotenots 71480 Cuiseaux.	Cam. 'Le Miroir',	tel. 85.76.71.78
C-8	Digoin 71160	Cam. mun. de la Chevrette, rue de la Chevrette,	tel. 85.53.11.49
F-3	Épinac 71360	Cam. mun. Le Pont-Vert, tel. 85.82.18.06	
D-4	Étang-sur-Arroux 71190	Cam. du Val d'Arroux,	tel. 85.82.32.35
D-7	Génelard 71420 Perrecy-les-Forges	Cam. du Pré-Châtelain. M. Lacroix,	tel. 85.70.21.73
E-9	Gibles 71800 La Clayette	Cam. du Château de Montrouant,	tel. 85.28.09.38
H-6	Gigny-sur-Saône 71240 Sennency-le-Grand.	Cam. du Château de l'Épervière	tel. 85.44.83.23
J-4	Lays-sur-le-Doubs 712110 Pierre-de-Bresse	Cam. 'des Pêcheurs',	tel. 85.72.82.32
J-6	Louhans 71500	Cam. mun. 'La Chapellerie',	tel. 85.75.19.02
D-2	Lucenay-L'Évêque 71540	Cam. mun. Mairie,	tel. 85.82.65.41

H-8	Lugny 71260	Cam. 'St-Pierre'	
H-9	Mâcon 71000	Cam. 'Les Varennes', Sancé,	tel. 85.38.16.22
F-9	Matour 71520	Cam. 'Le Paluet',	tel. 85.59.70.58
H-5	Ouroux-sur-Saône 71370 St-Germain-du-Plain	Cam. mun. Mairie,	tel. 85.47.01.12
C-8	Paray-le-Monial 71600	Cam. mun. 'Le Pré-Barré, bd. du Dauphin-Louis,	tel. 85.81.05.05
J-5	St-Germain-du-Bois 71330	Cam. 'de l'Étang-Titard', rte de Louhans,	tel. 85.72.01.47
G-5	St-Jean-de-Vaux 71640 Givry	Cam. 'de la vallée des Vaux',	tel. 85.47.11.98
C-4	St-Léger-sous-Veuvray 71990	Cam. 'La Boutière,	tel. 85.82.53.00
D-5	St-Nizier-sur-Arroux 71190 Étang-sur-Arroux	Cam. mun. de la Plage,	tel. 85.82.28.25
F-9	St-Point 71630	Cam. 'du Lac', 'Saint Point Lamartine',	tel. 85.50.53.06
G-10	St-Romain-des-Îles 71510 La Chapelle-de-Guinchay	Cam. mun.,	tel. 85.35.52.52
F-7	Salornay-sur-Guye 71810	Cam. 'de la Clochette'. Mme Gelin,	tel. 85.59.40.51
G-7	Savigny-sur-Grosne 71460 St-Gengoux-le-National	Aire Camping. M. Rebourg,	tel. 85.47.61.88
C-5	Thil-sur-Arroux 71190 Étang-sur-Arroux	Aire de Camp. Mme Chapey,	tel. 85.54.26.04
E-5	Torcy 71210 Montchanin	Cam. 'du Lac', plage des Sapins,	tel. 85.55.09.62
D-6	Toulon-sur-Arroux 71320	Cam. mun., route d'Autun. Mairie,	tel. 85.79.42.55
H-7	Tournus 71700 Tournus	Cam. mun. 'Le Pas-Fleury',	tel. 85.51.13.15
H-7	Uchizy 71700	Cam. 'Le National' 6,	tel. 85.51.10.90
I-4	Verdun-sur-le-Doubs 71350	Cam. mun. 'La Plage',	tel. 85.91.55.50